FIVE GENERATIONS

OF THE FAMILY

OF BURR HARRISON OF VIRGINIA

1650 - 1800

By John P. Alcock

HERITAGE BOOKS, INC.

Published 1991 By

HERITAGE BOOKS, INC.
1540E Pointer Ridge Place, Bowie, Maryland 20716
(301)-390-7709

ISBN 1-55613-378-2

VA
9292
ALC

A Complete Catalog Listing Hundreds of Titles on
History, Genealogy & Americana
Free on Request

To Joe, Nan, and Bud, each of whom has one-
thousandth of the genes of the first Burr Harrison

Table of Contents

Foreword

Our study of the colonial descendants of Burr Harrison (1637-97) originated in 1981 when Mariana Alcock and I moved to Monterey Farm near Marshall in Fauquier County, Virginia. The farm had belonged continuously to her direct ancestors since 1765, when Colonel Thomas Harrison bought a 1000-acre tract, of which Monterey was a part, to be his plantation "at the mountains." We wanted to know how and why the boundaries of the property had changed over the years.

That task turned out to be easily accomplished even by the rank amateurs that we were, because there were only a few deeds involved and all of these were available in the Fauquier courthouse in nearby Warrenton. Fortunately, Fauquier's records from 1759 to the present were intact, never damaged during the Civil War nor destroyed by a courthouse fire.

Emboldened by our success, we decided to take up the search for more information on Mariana's maternal ancestors, the previous owners of Monterey. That was a greater challenge, because the property had passed from a Harrison great-grandson of Colonel Thomas through daughters for each of five generations to the present.

We had the advantage that the Harrisons, Rectors, and Humes, that is to say the families of former owners, had all lived in northern Virginia since colonial times.

Their courthouse records are all within a hundred miles. The State Archives and the library of the Virginia Historical Society in Richmond are 110 miles away. Washington with its US Archives, DAR Library, and Library of Congress is only 50 miles down I-66.

To a degree we have divided the project; I took primary responsibility for the Harrisons while Mariana handled her other ancestral families. However, since we usually searched together, her help with the Harrisons has been invaluable.

I chose my part of the overall objective because, almost from the beginning, we could follow the Harrisons back to the seventeenth century. Having the distinctive name of the immigrant Burr Harrison coincide with that of an owner of the farm was a stroke of luck. Soon I became as interested in the history of the area during colonial times as in the genealogy of the early members of the family with its challenging puzzles.

Why did it take eight years to finish the job? In the first place genealogy cum history has been largely a winter avocation. One can't live on a farm without being very busy in spring and quite well occupied in summer and fall. But much time was consumed in "cracking nuts" hardened by the loss of many of the early records of northern Virginia and Maryland. Furthermore, we have learned many lessons that we shall benefit from in a new undertaking. Had we had a lap-top to use in the courthouses and libraries, an adequate computer program for filing and retrieving data, plus the numerous new indexed abstracts of northern Virginia records that have become available in recent years, our working time would have been shortened greatly.

I have attempted to reduce mistakes by going to original sources as much as possible, using secondary ones mainly to tell where to look. Though I now feel good about my accuracy in reading eighteenth-century script, I urge the reader to check any data that is important to his purposes. Some errors in copying may have crept in. I have tried to indicate where I have interpreted material or conjectured about its meaning.

I wish to thank especially our friends Berenice May Fuller and William Long for help with Burr Harrison of South Carolina (Chapter XIII), Gary Young for his help with Thomas Harrison of Kentucky (Chapter XI), Dorothy Thrawley for sharing her research on Lintons and Harrisons, Paul R. Lilly for his accurate and light-hearted correspondence about his Bullitt ancestors, and John Gott for his assistance and encouragement. Librarians and archivists must all have the patience of Job, because cheerfully and graciously from Annapolis to Chicago and Baltimore to Columbia, they have given invaluable help. My son, John Alcock, knows how grateful I am for his suggestions about content and his editing of a manuscript draft.

There remains plenty for genealogists to do on the Harrisons of northern Virginia. Perhaps the journal of the Reverend Thomas Harrison can be found. Someday somebody is going to solve the mystery of the origins of William Harrison of the West-Harrison-Pearson-Harrison Hunting Creek grant and make sense out of the tangle of Thomas and Burr/Burditt Calvert/Harris/Harrisons. I commend such projects to the reader. Good luck and happy hunting.

John P. Alcock
Marshall, Virginia
July, 1990

Chapter I

Burr Harrison (1637–1697), the Immigrant
(Burr 1, Cuthbert, Cuthbert)

Virginians as a rule have a deep appreciation of their heritage. No doubt this stems from the close geographical contact
that they enjoy with almost four hundred years of history and
from the special importance they and other Southerners attach
to family ties. "Kissing cousins" often know from whom they
share descent, even if they must go back four, five, or more
generations to reach their common ancestor.

Our own interest in family history was spurred by the "old
Harrison graveyard" located on our farm in Fauquier County. It
holds some fifty graves marked with rough-cut fieldstones, of
which only two bear legible inscriptions. Neither one is
complete enough to enable identification of the person buried
beneath. However, there is a monument inscribed with the
names of twenty-four persons buried in the cemetery. Heading
the list is a Burr Harrison, who was born on the farm about
1768 and died there in 1842.

The Burr Harrison buried on our farm was the great-great-
grandson of an immigrant with the same distinctive name.
Originally our purpose in tracing the first Burr Harrison and his
descendants was to solve some of the puzzles involved in the
genealogy of the family. Eventually as a by-product of that
objective, we obtained equal satisfaction in having the colonial
history of northern Virginia come alive for us through our study
of five generations of the family. We report on our searches to
show how the colonial Harrisons lived as well as how they were
related.

The founder of the family first appeared in Virginia in
Lancaster County. There on August 7, 1654, the county court
ordered that "Bour Harrison shall serve nine weeks at the
expiration of his time (per his indenture contract) for running
away from his master Tho. Meades." (1)

1

When Mr. Meades died less than a year later, the inventory of his personal estate showed only one servant, an unnamed maid who had two more years to serve. Evidently Meades had sold the contract of his refractory man-servant. (2) Harrison's new master was John Hallowes, a resident of the neighboring county of Westmoreland. In April of 1658 the Westmoreland court recorded that Elizabeth, the widow and administratrix of Hallowes, had assigned the indentures of five servants to Captain Thomas Cornwallys and William Hardige in payment of debts of her husband's estate. The transfer began:

> Wm. Baltrop for all his time
> Bushan Degnes, a Duchman, for all his time
> Jno. Addams for his time
> Burr Hallis for his time
> Wm. Crosier for his time
> together with all their wearing apparell
> and beds and coverings and bolsters
> thereunto belonging. (3)

Both Lancaster and Westmoreland counties are on the Northern Neck, the peninsula which lies between the Rappahannock and the Potomac rivers. The initial settlements in the region had been made only a decade before. Many of the earliest inhabitants, including Meades, Hallowes, and Cornwallys had come from Maryland. Meades had bought his Virginia plantation of seven hundred acres in 1653. He might have brought his teen-age servant, Burr Harrison, with him when he moved across the Potomac. Hope of finding an indenture or other trace of Meades or Harrison in the Maryland archives was thwarted by the loss of all early records of St. Mary's County.

On the same day that the agreement between Mrs. Hallowes and the creditors was registered, the court received a deposition from Humphrey Jones that he had heard the widow say she would consume as much as she could of her late husband's estate. (4) Poor Jones died within eighteen months, leaving all his belongings to his friend, John Vauhan, except for "one suit of broad cloath and one pair of shoes and stockings" which went to Rowland Evans. The will was witnessed "Bur Harris his marke." (5)

As might be surmised, Bour Harrison, Burr Hallis, and Bur Harris were one and the same person. Young Burr himself might have had some doubt as to whether his name was Harrison or Harris. Spelling of family names was not yet standardized. Lawyers writing documents and clerks copying them into

2

the record had no great incentive to get the correct name, since the important part of the validation procedure was acknowledgement of the document before the court by a principal or a witness. Later, after Burr had become established and was known by the officers of the court, the name was almost always written Harrison. ("Hallis" appeared only once. The clerk who made the notation formed the two l's shorter than others on the page and taller than his similar r's. Perhaps he hedged his spelling of the name.)

The vestry book (1745-1802) of Dettingen Parish of Prince William County contains a page taken from an earlier parish book stating that "Burr Harrison now or late of Chappawamsic ---- was baptized ---- the 28th day of December 1637" in St. Margaret's Parish, Westminster, England. (6) However, the original register of St. Margaret's, which is the parish church of Westminster Abbey, reads under 3 January 1637 (1638 new style) "christened Burre Harris, s. to Cuthbert." It also notes christenings of Cutbert Harrison, son of Cutbert in 1607; Alexander Harrison, son of Cuthbert and Susann in 1644; Thomas Harris, son of Cuthbert and Suzan in 1647; and Sarah Harrison, daughter of Cuthbert and Susanna in 1652. The burial records of the parish include only one of the family, that of Cutberd Harris in 1617. (7) (Spellings are those used in the registers. Prior to 1640 the name of the mother of the baptized infant is not given.) (8)

These English records indicating that the Harris/Harrisons had left St. Margaret's sometime after 1652 are consistent with the family tradition that Cuthbert brought his son, Burr, to the New World, but we have been unable to confirm this in Virginia or Maryland. In 1671 Governor William Berkley reported to England that there were forty thousand persons in the colony of Virginia. "Of these 2000 were black slaves and 6000 Christian servants. ---- Now [there are] not often unseasoned hands, as we term them, that die whereas heretofore not one in five escaped the first year." Very likely Cuthbert was one such who succumbed.

There is no trace of Burr's brother Alexander nor of his mother, Susanna, or sister Sarah. If the female members of the family came to America, they may have survived the dangerous voyage and the difficult period of acclimatization in the New World, because the maiden names of very few women of the time have come down to us. Marriage records were kept by the church rather than the state; no seventeenth-century register of a northern Virginia parish survives.

There are several references to one or more men named Thomas Harris or Thomas Harrison of unknown parentage in this period in Westmoreland and neighboring counties as well as across the Potomac in Maryland. A hypothesis that some of these pertain to Burr's brother, whose descendants used the family stock of Christian names, might explain the origins of some later Harrisons in the region.

Still, we have found nothing to indicate that the Harrisons from Westminster were related to any other of the Virginia Harrison families, including the Tidewater presidential one, which was already established and prospering in the colony well before young Burr arrived.

The earliest Westmoreland book has another record of interest: "Be it known unto all men that Burr Harrison doth give for his marke of cattle and hogges the swallow on the right ear and a cross with two slitts on the left ear. This mark was recorded the 20th of July, 1659." (9) Swallow referred to a brand that looks like a short-handled, two-pronged pitchfork.

Only a free man over twenty-one could act for himself in such legal matters. Therefore, Harrison must have completed the period of his servitude some time after April 1658 (when Mrs. Hallowes sold his contract) and this date of July 1659. If he was a poor orphan apprenticed to Meades by his mother or by the churchwardens, he would have had to serve his master until he had reached his majority at the end of 1658, plus the two months extra for running away. On the other hand, if his contract was to pay for transportation across the Atlantic, normally it would have been for four years. That term could also have expired in 1658 or 1659. So we can't tell now which type of indenture applied.

In 1661 Burr Harrison registered a different mark for his cattle; a "flower de leeze" on the right ear and a "half moon underneath and a slitt above" on the left. (10) Maybe he had found the original difficult to distinguish from that of a neighbor or easily altered by a rustler. The records from the seventeenth century hold many such registrations of brands. The region was then the northernmost frontier of the colony. As in the West two hundred years later, animals roamed unfenced in the woods making the recording of one's brand a prerequisite for setting out at farming.

There are additional references to young Harrison in the Westmoreland court books. In February 1664 he claimed his legally allowed compensation of 40 pounds tobacco per day for appearing as a witness on behalf of his employer, David Anderson, defendant in a suit brought by Colonel Valentine Peyton. (11) Anderson had become the fourth husband of Elizabeth Hallowes, three times a widow at the age of twenty-seven. As on all frontiers, there was a shortage of eligible females.

4

Young widows did not stay unmarried for long. They often lacked the means to support their children, and, if able to do so, they were considered an especially good catch.

Harrison asked for two days attendance and two days coming to and going from court, evidence that he resided in the distant northern part of the county, probably on Potomac Creek, where both Anderson and Peyton had plantations.

This area was made part of the new Stafford County, when it was set off from Westmoreland in 1664. From then until 1731 Stafford comprised all the territory of modern Stafford, Prince William, Fairfax, Loudoun, Fauquier, and Arlington counties except for a narrow strip on the northeast side of the Rappahannock, which was originally part of (Old) Rappahannock County. Before the division Westmoreland counted 614 titheables indicating a total population around two thousand. Something less than one-fourth of these resided in the new county, all of them within a few miles of the Potomac River. It took about twenty-five years for the titheables in Stafford to surpass 600. (12)

Subsequent Westmoreland and Stafford court minutes show that bad blood came to exist between Harrison and Anderson. An order in 1665 quoted Harrison's "humble petition ---- that David Anderson hath at divers and severall courts unjustly molested and troubled the poor petitioner about a sett of wedges borrowed of Mr. Sisson by the said Anderson's order in the time the petitioner was ---- Anderson's overseer, which wedges ---- Anderson pretended was conveyed away by the poor petitioner to his great scandall but have been all this while in the possession of ---- Anderson. ---- the poor petitioner humbly craveth reprivation as your worships shall think fitt for this his unjust molestation & refamation."

When the final jury verdict favored the plaintiff, the court ordered "Mr. David Anderson fourthwith pay unto Burr Harrison for damages 400 pounds of tobacco and cask." (13) A difference in social status was implied by use of the as-yet-undepreciated title of "Mr." for Anderson and its omission for Harrison. A Mr. ranked higher than the unprefixed commonality of people but lower than a suffixed Gent. As a vestryman Anderson rated the Mr.; if he had been a justice of the peace, he would have been styled Gent.

In Virginia an overseer operated on shares a farm located too far away to be managed by its absentee owner. The arrangement Harrison had with Anderson probably paralleled that of the contract between William Harris, a landowner, and John Burton, his overseer. By it Burton agreed to dwell at Harris's plantation of three hundred acres at Neapscoe for five years and

5

to plant corn and tobacco there. Harris was to put one of his hands there yearly and to allow two hundred pounds of meat for that man's upkeep, and Burton was to allow his helper a full share of tobacco and "Syder" produced in the orchard. Harris would stock the plantation with hogs and cattle; when settlement was made at the end of the five years, Burton would receive one third of the increase of hogs and a fourth that of cattle. Burton was allowed to slaughter two barrows in the first year but would have to repay them in kind at the end. He was allowed to put on two young sows of his own; Harris would get half their increase. If Burton himself wanted to buy additional cows later, Harris would match them, and they'd share in the increase equally. Corn produced would remain on the farm to feed the stock; that left on completing the contract or any excess during it would be shared equally. If Burton should happen to hire another hand to work on the place, half his wages would be paid by Harris. After the first year Burton could have provision for himself and one hand out of the increase in stock. Burton also promised to keep the orchard fence in good repair, to plant any trees that were wanting (these to be furnished by Harris), and to get timber for repairing the housing on the plantation. The "lease" was to expire at "xmas 1684." (14)

Returning to Burr Harrison we find he was in court as plaintiff or defendant in civil suits at least once during most years of his life. To modern eyes something appears wrong. Few of us are involved in the courts so often. However, in this respect Harrison did not differ from most of his contemporaries who owned any personal property. Disputes with neighbors, usually involving small sums, filled the order books of the county court. It met once a month for a three-day session, weather permitting. Cases were often continued many months and not uncommonly were dismissed due to the death of one of the parties. Settlements could be reached by agreement between the litigants out of court or decided by arbitrators appointed by the court with the consent of the parties. The disputants could ask for a jury to decide the matter or get the sitting justices to make a ruling, which could then be appealed to a jury or in the ultimate instance to the General Court at Jamestown. Why were there so many suits? Important factors were the paucity of written contracts due to the prevalence of illiteracy; the lack of adequate surveys of property lines; the limited amount of currency in circulation, which often necessitated that credit be given until the next harvest. Furthermore, it appears that sometimes a court action was taken to settle a minor misunderstanding between friends or even relatives, before it caused a serious falling out.

The first order book of the Stafford court covered the period from May 1664 through January 1668. Because the county archives were looted by souvenir hunters and vandals among the Union troops quartered in the vicinity of the courthouse during the Civil War, the next extant records cover wills, deeds, depositions, etc., for 1680 and then from March 1686 to February 1694, and court minutes from December 1689 to December 1693. Subsequently there is nothing until November 1699, when book Z begins. (15)

During the gaps in the court records, there remain only a few other documents relating to Harrison. One such showed up in a suit which started in 1769 and dragged on to 1790. Evidence entered in it traced the ownership of a tract from an original grant of two thousand acres in 1668 through all the changes for more than a century. The history began with the following letter:

Mr. Harrison my love remembered to you. This is to let you know that I do hereby testify that what you do concerning my land that I spake to you of when I was with you last I do hereby desire you to sell and dispose of it to any person or persons whatsoever and I do hereby bind myself for the same and whatsoever you shall do in and concerning the said land I will establish it in as large and ample manner as if I was there personally present myself and you may give as much warrant concerning the sale of it as need shall require. No more at present but love remembered to you and your bedfellow I rest your loving friend while I am Robert Horsington from Mastoun Parish. 24th October 1668.

This letter, accepted as a power-of-attorney, was followed by a 1673 instrument stating:

To all whom these presents shall come: Whereas Robert Horsington late of York County decd. had a tract of land of 2000 acres lying in Stafford County ---- and did give unto Burr Harrison 600 acres of the same and left the [rest] with --- Harrison ---- who sold 600 acres of the remaining 1400 for 7000 lbs. tobacco and whereas I Dorothy Horsington, late wife of John Horsington decd. ---- administratrix to my said husband

7

who was administrator to Robert his brother ----
know ye therefore that upon receipt of what
tobacco the said Burr Harrison stands indebted to
me I the said Dorothy Horsington do assign and
make over to the said Burr Harrison ---- my right
and title to the said 600 acres of land it being that
part that he is already seated on. (16)

The six hundred acres Harrison sold for Horsington went to a planter named Samuel Sneed in February 1669/70. It was this tract that was the subject of the suit.

Twelve months after Horsington's patent issued, twelve hundred acres "upon the main run of a creek of Oququon river" were granted by the Governor and his council to Will Harrys (the William Harris of the contract with Burton), Thomas Baxter, and Burr Harrys for "the transport of 24 persons." (17)

Such headrights of fifty acres per person brought into Virginia were given to encourage colonization. A movement across the Potomac from Maryland qualified equally with one across the Atlantic. The procedure for claiming the acreage was to present the names of the "transportees" to the county court with a description of the requested land. The court then certified the validity of the claim and availability of the tract to the authorities at Jamestown. One gets the impression that the Stafford clerk of court and the county surveyor at this time were not overly rigorous in their investigations. Rights could be bought and sold; so it is not to be inferred that the persons listed in the appendix to a grant were actually brought into Virginia by the grantees.

In this case, none of the partners claimed his own headright, although one for a Mary Harris was included. Baxter is among those claimed on a previous grant for land in Stafford, and more than one William Harris was brought into the region, but no listing for Burr or Cuthbert Harrison (or Harris) can be found in the files of the land office. Apparently, the record of the grant that their entry to the colony supported was lost.

When Charles II confirmed the Northern Neck Proprietorship comprising the territory north of the Rappahannock to Lord Culpeper in 1661, he prohibited the government in Jamestown from making new grants within its boundaries. In practice the colonial administration continued to do so until Culpeper himself arrived in the colony to take up the governorship in 1680. The last patent from Jamestown was made in 1679 to William Harris for three hundred acres in Stafford. After 1680 the Proprietor set up an office run by agents empowered to make land grants, collect quitrents, and otherwise look after his interests.

William Harris always was denoted in the Stafford court as Harris, never as Harrison. His tombstone, originally located south of the Occoquan, is now in the Pohick church yard. It reads: "Here lyes bodey of Liut. Williame Herris who died May 16: 1698 aged 65 years by birth a Britaine a good soldier a good husband and kinde neighbour." (18) Is it only a coincidence that the register of St. Margaret's Westminster notes that "William Harrison s. of Leonard" was christened 10 June 1632? If that baby grew up to be Liut. Williame Herris, he would have died just short of his sixty-sixth birthday. Thus, Will Harrys/Herris/Harris and Burr Harrys/Harrison might have known each other in England or even have been cousins.

A court case linking William Harris to Burr Harrison as a friend and possibly a relative took place in 1691. One Benjamin Lewis came to court testifying he had been a free Negro in England, but he had indentured himself for four years in return for his passage to Virginia. The ship captain had sold his contract to a man in (Old) Rappahanock County, and he had served about half his term there. Then he had been sold to William Harris for the remainder of it. When this was complete, he asked for his freedom, but Harris would not give it. Harris told the court that the indenture was forged, and that his purchase of Lewis as a slave had been warranted by the seller. Because he considered the man to be an "ingenious brisk fellow" whom he felt might be "careless and negligent of all manner of service," he had covenanted that Lewis should serve for fourteen years. He had registered the bill of sale and his compact with Lewis with the clerk of court eight months previously. Nevertheless, a jury ruled that the original indenture was valid, and the court, pronouncing that the second was a "fraud and deceit," ordered that Benjamin Lewis be given his freedom. Harris appealed to the General Court with Burr Harrison as his security to pay the costs of the appeal. (19) Record of this appeal, along with almost every action of the Governor's Council sitting as this highest court in the colony, was lost in a fire which destroyed the Government House at Jamestown.

The Lewis case is the only one that we have found involving a black man as either plaintiff or defendant in a civil suit in the Stafford Court during the seventeenth century. Significantly, it demonstrates that a black could obtain justice from both the jury and the magistrates.

Some years after his participation in the partnership with Harris and Baxter, Harrison purchased a property for his own account. Two letters in 1679 from the lawyer, William Fitzhugh, explained the situation to officials at Jamestown.

9

The first pretension of a title to the land in controversie was by old Capt. Brent who upon his pretended right settled severall tennants, to say Burr Harrison, Thomas Barton and one Bennet, whose widow this woman is that made such an exclamation about the house pulled down: Afterwards Collo. Washington as guardian to Gerrard Broadhurst sees and tries title about this land in Stafford County and recovered and the said tennants all turned to him and became his tennants as guardian aforesaid. After the tennants sue Giles Brent as son and heir of his father deceas'd for their said eviction and trouble and recover agst him. Afterwards Burr Harrison buys the land of Gerrard Broadhurst being of age ---- but here Harrison is kept out of his right, that is Barton's plantation, which he has sufficiently made appear to be his, without either action or answer and then contrary or only under the colour of a pretended title Matthews lays to it ---- For more than all that I have before informed you, this widow Bennet after Harrison's purchase did not only attune and acknowledge her new landlord, but delivered up her lease into his hands, and after[wards] she and a freeman that lives with her took the plantation from that time to the fall for the rent of one hhd. of tobo. At the expiration of which time, Harrison gives them two month's notice to provide for themselves, and before witnesses severall times forewarned them off, but their answer was they would neither go off nor pay the rent. Then and not before I advised him to pull down the house. (20)

Apparently Fitzhugh was unsuccessful in his claim on behalf of Harrison under the Broadhurst patent, because the next year, 1680, Harrison purchased five hundred acres from John Mathews, holder of the "pretended title." Mathews was the son and heir of Samuel Mathews, who had gotten a patent for 5211 acres in 1657 while he was governor of the colony. Its boundaries were delineated as abutting to the east on the Potomac River, south Chopawamsic Creek, west the "main woods," and north Quantico Creek. (21)

According to an abstract of the deed made by a clerk of court in the early 1800's, Harrison purchased from Mathews:

> *one tract and parcel of land containing 500
> acres having thereupon three plantations or tinna-
> ments one in the tenure and occupation of him the
> said Burr Harrison, one other in the tenure and
> occupation of Thomas Barton, and one other ----
> of Ralph Smith, the said land being part of a
> greater tract descending to me from my father
> Samuel Mathews late of this Colony, Esquire.*

We assume that Ralph Smith was the "freeman" living with the Widow Bennett and that William Bennett, whose deposition made in 1763 was filed in a nineteenth-century suit over the lines of the Mathews patent, was her grandson or great-nephew.

Unfortunately the papers of that suit did not include a survey plat that marked the location of houses along the Chopawamsic. However, an idea of the site of Burr's house (now within the Quantico Marine Base) can be gained from the report of William Perkins, Thomas Barton, and Thomas Norman appointed in 1687 to "view," i.e., lay out, a road "beginning at Mr. Mathew Thompson's quarter downe his plantation --- to Burr Harrison's plantation into the King's Highway (Route 1) past William Perkins's up to the Landing."

Possibly, Harrison was compensated by Broadhurst with five hundred acres on the south bank of the Chopawamsic that had been given to him in 1688 by his mother. The final Harrison plantation definitely included land on both sides of the creek.

Burr Harrison, now past his fortieth birthday, had come up in the world. First an indentured servant and next overseer on Anderson's plantation, he had progressed to tenant under Brent-Broadhurst and finally to yeoman farmer working his own land, or planter as that status was called in Virginia.

The parcel of miscellaneous Stafford court files for 1680 contains three references to Burr Harrison. One is an account submitted by Mathew Thompson of "charges (in pounds of tobacco) sustained by the running away of Wm. Williams:

To my own and Burr Harrison's trouble in Maryland after him
    --- 0200
To 400 Tobo pd Mr Baker for getting the sd. boy --- 0400
To 100 more pd Thomas Alcocke --- 0100
To dammages by his (absence at crop time) --- 2000"

Thompson brought his servant before a magistrate and proved that he had been away from July 31 to August 30.

11

The second is an example of the type of suit that filled the court dossiers of the time:

> *The deposition of Burr Harrison aged 43 years*
> *---- some tyme in March ---- being in the house*
> *of Richard Betham heard Thomas King make a*
> *bargain with Evan Jones for a young bay mare that*
> *was running in the woods ---- [Jones was] to pay*
> *King 1100 pounds of tobacco.*

The signature was copied as "Burr BH Harrison."

Four more depositions do not define the matter brought before the court, but do show that horse-trading was a common enterprise in the community. The bay mare purchased by Jones from King in March was sold by him a few months later to William Downing. This second transaction took place in Colonel George Mason's wheat field where Downing and Jones were part of a gang of reapers. When Downing asked the price, Jones replied, "You shall give me as she cost me being eleven hundred pounds Tobo. and take her as she runs in the woods." Downing said, "I will give it." A bit later Mary Downing was at George Lisle's house and told Lisle her husband had bought the mare of Jones for 1100 pounds tobacco and asked if Lisle would buy it. Lisle offered to pay an extra one hundred pounds for her husband's "bargain."

In the third instance Harrison and William Perkins testified to being present when a deputy sheriff executed a court order giving Thomas Odonnell possession of land "att Quantiquott" recovered from the lawyer Richard Gibson. (22)

The next notice of Burr Harrison came in 1683 when he sued Francis Meeke in the court of Charles County, Maryland for a debt of 500 pounds of tobacco. The suit is a reminder of how close the residents of Stafford County were to Maryland and how much traffic there was across the river in both directions. Meeke had lived in the Maryland county, but by the time of the hearing had moved to Stafford. For the Maryland court to have jurisdiction, the debt must have been incurred there on the northeast side of the Potomac. Then as now, lawyers were expensive, even more so in Maryland than in Virginia. The court set the fee of Harrison's attorney at 281 pounds; fortunately for Burr his attorney won the case, and the defendant had to pay all fees and court costs. (23)

Other court records involving the first Burr Harrison give an inkling of the economy of the period. For example, early in 1687 he must have had a dispute with a neighbor named Ralph Platt. Peter Beach deposed to the court that he had been at the

12

house of Burr Harrison some time the last summer and heard Platt offer to sell a mare to Harrison. When asked how much he wanted, Platt answered that for 1000 pounds of tobacco and cask, Harrison could have the mare and its unbranded colt. The two men had agreed on the deal according to Beach. (24) The horse was valued at twenty-five times the payment for a day attending court as a witness.

In another case David Strahan (Straughn) filed with the court a copy of his bill for lumber bought by Harrison. (25) Whether the sawmill both supplied and processed the timber or only sawed and planed logs cut by Harrison is not clear. Straughn made the following charges in pounds of tobacco:

950 feet white oak and poplar planks --- 950
300 feet black walnut --- 600
200 feet sweet gum --- 300
1 days work (illegible) & packing --- 30
2 hands 1/2 day carrying joyners waxe to the Landing --- 30

The court minutes also include an annual fiscal report setting out the expenses of the county government and the rate of the tithe (poll tax) to be collected. That Harrison truly lived on the frontier is demonstrated by these county accounts. With few exceptions he annually collected the bounty of 200 pounds tobacco per head for from one to as many as four wolves. One year, there is a notation "for his son," and in another instance "by an Indian," presumably his employee.

To qualify for this payment the claimant had to present the head of the wolf to a magistrate and make a sworn statement as to how, when, and where he had killed the animal. In the 1670's there were complaints to the General Assembly that this use of tax money benefited only those individuals who had horses roaming free in the woods. The law was even changed to collect a special fee from owners of horses to pay the bounties, but the original act was reinstated after a brief period. A 1691 revision set the subsidy at 300 pounds of tobacco if the wolf were taken by "pit or trap" and 200 by gun or other means.

As all these transactions make evident, the standard currency of colonial Virginia was tobacco. The colony maintained official warehouses, where inspectors graded the product and issued certificates of the quantities they held belonging to each planter. Casks holding 1000 pounds of tobacco leaf had the identifying mark of the grower. The certificates were legal tender. In some cases actual tobacco changed hands. Payments were also made with notes from tobacco merchants in Britain or the colony. The exchange rate in the latter part of the seventeenth century for payment of quitrents to the Proprietors was 6 shillings per 100 pounds of tobacco (or 5 shillings per Spanish piece of eight, also used as money by the colonists).

Early in the Spring of 1689, ten years after his difficulties with Thomas Barton and the Widow Bennet, Harrison got himself into big trouble related to England's Glorious Revolution, which deposed King James II and installed the firmly Protestant William and Mary. Prince William of Orange was married to Mary Stuart, the elder daughter of James and his Protestant first wife. The proximate cause of the Revolution was the birth of James's son by his Catholic second wife. The child had replaced Mary as heir to the throne. An earlier aborted revolution led by the Duke of Monmouth had resulted in the execution of thousands of his adherents. Although William had arrived in England in December 1688, news of the outcome of the revolt, largely fueled by anti-Catholic sentiment in England, had not yet reached Stafford County.

Nicholas Spencer, Secretary of the Colony, writing to the Colonial Office in London after the event involving Harrison gave the official point of view.

> *The Revolution in England had such an effect here that for some time peace and quiet were doubtful, unruly and disorderly spirits laying hold of the motion of affairs and that under the pretext of religion. On these false glosses they betook themselves to arms, particularly at the heads of the Potomac and Rappahannock, from the groundless imagination that the Papists in Maryland ---- had conspired with the Seneca Indians to cut off all Protestants. This was taken from the declaration of an Indian [to Burr Harrison] and though groundless took so good belief, being improved by some evil members who desire to fish in disturbed waters that the inhabitants of the North drew themselves together for defence ---- matters were pressingly leading to a rebellion but, thank God, speedy care and timely remedies quieted them down again. Suspecting the reality of the Indian's information I ordered him to be secured, not doubting but by reexamination to discover the certainty of the designed forgery; but the notorious persons who set the Indian to work prevented a detection of their villainy by privately destroying him. The party sent to apprehend him weakly*

14

entrusted him to West and Harris [Burr Harrison] who offered to bring him in; and he has since been discovered murdered in the woods by West, who had best reason to know where to find him. He and others are to answer for their part in the matter. (26)

The affair gives us a glimpse into the mind-sets of the people of the region, of their relations with the Indians, of their religious prejudices, and of their muted conflicts with the ruling class of wealthy and powerful landowners, some of whom, especially in Maryland, were "Papists."

Rumors must have circulated wildly throughout the winter, but the commotion in March was inflamed by Harrison's "examination" of some Piscataway Indians at the order of the Stafford court.

The results were reported as follows:

Here being some discourse that was talked by the Indians it was ordered by the Commision of Stafford Court that Mr. Burr Harris ---- come to the house of John West to examine them and the Indians doth declare that the great men of Maryland hath hired the Seneca Indians to kill the protestants nameing Coll. Darnall, Coll. Pye, and Mr. Boarman and further did sweare God Dam Mr Boarman he is all one [with] the Senecas. ---- Boarman did tell the Indians that the English would first of all kill the papists and then would kill all the Indians ---- and that they must make haste and kill the protestants before the shippes come in for after ---- the protestants would kill all the papists and then all the Indians.

The paper was dated March 16th 1688/9 and signed Burr BH Harris, Ralph R Platt, John West. West and Platt took several copies over to Maryland adding: "This is to give you all notice of a blow that will be given suddenly if not prevented by the Lord."

A few days later "further information given by Burr Harris as he returned from examination of the Indians" was supplied the Marylanders:

on Saturday last he met with a boate goeing up the River that came lately from St Maries and after inquiry what newes in those parts they told

*him that Coll. Pye was lately heard to say that he
did hope before Easter Day to wash his hands in
the protestants blood and that if he had the prince
of orange there he would thrust his sword up to the
beame in him.   And further ---- two or three
masters of shipps [were] looking out for Coll. Pye
to ---- transport him for England.   [The Puritans
in Boston did just that with their governor, Sir
Edmund Andros, when they received the "good
news" of the overthrow of James II.] ---- "yes-
terday came over from pomonky [in Charles
County] with him an Indian called Chicarter a
warr captaine that was going to Capt Brents and
told him Capt [George] Brent [a Catholic] had
sent for him. ---- the Indian told him that they
did heare the Englishmen in England had cutt off
their Kings head and ---- [an] abundance of
dutchmen [were] comeing ---- and that they
should bring abundance of Matchcoats and other
things with them.*

The account was signed Burr BH Harris at Potomacke
Creeke 19 March 1688/9.

Meanwhile in Stafford the residents took the situation so
seriously that they abandoned their farms and sought refuge in
the fort built and maintained for their protection during such
times of trouble.   A Maryland Councilman reported to his
colleagues "the people enfort themselves in Stafford ---- we
doe dayly here the beating of drums and vollyes of shott ----
they are all in armes [over] there." (27)

The final outcome of the matter is furnished by the minute
of the meeting of the Governor's Council on April 26, 1689.

*Whereas divers wicked and ill disposed persons
of the Counties of Stafford and Rapp. laying hold
of some false and extravagant reports ---- that
tenn thousand Seneca Indyans together with nine
thousand Nanticoaks were all landed & joyning
their forces with an immediate purpose of distroy-
ing all the Protestant inhabitants of Virg. and
Maryland ---- and forasmuch as John Waugh,
clerke, is reported to have been very instrumentall
in possessing the people with those imaginary
feares ---- and Bur Harrison and John West being
suspected to be the first contrivors & designers of
all those false and evill reports ---- It is ordered*

16

that Jno. Waugh, clk., Bur Harrison and Jno.
West be taken into custody of the Sheriff of Staf-
ford County in order to their being carried on
board his Majesties Ketch the Deptford" ---- to
determine whether they should be taken by the
ship to Northampton County or "committed to the
gaol at Stafford or let at liberty with good security
for their good behavior and appearance ----- at
the next General Court at James City.

The three accused were granted "bayle." Waugh is known to have made the required formal public apology at Jamestown, and probably West and Harrison did also. The minute continues:

forasmuch as it is vehemently suspected that
Capt. George Mason countenanced and encour-
aged these factious mutinous dangerous reports
---- resolved he be removed from being a Justice
of the Peace and discharged from his command in
the militia. (28)

Fairfax Harrison, an eminent amateur historian of northern Virginia, resurrected the episode in an article titled "Parson Waugh's Tumult" published in 1922. (29) This latter-day Harrison, not a descendant of Burr, took the side of law and order in his account. One can wonder, however, whether Spencer's report was not somewhat biased and self-serving. He had been named to his high post by his relative, Lord Culpeper, whom James II had appointed governor of Virginia and confirmed in the Proprietorship of the Northern Neck. Secretary Spencer must have been a bit uneasy about how the new authorities would treat him.

Definitely, local political differences were mixed in with the religious sentiments. For example, in 1680 a Stafford man related that he was at

Chopawamsick Church which is kept at Thomas
Barton's several of the company being together
before the sermon ---- some asked Mr. Waugh
[the rector] what newes from towne. Mr. Waugh
replied we had chosen Mr. Fitzhugh a Burgess
---- that he was for his own self-interest, for he
was one of the first which sided with the Governor
and Council about the 2 and 3d phhd [two shil-
lings threepence per hogshead of tobacco] to give

17

to the King and did neglect all the countrey's grievances. (30)

Before the year 1689 was out, both Spencer and Culpeper died. Nothing was ever done about the charges of murder and treason against Harrison and West. By the next year the Tory, William Fitzhugh, had been forced to resign his position as presiding justice of the Stafford court, and George Mason had become the second ranking member of that tribunal. Not long after, Mason was made commander of the militia. John West, Harrison's "partner in crime," soon afterwards was appointed an ensign in the militia.

Harrison may have had more than political differences with Fitzhugh. When the latter had been the lawyer in the attempt to eject Thomas Barton and the Widow Bennet from the Chopawamsic plantation, he began one letter: "Once more at the instance of Bur Harrison, I take opportunity to write to you." Another (to Secretary Spencer) commenced: "I am informed by Burr Harrison that you tax me of rashness in counselling him" to tear down the widow's house. It ended: "The man's importunity and my own vindication has drawn this letter to this prolixity." As far as is known, Fitzhugh never represented Harrison again.

Furthermore, a world of difference existed at the time between the social and economic status of a "planter" and that of a "Gentleman." Consider the account of a visit to Fitzhugh's house made at Christmas time in 1686 by Ralph Wormely, a member of the Governor's Council and the owner of an extensive estate on the Rappahannock. He was guiding two visitors, one of whom was an English lord and the other a French Huguenot, who wrote the account.

> *Mr. Wormeley is so esteemed in these parts that all the gentlemen of consideration in the countryside we traversed came to meet him and, as they rode with us, by the time we reached Col. Fitzhugh's we made up a troop of twenty horse. The Colonel's accomodations were so ample that this company gave him no trouble at all. We were all supplied with beds though indeed we had to double up. Col. Fitzhugh showed us the largest hospitality. He had a store of good wine and other things to drink and a frolic ensued. He called in three fiddlers, a clown, a tightrope dancer, and an acrobatic tumbler and gave us all the divertissement one could wish. It was very*

18

> *cold, but no one thought of going near the fire,*
> *because they never put less than the trunk of a*
> *tree upon it and so the entire room was kept warm.*

The partying went on "well into the afternoon" of the next day. It broke up only because the titled Englishman had an appointment in Maryland.

> *Col. Fitzhugh was hospitable to the last. He*
> *not only brought a quantity of wine and bowls of*
> *punch down to the shore there to serve us a parting*
> *glass but he also lent us a sloop. (31)*

As we have noted, the matter of the "Tumult" also gives an insight into relations between the colonists and the Indians. The choice of Harrison by the Stafford Court to "examine" the Piscataway tribesmen implies that he had some facility in the Algonquian Indian language or at least he had more acquaintance with members of the tribe than many other residents of the County. There are a few other supporting glimpses in the records, such as the bounty for a wolf killed by an Indian, payment in the county levy for a trip undertaken at the behest of the court "up-river" (no one but Indians lived more than twenty-five to thirty miles up the Potomac from Quantico), and the fact that one of his sons a decade later seems also to have known Algonquian.

There is no doubt that the average contemporary of Harrison feared the Indians greatly. We can be pretty certain that most of them subscribed to the adage that the only good Indian was a dead one, even though the governments at Jamestown and St. Mary's did attempt to protect Indian rights, especially those of such tribes as the Piscataways that had put themselves under the protection of the English.

However, the degree of justice afforded these wards of the state is suggested by an incident involving a neighbor of Harrison's a couple of years before the "Tumult." An Indian was discovered dead on the banks of the Chopawamsic. He had been shot in the back; hoofprints of a horse were found in the mud of the bank where he lay. At the inquest, the head-men of the tribe accused Thomas Norman of the deed. They pointed out that Norman was the only person who went hunting on horseback; an Indian would have used a tomahawk rather than a gun. The testimony was sent to the governor for disposition. His answer that the evidence was insufficient to prosecute Norman seems reasonable, but he might have refrained from adding that anyway the murdered man was not a Christian. (32)

One of the first acts of the newly formed Stafford court in 1664 had been to pass the following order:

> many sad accidents have happened by the Indians hunting in the woods as by firing the same [either to drive game in their direction or to clear land for planting] and particular persons do harbor them [as huntsmen or servants?]. The court doth order that no Indian by any person whatsoever shall be suffered to (enter) any part of the English habitation. (33)

Although this ordinance was later reversed so as to comply with an act of the Assembly, still during the Tumult Secretary Spencer with Richard Lee and Isaac Allerton, both also residents of Westmoreland County and members of the Governor's Council, wrote William Joseph, "president of the province of Maryland" asking him and the Maryland Council to

> forthwith order the Indians of your province of Maryland now ranging in Stafford County to re-paire to their respective Indian Townes and also please to command them not to pass over to the west and south side of potomack River and this request we make to satisfy the present feares and disquiets of the Inhabitants. (34)

Burr Harrison may have kept out of the limelight after the Tumult, but he did not stay out of court. A suit was brought against him by Robert Brent, a lawyer and a Catholic, whose life had been threatened by the rioters. It claimed that Harrison had appropriated three cattle "big with calf" that had belonged to Richard Nixon, in a conspiracy to hide them while Nixon fled the county. Brent had obtained a judgment against Nixon and had attached all his property. When Harrison produced a bill of sale by Nixon in payment of a debt of 2500 pounds tobacco, the justices ruled that his purchase had been made before the attachment and thus was "good, authenicke and valid in law." (35)

Undoubtedly, the same cows were those that Richard Gibson, another lawyer, charged Harrison with having spirited out of the county. Gibson had cosigned Nixon's bond for the administration of the estate of Richard Holmes, whose widow had married Nixon. Later, the man had departed the county, leaving the estate without assets. Gibson, as security, had been ordered to pay off the creditors, but given time to look for anything the man might have left behind. One result of the search was the complaint that

> before the inventory and appraisement had been returned, Burr Harrison fraudulently combined and conspired for avarice sake with the said Nixon to waste and embezzle the said [Holmes] estate and to that effect did take and accept from the said Nixon a bill of sale for all the said cattle ---- and all the consideration for this bill of sale was for a while to conceal the said Nixon in the county and then to provide the means for his escape. (36)

A deposition by Nixon's wife stated that "after Nixon was running away the said Burr Harrison sent his sonnes Thos. and Burre to drive away the cattle," but she added that Harrison had talked to Holmes, her previous husband, about buying the animals. (37)

After the justices ruled against him, Gibson demanded a jury trial. When this too exonerated Harrison, Gibson appealed the case to the "Lt. Governor and Honorable Council at Jamestown City." The final outcome is not known, but at least Gibson had succeeded in holding off the creditors of the estate for more than two years.

The variance between our modern concept of lawsuits as totally confrontational and that of colonial Virginians is epitomized by these two cases. Strange as it seems, when Harrison's lawyer died while conducting the defenses against Brent and Gibson, Brent took his place in the Gibson suit, while Harrison managed his own pleadings in the Brent suit, appearing "in persona" before the court. Furthermore, Gibson and Harrison were not only neighbors, but apparently friends, as indicated by a deposition made by William Borne during the period that the Gibson suit was before the court. Borne recounted that cider he had purchased from Matthew Dyke and failed to pay for had been drunk on the occasion of one of several back-and-forth visits made between people of Maryland and Borne, Richard Gibson, "Burr Harrison and his wife and all his family and Thomas Barton and his family." (38)

In 1688 the Nixons had sold Harrison two hundred acres on Great Hunting Creek including a large marsh. The land is in what is now the city of Alexandria. In fact its northern line eventually became a section of Duke St., a principal thoroughfare in the city. The transaction resulted in a suit brought by

Harrison in 1694. Elizabeth Nixon had been bequeathed the land by her father, John Alexander. Robert Alexander, her brother, had put off attempts by Harrison to get the parcel divided out of a larger tract. After more than four years had passed, a survey was started, but the next day Alexander refused to allow the county surveyor to complete the work, claiming that his father's will was invalid. If true, Robert, the eldest son, would have inherited the entire property under the law of primogeniture. The court ruled that the will was authentic, but then the defense claimed that the suit should have been brought against Robert and a brother, since the will had devised the other part of the tract to them jointly. In the end the court also rejected this argument and ordered the sheriff "to put Burr Harrison into quiet possession of his land." (39) The absence of favoritism on the part of the court is demonstrated by the fact that Alexander was one of the justices. He would have stepped down in a case in which he was involved, of course. Robert Brent, lawyer for the defense, had himself witnessed the deed to Harrison from the Nixons.

Most of the published genealogical data on the immigrant Burr Harrison assert that he died in 1706. Very likely, this conclusion dates back to the 1915 genealogy in the *Virginia Magazine of History*, which said, "... one account giving an impossible date as he was alive after it, states that he died in 1697 and another no doubt correct, gives it as in 1706. No will remains and no positive proof remains as to the date of his death." (40) Nevertheless, we now know that Harrison did die in 1697.

The confusion arose through ignoring the existence of a "Burr Harrison Jun'r" who in September 1692 won his suit against David Straughn. In the same session of the court, it was ordered that "Burr Harrison Sen." be paid for attendance in a case between Elizabeth Minithorne and John West.

The two suits provide further insight into the mores of the time. The occasion of the former is evinced by:

> the deposition of Anne Barton aged about twenty seven years beinge sworne ---- David Strahan and Burr Harris Junr. being at the sd deponts house went to cards and playing att putt at 60 or 70 per game a considerable time butt at length leavinge off David Strahan was six hundred poundes of tobacco looser wch the sd Strahan said he would pay to the sd Harris saying he [the winner?] had made a good after noons worke.

22

The reason for the elder Harrison's involvement in Minithorne vs. West is manifest in the formal complaint of the plaintiff:

> *Elizabeth Minithorne Widow complains*
> *against John West in plea of trespass for that the*
> *plt. hath long lived in this county in good fame*
> *and credit and hath retained the love and esteem*
> *of her good neighbors until Mr. John West of his*
> *malice aforethought minding not only to destroy*
> *her good name fame and reputation but also to*
> *bring her to an untimely & ignominious end did*
> *speak and utter these false scandulous and crimi*
> *nous words Vizt that your Pet[itione]r was a damd*
> *whore and had poisoned her husband Richd.*
> *Minithorne which words the deft. did often speake*
> *at divers places ---- and more particularly ---by*
> *way of dissuasion to Mr. Burr Harrison whom he*
> *thought to make love to your petitioner so that she*
> *is not only especially damnified in the advance of*
> *her fortune but also if the words were true lyable*
> *to suffer death ----.*

A jury awarded Mrs. Minithorne damages of 5000 pounds tobacco.

If the Widow Minithorne hoped to "advance her fortune" by marrying Harrison, it would mean that the previous Mrs. Harrison had died sometime in the two years that had elapsed since she had attended the parties with the Marylanders.

In March 1693 Burr Jr. entered a complaint against Jonathan Parker. Two months later Parker filed a suit against Burr Harrison Sr., claiming payment for cider bought of the deceased first husband of his wife. When the defendant refused to take an "oath upon the holy evangelists of almighty God that he had never received any sider," he was ordered to pay 295 pounds of tobacco. (41)

In colonial times and even later, senior and junior were used to distinguish between two men of the same name, not necessarily father and son. When one died, the appendage of the other was discontinued. After February 1694, there were no surviving court records until November 1699. Thereafter only a plain "Burr Harrison" remained.

That the elder Burr Harrison had died before November 1699 is proved by a 1741 deed in Prince William registering a division of the 1200-acre tract on the Occoquon that William Harris, Thomas Baxter, and Harrison had obtained in 1669. It recites that William Harris claimed "by survivorship" 450 acres of this tract that had not been sold previously, and by his will dated 24 March 1697/8 devised this land to his grand-daughters, Jane and Ann Owsley. (42) The law provided that a jointly owned grant could be sold in parcels or divided among the partners by new deeds. However, any part that remained unsold or undivided passed entirely to the surviving partner. Clearly, both Baxter and Harrison had died before Harris made his will. An accounting by the executor of Baxter's estate in 1699 has survived, but the books which would have shown the wills of Harris and Harrison, appointment and bonding of executors and their reports, and naming of appraisers and their inventories have all been lost.

In addition to this support from the will of William Harris, the family Bible of a great-grandson directly corroborates that the first Burr Harrison "departed this life in 1697." (43)

Unfortunately, no contemporaneous records remain with any information about Harrison's wife. Not even her first name is known, although a report claiming to be based on a journal of the Rev. Thomas Harrison, a great great-grandson, says she was Sarah Frances Burdette. (44) We have been unable to find the journal.

The absence of information about Mrs. Harrison is not unusual, since married women could not own real estate nor take legal action except through their husbands. Marriage records were kept by the parish church, not by the county. Indeed, the Act of Parliament requiring parishes of the Established Church to maintain registries of baptisms, marriages, and burials did not come into effect until 1664.

The couple had at least three children: sons Thomas and Burr Jr. named in Elizabeth Nixon's deposition, and a daughter Sybil known from a 1734 deed recording a sale from Thomas Whitledge of "200 acres on the south side of Chappawamsick run being land that his grandfather, Burr Harrison, bought from Maj. Richard Heabeard and willed to his mother, Sybil Whitledge." This deed also establishes that the immigrant died testate. The purchaser of the acreage was another grandson. (45)

It is likely that there were other children, for women married early and commonly had more than three children, if they lived long enough. Some genealogists have hypothesized that a William Harrison, who appeared in the Stafford records for the first time in 1700, was another son. This man was a partner of Burr's son Thomas in a 1707 land grant, but we have not been able to validate his parentage. (See Chapter XX.) Two other daughters are indicated by the use of the name Burr in the proper time frame to be grandchildren. Thomas Barton Jr., son of the man who questioned Harrison's title to his Chopawamsic plantation, had a son called Burr born after the turn of the century, too late to have been a godson of the immigrant, although he could have been sponsored by Burr Jr. Similarly, a Burr Wallis who died in 1736 may have been a grandson of the immigrant Burr. He was the son of John Wallis, who lived near the Chopawamsic. (Chapter XVII.) Another hypothesis has Sarah, the first wife of the John West of Waugh's Tumult as a daughter of Harrison. None of these proposals has ever been proved or disproved.

Reports that Burr Harrison was a justice of his county and even a burgess are without foundation. He was never referred to as Gentleman or by a military title, as were all the justices of his century. Furthermore, Harrison, despite the capacity that his accomplishments demonstrate, never learned to write. His signature as witness to the Jones will in 1660 was recorded as "Bur Harris his marke." All other known documents with a copy of his signature showed it as "Burr BH Harrison"; nobody of the period would have confused the "BH" with initials of middle names.

On the other hand, his sons, Thomas and Burr Jr., were both literate men who held important positions in the county. We wonder who educated the two. Could it have been their mother? More likely for the era, it was someone living nearby who had taken an interest in the boys. (46)

In summary, the first Burr Harrison was an unusually successful frontiersman, who improved his condition in life by his own efforts without the help of formal education, inherited wealth or social status, or a patron who would see to his advancement. On the base of his achievements a son would reach the highest position in the county. Many of his descendants, including several whose first name was Burr, have had distinguished careers. He may not have been a grandson or otherwise related to a Sir Thomas Harrison, Lord Mayor of York, or to a General Harrison of Cromwell's army executed for his part in the trial and beheading of King Charles I, as some descendants have hoped, but in his own right he can be counted among the founders of Virginia.

Notes:

1. La 1-152, 1654. This is the only reference to Burr Harrison in Lancaster. When Mr. Beverley Fleet wrote his *Virginia Colonial Abstracts*, Vol. 22, he commented in a note: "I must say that that entry took my breath away for an

instant." The only other reference to any Harrison in Book 1 (p. 146) is to a Ha. (Hannah or Harriet?) Harrison. Two months earlier William Nesham had been ordered to lodge her "until the next court when Geo. Beach is to appear and answer misdemeanors towards her and her brother."

2. La W-2-76, 1655. The inventory had a total worth of 17,502 pounds tobacco, 70% of which was the value of live-stock (4 draft oxen, 1 bull, 5 cows, 9 heifers, 1 steer calf and 1 cow calf, 4 sows, 18 shoats, and 8 pigs). La W-2-12, March 1654/5, pr. June 1655. Meades's will mentioned his wife, sons Thomas and John, and daughters Mary, Margaret, Joyce, and Anne, the last-named cut off with a bequest of one shilling. Son Thomas was living in Essex County in 1716.

3. W Records 1658-1661, p.103a., 1658. Hallowes had come to Maryland in 1634, moved to Virginia ten years later, and died in 1657. He had married Restituta Tue in 1639, before marrying Elizabeth, the widow of John Shurman. We have not seen the report on the archaeological excavations of his Westmoreland home, probably the site where Harrison served.

4. Ibid., p.104, 1658. Jones confirmed the testimony of John Dalton.

5. Ibid., 10/23/1660. Jones was 32 and had come to Virginia about 1648. Both Jones and Vauhan were planters; the latter died testate in 1663 leaving two minor sons, Samuel and William, and a son-in-law, John Watts.

6. G.H.S.King; *Records of Dettingen Parish, Prince William Co., Va. 1745-1802*, p.124. A page had been taken from the Overwharton Parish Register in the 18th century and attached to the first page of the Dettingen book, most likely by the immigrant's grandson, another Burr Harrison, who was named clerk of the vestry, when Dettingen was formed in 1741.

7. The originals and printed indexed copies of the registers are available in the library of Westminster Abbey.

8. In the parish of St. Martin's in the Fields, which adjoins St. Margaret's, the burial of a Cut'b't Harrison who died of the plague in August of 1563 and the marriage of Cutbertus Harrison and Agnete Ley in 1600 are recorded. Probably the younger Cuthbert was the grandfather of the immigrant Burr. The register of St. Margaret's notes burials of Thomas Harris who died of the plague in July, 1666 and Susan Harris who died in 1668. They may have been respectively the brother and mother of Burr, but the register gives no further information. One may guess that Burr was

26

the maiden name of the mother or a grandmother of the immigrant; the only references to a possible ancestor are burials of Robertus Burre in 1624 in St. Martin's and of Richard Borre in 1653 in St. Margaret's. However, neither Robert nor Richard was a name used by descendants of the immigrant Burr.

9. W Deeds and Wills, No. 1, pages unnumbered.
10. Ibid. 8/9/1661.
11. W Records, 1661-64. David Anderson lived at this time at Nominy, but he sold his plantation in 1664 to Col. John Washington and moved to Stafford. The tract purchased by Washington became part of Wakefield, the birthplace of the first president. Valentine Peyton, a justice and burgess of Westmoreland, died in 1665 without progeny. Later men of this name were descendants of his brother Henry.
12. Sarah K. Gilliam, *Virginia's People*, estimated that the population of the colony increased from 17,000 in 1650 to 33,000 in 1660 and 49,000 in 1680.
13. W Records 1661-64. 2/24/1663/4, 5/25/1664. St Records 1664-8, pp.21, 22, 25 and 31.
14. St Records 1680, p.21.
15. The St records book covering the period from 1686 to 1694 lost during the Civil War was recovered from a dealer in 1984 and is now in the State Archives in Richmond.
16. PW Land Causes, October 1790, p.42-43. Horsington's 1668 patent was on the south side of Powells Creek. 800 a. (2000 less 600 to Sneed and 600 to Harrison) was willed to his brother John, who devised it to his daughter Mary. When she died without heirs, the land "escheated" and was taken up in 1690 by George Brent and William Fitzhugh, the Proprietor's agents managing the land office in Stafford. Horsington resided in York County. We have been unable to determine how he became friendly with Harrison, although a daughter of a Giles Horsington was christened at St. Margaret's in 1649.
17. Nugent, *Cavaliers and Pioneers; Abstracts of Va. Land Patents II-75*, patent 6:295, 10/25/1669. Next year Harris and Baxter were granted 3000 acres on the Occoquan. Baxter died in 1692, aged fifty-five, survived by a son Thomas and wife Mary. Might she have been the transportee Mary Harris? Baxter was on the list of headrights for a 1655 Westmoreland patent. In 1677 he owned land on Powell's Creek and probably lived there.
18. W1 4-195. The large horizontal stone moved to the Pohick churchyard by the descendants of Harris's daughter Ann Owsley is still legible. "Herris" for Harris parallels the

British pronunciation of clerk, derby, and Berkeley.

19. St Records 1686-94 p.166, 1690. Bill of sale of young Negro man named Benjamin to serve Harris during his natural life and Harris's commutation to fourteen years of servitude signed "Benjamin negro seale" acknowledged and recorded. St Records 1689-93 p.145, 1691. Court order Lewis vs Harris.

20. *William Fitzhugh and his Chesapeake World, 1676-1701,* ed. Richard B. Davis, pp. 73-77. The lawyer Fitzhugh (1651-1701) came to Virginia about 1673. He took full advantage of his position as land agent of the Proprietors leaving at his death in 1702 54,000 acres to his sons. Capt. Giles Brent Sr. arrived in Maryland in 1634 and was once acting governor there. He resettled on the Virginia side of the Potomac about 1646. Although a Catholic and thus disqualified from holding any public office, he and his relatives were generally undisturbed in the community. He died in 1671. He had married the twelve-year-old daughter of a Piscataway chieftain, who had sent her as hostage for the tribe's allegiance to the English to a Jesuit mission at the Maryland capital, St. Mary's. Their son, Giles Jr., died in 1679 or 1680. His son, Giles III, died as a child. The Brent patent (4-402, 1662) for 1000 a. on Chopawamsic above the land of Walter Broadhurst renewed a 1658 grant. Thomas Barton remained a neighbor of Harrison purchasing land near the Chopawamsic on Quantico Creek in 1678. The other tenant could have been a Thomas Bennett who registered his mark for cattle in 1658 or a Jonas Bennett who resided in Stafford in 1666. Bennetts continued to live in the Quantico area through the 18th century. Gerrard Broadhurst was the son of Walter (1618-1659). His mother was Ann (Gerrard) Brett Broadhurst Washington. She married the widower Col. John Washington, a third marriage for each.

21. PW Land Causes 1833-44, pp. 13, 50, 71, etc. After the sale to Harrison, John Mathews either directly or by power to Capt. George Brent sold 260 a. to Ralph Smith, 100 a. to Thomas Meredith, 300 a. to John Waugh, 500 a. to Peter Beach, and 100 a. to Roger Davis. His son Samuel sold Ralph Smith 200 a. in 1706. All this land fronted on the N side of the Chopawamsic. The 5211 a. grant less 2000 a. was sold to John Holloway in 1715 and reassigned in three months to Robert "King" Carter. A suit by Carter's grandson in 1763 and another by the latter's heirs ending in 1839 produced surveys and depositions relating to Harrison's land, but the plats that might have shown more were not

filed with the court papers. St Records, 1686-94, pp.7, 58. Order for the road. Mathew Thompson was appointed a justice of Stafford in 1686. William Perkins died about 1705.
22. St Records, 1680, pp.16, 23, 26.
23. Charles County (Maryland) Liber M, pp.176 and 189.
24. St Records 1686-94, p.38, 1686/7. Both Platt and Beach were close neighbors of Harrison. Platt who had played a role in Parson Waugh's Tumult died childless in 1690. The estate account of Peter Beach was submitted in 1707. He was probably the son of William Beach, who owned land on the Chopawamsic in 1666.
25. Ibid., p.74, 1688. In 1692 Straughn was the lieutenant commanding the Rangers, a troop of ten horsemen who "ranged" over the back-country in times of trouble with Indians.
26. *British Colonial Papers, America and West Indies*, 13-32, items 92 & 93. John West was the oldest son of John and Susanna (Pearson) West. Parson John Waugh (1630-1706) was the controversial rector of Potomack (Stafford) Parish. He was involved in two scandals which reached the Stafford court. One was for marrying a widower to a nine-year-old girl, who obtained an annullment when she became 13. In the other Waugh's wife Elizabeth complained about Abram Beckington, who in front of witnesses at Waugh's house, when the Parson was away in Jamestown, called Mrs. Waugh a whore and claimed that he was the rightful father of her child. George Mason, the second of the name in Virginia and grandfather of the author of the Bill of Rights, was following in his late father's footsteps as one of Stafford's leading citizens. The first George Mason (1629-1686) arrived in Virginia before 1653 and achieved the offices of presiding justice, county lieutenant, and burgess in Stafford. The son also held these positions at various times before his death in 1717.
27. *Maryland Archives VIII*, pp.76-90.
28. Public Record Office, Kew, England. Ref.CO5/1405.
29. Fairfax Harrison, *Landmarks of Old Prince William*, p.127.
30. St Records 1680.
31. Fairfax Harrison, *Travels of a Frenchman in Virginia*, p.67. Translation of the journal of Eugene Durand.
32 St Records 1689-93, pp. 80, 85.
33. St Records 1664-68, p.12.
34. *Maryland Archives, VIII*, p.82.
35. St Records, 1689-93, pp.1, 9, 21, 35, 70, 91-93, 102, 153, 164 and 167 and 1686-94, p.190. Robert Brent was the

nephew of old Captain Brent and brother of Captain George Brent, William Fitzhugh's law partner. In 1692 he represented more clients than any other lawyer practicing in Stafford.

36. Ibid., pp.35, 98, 132-133, 137 and 192. Richard Gibson was the second busiest lawyer in Stafford at the time. He tried unsuccessfully in 1690-92 to require Brent to take the "oath" that he subscribed to the Church of England's doctrine on the Eucharist rather than the Roman Catholic belief. If Brent did not elect thereby to renounce his Catholic faith, Gibson wanted him barred from practicing in Stafford court. Both men lived near Harrison, and both died in 1696.

37. St Records 1686-94, p.170, Nov. 1690.

38. Ibid., p.190. Cider was evidently a favorite drink of the colonists, one of the items sold in taverns at prices fixed by the court.

39. Ibid., p.103. Also St D P-178. Capt. John Alexander, for whom the city of Alexandria is named, was on the first commission of peace for Stafford in 1664. He died in 1677 and his son, Robert, died in 1704.

40. V 23-214 ff. Other genealogies of the descendants of the immigrant Burr Harrison were published in the Richmond Times-Dispatch genealogical column of 9/13/1908; Hayden, *Virginia Genealogies*, p.512; and H.T. Harrison, *A Brief History of the First Harrisons of Virginia* (1915).

41. St Records 1689-93, p.263 (Barton deposition), p.294 (Minithorne), p.296 (Straughn), all in 1692; p.324 (B.H. Sr. and Parker) in 1692/3; p.334 (B.H. Jr. and Parker) in 1693. Ann (Green) Barton was the wife of Edward Barton.

42. PW D E-305. Jane and Ann Owsley were the daughters of Thomas and Ann (Harris) Owsley. He was clerk of court in Stafford when he died in Oct. 1700.

43. *Kentucky Bible Records*, Kentucky Genealogical Records Committee, DAR. 1948, pp. 10-22. The Bible belonged originally to Cuthbert Harrison, a great-grandson. (See Chapter IX.)

44. G.H.S. King papers, Virginia Historical Society, Mss 1k5823a, has a page of notes headed children of Burr Harrison--Sarah Frances Burdette, sent him in the 1930's by a Mrs. McFarland who quotes a letter to her by a Mrs. L.C. Hardy: "All of my notes and dates are from very old diary of my great-grandfather Rev. Thomas Harrison, who was born 1750, educated in London, Eng." Mrs. Hardy was Colonial Dame #1746. We have been unable to locate either the original journal or a copy.

45. PW D B-263, June, 1734. The grant to Richard Heabeard

of this tract is recorded in Patent Book 6:2, 10/26/1666. Heabeard was one of the first justices of peace for Stafford in 1664, and later was a vestryman along with John and William Heabeard. A John Heabeard was baptized in 1647 at St. Margaret's. Were the Heabeards instrumental in bringing Burr Harrison to America?

46. The magistrate Mathew Thompson, whose property adjoined that of the Harrisons, may have arranged for the education of the boys. Other possibilities include Robert Brent or his wife Anne, one of the few literate women of the period, Richard Gibson, the Rev. John Waugh, and John West Sr., the last two less likely since they lived farther away. Most of the other people who dwelt near-by were themselves illiterate.

Chapter II

Burr Harrison Jr. (ca.1668–ca.1715)
(Burr 2, Burr 1)

Until recently genealogists studying the immigrant Burr Harrison and his descendants did not have available a missing Stafford county record book recovered in 1984. So they did not know about the deposition made in November of 1690 stating that Burr Harrison sent his sons Thomas and "Burre" to drive off some cattle. Almost without exception they overlooked the existence of the second Burr Harrison, even though two men of that name, who had to be differentiated by the terms Junior and Senior, did show up in the Stafford court records in 1692 and 1693. The four extant cases of these designations appeared within a few pages of each other in the court minutes; the books for 1694 to 1697, which might have presented more, were lost.

Having missed these obscure data, some genealogists were forced to ascribe to the immigrant Burr Harrison Sr. astounding deeds for a man who, if alive, would have been in his sixties. He was assumed to have married at this stage in life a young widow, who died shortly afterwards. Almost immediately he married another widow. He became a junior officer of the Rangers charged with patrolling the outer limits of English settlement on the lookout for hostile Indians. He undertook an arduous journey to the uppermost end of the county in the company of a man who would have been less than half his age. In reality, these were not the deeds of the first Burr Harrison, for he had died. Instead, they were the actions of his son, Burr Harrison Jr. The original mistake was understandable; unfortunately, it became accepted as fact in several later genealogies.

In two related land grants issued in 1699 by the office of the Proprietors of the Northern Neck, the son was referred to as plain Burr Harrison with no Junior. The need for the special denomination had ended with the death of the father. The first patent stated:

> *William Mansbridge in 1697 died seized of a parcel of land situate on Quanticott [Quantico] Creek containing 200 acres. The same Mansbridge died without heir or disposing of his land otherwise than to Mary, his wife, for life, with whom the said Harrison hath intermarried and therefore the land escheats. The said Burr Harrison prays to be admitted tenant.*

The other grant was for an adjoining lot of 100 acres that also had belonged to Mansbridge. (1) Since Quantico Creek runs into the Potomac a couple of miles north of the mouth of the Chopawamsic, the tracts were close to the Harrison home plantation, on which Burr had grown up.

These two grants followed a common procedure for obtaining land from the Proprietors, who at this date were Marguerite, Lady Culpeper, the widow of Governor Culpeper; Thomas, 5th Lord Fairfax; and Catherine, his wife, sole heir of the late governor. Their agents in Virginia were William Fitzhugh and George Brent. When the holder of a grant died without a will and without legal heirs, as happened quite often in a period when wills were usually written on deathbeds, the grant was said to escheat, thereby reverting to the Proprietors. The widow had a right to use of the property during her lifetime, but could not dispose of it by sale, lease, or bequest, unless she had obtained a new patent on it in her own name. Buyers were on the lookout for such escheated lands; often they were picked up by the Proprietor's agents, themselves, who were in the best position to know what had become available. Neighboring landowners were also common purchasers. In this case Harrison had an inside track. Having married the widow Mansbridge, he did not have to wait until her rights had expired. He did have to pay the composition, basically a one-time payment for the patent, and any arrears of the annual quitrents pertaining to the tract.

Harrison's marriage to Mary Mansbridge was his second. Previously, he had been married to Lettis (Green) Smith, the widow of Edward Smith. Burr and Lettis were wed sometime in 1695 or 1696. She died in 1699, possibly in childbirth. In the 1940's a tombstone was found by Mr. George H.S. King near Woodbridge, Virginia on the south side of the Occoquan. (2) In a photo taken by Mr. King and now in his papers at the library of the Virginia Historical Society we saw:

```
TTIS  ERIS   TH
DAVGHTER  MR BV
RISO   DIED  MARC
THE  2  1698  AGED
16  DAYES
```

We think filling in the eroded letters would yield LETTIS
HERISON THE DAUGHTER MR BUR HERISON DIED MARCH
THE 2 1698 AGED 16 DAYES. Mr. King translated the inscription: "Lettis Harrison, Daughter of Mr. Burr Harrison, Died
March 2, 1698, Aged 16 Days."   New style the year would be
1699.

By her first husband Lettis had had three children; William, Edward, and Katherine. After his remarriage, Burr petitioned to be appointed guardian of the Smith orphans.   (3)
Later he posted a bond of 30,000 pounds of tobacco for the
management of the children's share of the estate of their
maternal grandmother. (4)

In November 1699 the widow Anne Carmalt indentured two
of her children to her "loving and good friend, Burr Harrison."
Bridget, seven years old, was to serve until she was seventeen,
unless she married before that birthday. Henry, aged five, was
bound until he came of age. The contract specified that the
children were not to serve anyone else, if Harrison should die.
(5) As in the case of the Carmalt children, poor orphans, if
boys, were apprenticed by their mother or by the churchwardens
of the parish to persons who could teach them a trade; if girls,
they were placed as household servants. In contrast, underage
heirs of a well-to-do man, such as Edward Smith, had guardians appointed by the courts to care for them and their estates.
An orphan boy, aged fourteen or older, could request the court
to name a guardian of his own choosing.

As we have noted, Burr Harrison Sr. probably had employed
Indians as hunters and servants and had acted on at least one
occasion as an interrogator of some friendly tribesmen.   Thus,
the younger Burr may have learned to speak Algonquian.   That
may be a reason he was chosen with a companion to undertake
a mission to the Chief of the Piscataway tribe.

The crisis that necessitated a journey to the Indian camp
had begun late in 1698, when the residents of Stafford, including Harrison, petitioned the governor and the General Assembly
sitting at Jamestown demanding that the "bloody villain,
Esquire Tomm ---- be brought in by the Emperor of Piscataway who entertains him and protects him from condign punishment." "Squire Tom" was a Pamunkey Indian who the year

before had killed the wife of William Wigginton. (6)

Governor Nicholson in answer ordered the justices of Stafford to send one or more messengers to the Emperor, "who had fled from his Majesty's province of Maryland with his nation of Indians about two years ago." They were to command the chieftain to appear before the governor in two months' time and to give a full account of their journey and their observations at the Indian fort. (7)

Immediately the justices replied that they had selected "two substantial persons inhabitance of this county to wit Mr. Giles Vandecasteel and Mr. Burr Harrison" to be the emissaries. (8) The two "ambassadors" submitted a full report, as soon as they got back from their undertaking.

> *In obedience to his Excellency's [the governor's] command and an order of this court we, the subscribers, did meet with the Emperor of Piscattaway at his fort [stockade] and did then command him, in His Majesty's name, to meet his Excellency in a General Assembly of this his Majesty's most ancient colony and dominion of Virginia the first of May next or two or three days before with some of his great men. As soon as we had delivered his Excellency's command, the Emperor summons all his Indians that was then at the fort ---- being in all about twenty men. After consultation of almost two hours, they told us they were very busy and could not possibly come or go down, but if his Excellency would be pleased to come to him, some of his great men would be glad to see him and then his Ex'lly might speak what he hath to say to him & if his Excellency could not come himself, then to send some of his great men, for he desired nothing but peace. They live on an island in the middle of the Potomac River; it's about a mile long or something better and about a quarter of a mile wide in the broadest place. The fort stands at the upper end of the island but not quite finished & there the island is not above two hundred and fifty yards over; the banks are about 12 feet high and very hard to ascend. Just at the lower end of the island is a lower land and little or no bank; against the upper end of the island two small islands, the one on the Maryland side, the other on this side which is about four acres of land & within two hundred yards of the fort, the other*

35

smaller and something nearer, both firm land &
from the main [riverbank] to the fort is about four
hundred yards at least ---- not fordable except in
a very dry time; the fort is about fifty or sixty
yards square and there is eighteen cabins in the
fort and nine cabins without the fort that we could
see. As for provisions they have corn; they have
enough and to spare. We saw no strange Indians,
but the Emperor says that the Genekers [Senecas]
live with them when they are at home; also adds
that he had made peace with all the Indians
except the French Indians; and now the French
have a mind to lie still themselves, they have
hired their Indians to do mischief. The distance
from the inhabitance is about seventy miles, as we
conceive by our journeys. The 16th of this instance April, we set out from the inhabitance and
found a good track for five miles, all the rest of
the day's journey very grubby and hilly, except
some small patches, but very well for horse, though
not good for carts, and but one run of any danger
in a fresh, [freshet] and then very bad; that night
lay at the sugar land [an area along the river
where the Indians made maple sugar] which judge
to be forty miles. The 17th day we set the river
by a small compass, and found it lay up N.W.B.N.,
and afterwards set it and always found it near the
same course. We generally kept about one mile
from the river and about seven or eight miles
above the sugar land we came to a broad branch
[still known as Broad Run] of about fifty or sixty
yards wide, a still or small stream, it took our
horses up to the bellies, very good going in and
out; about six miles farther came to another great
branch [Goose Creek] of about sixty or seventy
yards wide with a strong stream making fall with
large stones that caused our horses sometimes to be
up to their bellies and some times not above their
knees so we conceive if a fresh then not fordable;
thence in a small track to a smaller run, about six
miles indifferent very, and so held on till we came
within six or seven miles of the fort or island and
then very grubby and great stones standing above
the ground like heavy cocks [haystacks], they
hold for three or four miles and then short ridges
with small runs until we came to ye fort or island.

36

*As for the number of Indians, there was at the fort
about twenty men & about twenty women and
about thirty children, & we met four [en route].
We understand there is in the inhabitance [Eng-
lish settlements] about sixteen. They informed us
there was some out hunting but we judge by their
cabins there cannot be above eighty or ninety
bowmen in all. This is all we can report, who
subscribe ourselves*
    Your Ex'lly most dutiful servants,
    GILES VANDECASTEEL   ·
    BUR HARISON   *(9)*

The report allows the route taken by Vandecasteel and
Harrison to be traced. Their point of departure was apparently
north of the Occoquan river in what is now Fairfax County. The
sugarland where they camped the first night is some twelve
miles southeast of Leesburg. Sugarland Creek retains the
name. The Indian village probably was on what is now called
Heater Island near Point of Rocks, Maryland.

The following November, David Straughan and Giles Tillet
repeated the journey, finding conditions much the same. The
Emperor said he and his people would like to live among the
English again, but he was afraid that "strange" Indians urged
on by the French would follow them and "do mischief amongst
the English," for which he would be blamed. (10)

His fears of an attack on the colonists by foreign Indians
were justified. Within six months Colonel George Mason, the
man removed from his captaincy in the militia during Parson
Waugh's Tumult but now the county lieutenant commanding the
whole force, had to send the following urgent report to the
governor:

*On Sunday the 16th [of June 1700], about 3 of
the clock in the afternoon came about twenty or
thirty Indians to Thomas Barton about 20 miles
above my house. The man and his wife and brother being abroad, & left his 3 children & an orphan
boy at home, & had got a man and his wife &
children from a plantation of mine, about 2 miles
from him, to stay to look after his house until they
came home. The Indians fell on them & killed
Barton's 3 children, the man and his wife & his 3
children. The orphan boy ran away, he being out
at play, blessed be God, got to a neighbor's house
& is safe. They killed them with arrows & wooden*

37

*tomahawks;------. This murder was the horrablest
that ever was in Stafford-----has almost frightened our people out of their lives and interests, &
besides, the Emp'r & his Indians being still out,
w'h did as surely done the murder as God's in
heaven. (11)*

Governor Nicholson was not ready to accept Mason's charge
that it was the Piscataways who had committed the outrage.
Two representatives sent under his direct orders reported that
the emperor spoke in English as well as the Indian tongue,
exhibited considerable dignity and intelligence, as could be
deduced from his handling of the command carried by Vandecasteel and Harrison, and insisted his people did not perpetrate
the massacre. (12)

Early in July Mason reported that he had placed six men
and Ensign Giles Vandecasteel to range from Pohick to the
uppermost inhabitants (in the area now Alexandria) "and Cornet
Burr Harrison from Occoquon down to Potomac Creek with two
officers and men doth give good content. ---- The inhabitants
still continue from their houses [presumably in the fort] but
abundantly better satisfied" now that the Rangers were active.
(13)

Forts for protection from the Indians had been constructed
on both the Rappahannock and the Potomac before 1671. The
Rangers were established about 1690. A troop at the head of
each large river consisted of one lieutenant, eleven soldiers
and two Indians. The lieutenant was paid 5000 pounds tobacco
per year, the soldiers three thousand. Each had to furnish his
own horse, arms, ammunition, and provision. The Indians were
paid eight yards of "duffils" (a coarse woolen cloth) and two
barrels of Indian corn annually. The lieutenant was charged
with procuring a horse, bridle, and saddle for each Indian.

Just how long Harrison's troop continued its rounds, which
had been started at four days a week, is unknown, but there was
no more trouble that year. As far as we know, Squire Tom was
never captured, nor were the Indians who killed the innocents at
Barton's plantation ever identified. Apparently, the Piscataway
sachem was absolved of complicity in either crime. Descendants of his nation's people still live in an isolated region along
the upper Potomac.

Both Burr and Mary Harrison must have been relieved when
these taxing duties in monitoring the Indians were over.
Perhaps a crop failure occasioned by the Indian troubles or
maybe just the expense of maintaining a wife and three orphans
left Harrison short of cash. Whatever the reason, in December

38

1700 he sold six hundred acres of land on Powells Creek for 7000 pounds of tobacco. (14) This tract was the one his father had been given by Robert Horsington in 1668. Surprisingly, the price that the first Burr obtained for the adjoining six hundred acres that he sold for Horsington in 1670 was also 7000 pounds tobacco. Evidently land in the area had not appreciated in terms of tobacco in thirty years.

As required by law, Mary Harrison relinquished her "dower rights" to one-third of her husband's land. For this purpose, an impartial witness was required to interview her out of the presence of her husband. Her release was appended to the deed. "I, Mary Harrison, wife of Burr Harrison, by these [presents] authorize David Straughan to acknowledge my third of 600 acres on the so. side of Powell's Creek to James Bland living at Poplar Hill in St. Mary's county." Mrs. Harrison made her mark.

Other references to the second Burr Harrison include a power-of-attorney given him in 1705 by Margaret Chapman, the wife of Thomas Chapman Sr. Through her dower rights in a third of the property of her first husband, William Perkins, the Chapmans had an interest in a tract of land known as Freestone Point. They were relinquishing their claim in favor of William Perkins (Jr.), undoubtedly her son. We suppose Mrs. Chapman was unable to appear in the court and appointed her friend Harrison to act for her. (15)

In another instance, Richard Hatfield, an Indian, indentured himself to Harrison for seven years. He was to serve his master as if he were an "imported servant" at whatever "lawful" work he was set to do. If he ran away or otherwise failed to live up to the contract, the customary penalties (mainly a punishing extension of the term of servitude) would apply. Harrison was to furnish Richard good and sufficient meat and drink, washing, and lodging, a horse, a suit of clothes, two shirts and a pair of shoes. A further condition of the contract was that Hatfield be taught to read and write in English. (16)

One of the last known records of Burr Harrison Jr. is found on an indenture by the churchwardens of Overwharton Parish of a newly born bastard mulatto child named Mary Allenson, "until she shall accomplish the years of 31." To modern eyes, this appears to be harsh and unjust, but the participants thought it an act of kindness (mixed maybe with a little self-interest). The document begins:

> whereas the law directs that care be taken by
> the churchwardens or overseers of the poor that the
> poor children whose friends are not able to main-

*tain them or otherways may happen to have no
friends at all to look after them and lest they be
brought up in idleness as wandering beggars and
become chargeable to this parish.*

George Mason Jr. was the person to whom the baby was
entrusted. The indenture was signed by the churchwardens,
Edward Mountjoy and John West, and witnessed by Burr Harrison and George Mason, who likely were vestrymen as care of
the poor was the responsibility of the parish vestry. (17)

The final traces of Burr Jr. were three appraisals made in
March 1708/9 of the estates of James Bland, Andrew Delaps,
and Mathew Perkins, and a supplemental inventory of Bland's
taken two months later. None of the three had any slaves or
indentured servants. Bland, the purchaser of the land on Powell's Run, had left personal property worth about 25,000 pounds
of tobacco, including a crop of tobacco valued at 8105 pounds.
The other two appraisals were for only 3264 and 2100 pounds
respectively. Perkins was probably the son of Margaret
Chapman, for his estate account was presented by William
Perkins. Against his meagre inventory, the account showed
expenses of 500 pounds tobacco for attention in his sickness
and dinner for people at his burial, 200 for a shirt and sheet in
which to bury him, 400 for a coffin, and 250 for fees paid to
settle the estate. The account for Jacob Gardiner presented at
the same court session noted that his widow paid 1000 pounds
for a "coffin, sheets, and other expenses at his funeral" out of
a total estate of 3834 pounds. (18) No wonder widows remarried quickly.

From September 1709 until 1721 all Stafford court records
have been lost. Harrison must have died between those years.
That he had made a will is evident from a 1739 deed describing
that he had left two hundred acres on the north side of Quantico
Creek to George, Burr, and Thomas Calvert alias Harrison.
The tract was the one he had acquired after marrying Mary
Mansbridge. (See Chapter XV.)

Harrison's Smith stepchildren survived to adulthood. William received a bequest of land from Martin Scarlett Jr. in
1725. Edward became a mariner. Katherine married John
Hancock. One wonders what became of Mary Mansbridge
Harrison, the Carmalt children, and the Indian, Richard Hatfield. Either history passed them by without further mention or
the vandalizing of the Stafford court records eliminated any
chance of knowing more about them. The second Burr Harrison
almost shared their fate of being lost to posterity, even though
he was a literate, responsible, and respected member of his

community. His history deserves a place in the memory of his descendants.

Notes:

1. NN 2-305, 1699/1700. William Mansbridge had purchased both lots from Thomas Days. In one deed the name of the latter is spelled Dyass, which may give a clue to its pronunciation in the seventeenth century. One of the two lots adjoined land of Thomas Barton Jr. For some reason Harrison did not request a patent on another near-by 100 a. that Mansbridge had bought in 1687. It was not until 1729/30 that Richard Britt obtained an escheat grant of the land.
2. G.H.S. King Papers, Collection in the Virginia Historical Society Library. The late Mr. King was a careful genealogist who studied various colonial families of northern Virginia for over forty years. He recognized the existence of Burr Harrison Jr., but uncharacteristically assigned him a death date of ca. 1721 based on the reference to "Harrison's will" on page 99 of lost Liber L in the General Index of Stafford Wills. There is little doubt this pertains to William Harrison Sr. Mr. King's papers are an invaluable source for any genealogist working in the area.
3. St Z-63, April, 1699. Lettis (Green) Smith Harrison was the daughter of William and Ann Green. Her father had arrived in Stafford Co. before 1670, when he received a grant of 1150 acres on Pohick Creek for the transport of twenty-three persons including himself and his son of that name. He died before 1685, and his widow married Martin Scarlett, a political rival of William Fitzhugh. Edward Smith, Letiss's first husband, died about 1695. When Ann Green Scarlett, grandmother of the Smith children, died in 1698, she named her son Joshua the executor of her estate. But in quick succession he and his widow, Jane Green, also died. George Mason was appointed Jane's executor. Mrs. Scarlett in October 1696 had deeded Joshua a tract on Occoquan Bay with the proviso that if he died without heirs, it was to pass to his sisters Ann and Lettice. Their husbands, Burr Harrison Jr. and Edward Barton, witnessed the deed.
4. St Z-149, Oct. 1702. Edward Barton had signed a similar bond for his children by Ann (Green) Barton, one of the sisters of Lettis Harrison.
5. Ibid. Z-3, Oct. 1699. The Widow Carmalt indentured her 11-year-old son John to Edward Barton at the same time.

41

6. *Calendar of State Papers*, 1–60, Nov. 1698. Although Burr Harrison signed with no "Jr.," he did not have to make his mark; thus he was the son and not the immigrant, who had died the previous year.

7. Ibid. 1– 62. See also Goolrick, *The Story of Stafford*.

8. Ibid. 1–63.

9. Ibid. 1–64. The reference gives Vanderasteal and in another place Vandicastille as the name for Harrison's companion. The spelling we have used seems to be the most common in original records. The will of Vandecasteel was proved in March 1699/1700, less than a year after the mission. Vandecasteel lived just north of the Occoquan on part of the "Harrys–Baxter–Harrys" patent.

10. Ibid. 1–67, 1699.

11. Ibid. 1–69, 1700. This Thomas Barton could have been either the one who may have married the sister of Burr Harrison Jr. or the orphaned son of Nathan Barton. (See Chapter XVII.)

12. Ibid. 1–70, 7/3/1700.

13. Ibid. 1–71, 7/10/1700

14. St Z–108, 1700.

15. St Z–279, 1705.

16. St Z–315, 1706.

17. St Z–390, 1707. The term of the indenture, until age 31, was fixed by the Assembly for illegitimate mulatto children. George Mason Jr. was not the son of the witness, Colonel George Mason II, but instead was George Mason of Aquia, whose relation to the Masons of Gunston Hall has not been determined. Hayden gives 1690 as the date of birth of George Mason III. At age seventeen he could not have signed the indenture.

18. St Z–464 (Bland), 465 (Delap), 466 (Perkins). Only Bland owned land. The Bland family continued to own the 600-acre part of the Horsington patent at the mouth of Powell's Creek on its S side; in 1770 it belonged to Davis Bland Jr.

Chapter III

Thomas Harrison (1665-1746) of Prince William
(Thomas 2, Burr 1)

The page of the vestry book of Dettingen Parish that gives the date of birth for the immigrant, Burr Harrison, also notes that "Thomas, the son of said Burr Harrison, was born September the 7th day, 1665 and departed this life on the 13th day of August at 2 in the morning, 1746." This man's lifespan of eighty-one years covered almost half the period between the first settlement at Jamestown and the Declaration of Independence. In his lifetime, the population of Virginia increased sevenfold from 35,000 to about 235,000. The frontier in northern Virginia moved from the area where he was born, a few miles from the Potomac, across the Blue Ridge into the Valley of the Shenandoah. Having begun life as the child of a small farmer working rented land, Thomas Harrison became the largest grower of tobacco in his county and reached the posts of commander of the county militia and presiding justice of its court. His career demonstrates that upward social mobility on the frontiers of America began well before the Revolution.

In following the life of this Thomas Harrison, the problem is how to distinguish him from contemporaries of the same name in the region. A Thomas Harrison purchased land in Stafford from William Green in January 1685/6. (1) The buyer could not be Burr Harrison's son, who was not yet twenty-one and therefore could not buy real estate. When Sarah Matheney was ordered in November, 1690 to pay Thomas Harrison 80 pounds tobacco for two days attendance at court, it is impossible to ascertain which man was the witness. (2) When the lengthy legal struggles of Burr Harrison Sr. with Robert Brent and Richard Gibson were decided in 1691, Thomas Harrison, obviously Burr's son, was paid for his attendance as a witness in the Brent case. However, in the other suit, Gibson subpoen-

43

aed him to testify to what he knew of the matter, and when he did not appear, he was fined 350 pounds tobacco. (3)

Because so many of the Stafford records are missing, the next mention of Thomas Harrison is found in 1700, when he signed a petition to Governor Nicholson from the civil and military officers of the county requesting "a forse to range and scoute on the fronteares." (4) Harrison was one of four militia captains under the command of Colonel George Mason, Lt. Colonel Rice Hooe, and Major William Fitzhugh. The other captains were Charles Ellis, George Anderson, and John West. (5) From then on Thomas, the son of Burr, was usually referred to as "Captain"; after 1731 as "Colonel." In court documents he was termed Gentleman, distinguishing him from others of the name who were "planters." He and his son were the only Thomas Harrisons of the period in northern Virginia who could sign their names; three others made their marks.

Several records naming Captain Thomas Harrison add to the picture of life in the first decade of the eighteenth century. He was among the buyers at an "outcry" (auction) of William Betty's estate. (6) Such sales of part or all of the deceased's personal property were common, especially when the assets of an estate were insufficient to satisfy the creditors. Captain Thomas witnessed a deed, whereby a young neighbor, Samuel Gibson, aged twenty-two, sold land inherited from his father, the lawyer Richard Gibson. (7) The county accounts for 1701 showed he was paid 800 pounds tobacco for the heads of three wolves; one each killed in a trap, by gun, and by pit. The Captain was one of twenty-two prominent citizens of Stafford signing a memorial of condolence to Queen Anne on the death of her brother-in-law, King William of Orange. (8) In 1706 Charles and Mary Christmas apprenticed to Harrison her son, Thomas Cross, until he reached the age of twenty-one. A codicil to the indenture required "Harrison and his heirs to bring this said Cross to read." (9)

About 1700 Captain Harrison left the Chopawamsic area to live at Hunting Creek, twenty-five miles or so to the north within the present city of Alexandria, on the land bought by his father from the Nixons. That this area was less settled than the older parts of the county may explain why Harrison collected the bounties on so many wolves. There is a bit of a mystery about his move. Why did he leave his late father's plantation on the Chopawamsic, to which he returned after only three years and which he bequeathed to his eldest son? Maybe his mother was still alive and utilizing her dower rights to the family's home plantation. Harrison had recently married, and his bride may have wanted a home of her own. They might

44

have returned after the mother died.

Soon after his return from Hunting Creek, Captain Thomas began a flurry of land purchases from the Proprietors. Their agent in Virginia was now Colonel Robert "King" Carter, king because of the enormous land holdings he arranged to obtain for himself and his family through the office. In 1705 Harrison in association with Thomas Walter received a grant of 112 acres on the Occoquan River and Morumpsco Creek "just below the main road." (10) His next purchase was made through a syndicate composed of John West, William Harrison, Thomas Pearson, and himself, which was granted 4639 acres on Hunting Creek in 1706. (11) Fairfax Harrison in *Landmarks of Old Prince William* opined that the partners were kinsmen and that John West was probably married to a daughter of Burr Harrison, the immigrant. West and Pearson were definitely cousins, West's mother being a Pearson. According to family tradition, the two Harrisons were brothers, but this has not been confirmed (nor refuted). Similarly, no proof has been found that West or Pearson was an in-law of either.

A plat of this property has survived showing how the partners divided the tract into eight equal pieces. Each partner received two of these, those of Thomas Harrison being on the opposite uppermost corners of the U-shaped plot. Harrison sold half of each of his pieces to Captain Simon Pearson, son of the partner in the patent, in 1718. (12)

The survey for the division started at a "pickhiccory" (pignut hickory) and ran through twenty-seven angles, most of which were marked by trees; there were seven white oaks, four red oaks, four "Spanish" (southern red) oaks," three black oaks, two hickories and one maple. (13) They were probably representative of the composition of the virgin deciduous forest covering the region at the beginning of the eighteenth century.

After the grant to the partnership the Captain on his own account obtained 294 acres in the fork of the Chopawamsic main run adjoining land belonging to William Brent, on which Harrison held a "lease-for-lives." (14) A year later with Abraham Farrow he patented 800 acres on branches of the Chopawamsic and Quantico Creeks. The deed mentioned a path which went from Thomas Harris's to Quanticutt (Quantico) Mill. (15)

Captain Harrison received his last patent from the Proprietors in 1710 in partnership with his brother-in-law, Thomas Whitledge, husband of his sister Sybil. (16) The 938 acres on Cedar Run were later split into quarters, two non-adjacent ones going to each partner following the pattern of the Hunting Creek division. (17)

In 1724 the register of Overwharton Parish has a list of quitrents paid to the Proprietors. Capt. Thomas Harrison paid on 1639 acres. On 200 acres more the fees were paid by his eldest son Burr with the notation that the land belonged to Capt. Harrison. (18) His share of the five land-grants less the sale to Simon Pearson totalled 1799 acres. Since title to the lands held by the first Burr Harrison traced back to original grants by the administration of the colony rather than ones by the Proprietors' office, property that Captain Thomas had inherited was probably not subject to quitrents to the Proprietor. The difference of only 40 acres suggests that the grants accounted for almost all his acquisitions of land.

Also in the Overwharton register is a census of tobacco planters made in accord with a 1723 law regulating the planting of tobacco in an attempt to maintain its value as the principal export of the colony. The statute limited production to no more than 6000 plants per laboring person plus 3000 per male between the ages of ten and sixteen. The type of tobacco grown is given as Arronoco. In the part of the parish between Aquia and Quantico Creeks, Harrison was growing 44,929 plants with six men and four boys, including himself and his son Thomas Jr. Two of the men and two boys were Negroes. He was the largest grower in the area. His married son Burr and two men working a separate farm had 11,042 plants. (19)

This tobacco census confirms that by 1723 new immigrants paying for their crossing of the Atlantic by an indenture contract had become difficult to obtain. Convicts exiled from Britain were the major new source of agricultural labor. Slaves, mostly coming from the British West Indies, were not yet common in the region north of the Rappahannock. In contrast, when a son of the Captain died fifty years later, his estate counted more than seventy-five slaves.

The public career of Captain Thomas, except for his militia service, did not begin until he was fifty years old. Infrequent lists of the commissions of peace for Stafford County show he was not a justice in 1714, but had become one by 1726. In 1729 he was second in the commission after Dade Massie. (20)

When the new county of Prince William was formed out of Stafford in 1731, with the Chopawamsic being its southern boundary, Harrison, now sixty-five, headed its list of thirteen magistrates. (21) In addition, the governor appointed him county lieutenant, commander of the militia with the rank of colonel. He continued as the presiding justice until his death, although in the final years of his life the designation was evidently honorary. In fact, Dennis McCarty, number two in rank officially, was called first justice on a receipt for an administrator's bond in 1740. (22) In the commission named for Prince William in 1742, after Fairfax County had been split off, Harrison remained as first justice with Robert Jones and Thomas Harrison Jr. following in order. (23) On a 1743/4 bond Jones was termed first justice. (24) Because the court order books for the period from the formation of Prince William in 1731 until 1750 have been lost, we cannot tell when or to what extent the state of the old gentleman's health allowed him to attend the monthly court sessions or prevented him from doing so.

Harrison's service as the commander of the county militia was interrupted in 1741, when William Fairfax came to reside in the county. Fairfax, who was a relative of the Proprietor, Lord Fairfax, and his agent in the land office, was made the county lieutenant. The next year he became the first county lieutenant of the new Fairfax County, set off from Prince William, and Harrison was restored to the position in Prince William. Presumably, this time the office was given to recognize his long service and to avoid political problems in choosing among the younger leaders of the county. When Harrison died in 1746, he was succeeded as presiding justice and as county lieutenant by his son Thomas.

In 1732 the now Colonel Harrison faced an uprising similar to that in which his father had been accused of being a ringleader forty years earlier. Ironically, this time he was the person charged with restoring order. A minute of the Governor's Council noted receipt of an express letter from the colonel advising that "a number of the meaner sort of people of that county [Prince William] consisting of fifty men were got together in arms designing to destroy the public warehouses in that and the adjacent counties expecting to be joined by other malcontents from the neighboring counties." To suppress the insurrection, the Council ordered that the commanding officers of the militia in the counties of the Northern Neck should call together their troops, read the Act establishing the militia and inform them that they were bound to march against the mutineers, if the rebels did not lay down their arms. (25) Evidently, these orders were successful, for nothing more was heard of the affair in the proceedings of the Council.

In 1737 the Council noted "whereas information is given to this board that Colo. Thomas Harrison of Prince William County may be a material witness to prove the boundarys between His Majesty and the Lord Fairfax as the same have been constantly held and respected since the granting of the Northern Neck, it is ordered that the Clerk of the Council write"

Harrison asking him to attend the next court in Williamsburg and assuring him that his expense and trouble should be amply repaid. (26)

The dispute between the government of the Colony and the sixth Lord Fairfax, who was now sole Proprietor of the Northern Neck and had come over to Virginia to look after his interests, began when Governor Spotswood made a land grant in the northern Shenandoah Valley to set up a buffer against the Indians. The boundaries of the Proprietorship had been fixed by its charter as lying between the Rappahannock and Potomac Rivers from their headwaters to their confluence. When King Charles II made the gift to his friends in 1664, no one had the least idea where those headwaters were, nor did they in 1689 when King James II reconfirmed the charter. A commission was set up comprising representatives of each side, with Colonel William Byrd of Westover heading the colonial government's group. By 1737 it had been agreed that the Rappahannock began at a spring in the Blue Ridge in what is now Madison County, Virginia. This spring discharges into the Rapidan, which is the southern fork of the Rappahannock. The government side argued that the headwaters of the Potomac were at the confluence of the Shenandoah and the Potomac, now Harpers Ferry. Their main justification was that the Indians used the name Potomac only to that point, calling the two branches by other names, Sherando and Coonemara.

Harrison's testimony was intended to strengthen the government's case. He stated that he had lived "ever since he was a child" on the plantation where he was then living on Chopawamsic Run about forty miles below the falls of the Potomac, except for three years when he lived at Hunting Creek. In 1675 that creek, some fifteen miles below the Falls, was roughly the upper limit of settlement on the Potomac, but the few families living there had been forced to withdraw back down the river during the war with the Susquehanna Indians. He had first heard of the Falls about ten years later, but it was not until he himself moved to Hunting Creek "about 36 or 37 years ago" (i.e. around 1700) that people began to venture to the Falls to fish. Before then the Indians had frightened off anyone who had attempted to go so far. The point was that when James II had confirmed the charter, people knew only vaguely of these falls, still a very long way from where the Potomac began. Harrison was paid five pounds, seven shillings, sixpence for "attending at Williamsburgh."

The final verdict was given in England in 1745. It very much favored Lord Fairfax. With respect to the beginnings of the Potomac, the North Branch (which divides Virginia and

West Virginia from Maryland) was chosen. From its headspring (located on today's maps as the southwesternmost point in Maryland) a west-east line was drawn to the spring in the Blue Ridge fixing the area of the Proprietorship at 5,282,000 acres. Part of the dividing line is visible on current maps as the northern boundary of Rockingham County. The solution avoided problems with the governor's numerous grants south of the line in Augusta County, of which Rockingham was then a part. The governor no longer was permitted to authorize grants to the north of the line. Lord Fairfax was supposed to honor the few that already had been made there, but he did not comply, nor did he correct a few grants he had made just south of the line. Some of the resulting law suits dragged on until the turn of the century.

Harrison's clear deposition coupled with the fact that he was able to undertake the journey to the capital demonstrate that he was still physically vigorous and mentally capable at age seventy-two. During his long life he had made and kept several good and loyal friends. One of them was John West, partner in the land purchase and the man who had been charged as co-conspirator with Harrison's father in Waugh's Tumult. West was commissioned ensign about 1690, made lieutenant in 1692, and became captain some years before Harrison in the 1690s. Eventually he reached the rank of major. He was a few years older than his friend, as he had a son born before 1683, when Harrison was only eighteen. West died early in 1717. In his will he asked his friends Capt. Thomas Harrison and William Simon to assist his wife in administering his estate and in bringing up and educating his son John "in the reformed religion according to the Church of England." Apparently he had reason to be worried about the religious aspect of this charge. His young widow had been married first to a Turley, and the Turleys were Catholics. Thirty years later the Fairfax County list of titheables noted that John West (the son) was formerly a "Papist" but lately a vestryman.

Besides witnessing to the esteem in which West held Harrison, this will provides the only remaining record of the given name of the Captain's wife. Among the bequests is one to "Seith Harrison, the wife of Captain Thomas Harrison," of 500 pounds tobacco to buy a mourning ring. Such rings of gold or silver had an enameled band with the name of the deceased, his age at death, and the date of death. Bequests for this purpose by wealthy persons were a fairly common practice in Virginia as well as England during the eighteenth century. Other dispositions in West's will included a young horse to Will Harrison Jr. (son of the partner in the land grant); the gun that "I commonly use" to Burr Harrison, the son of Captain Thomas Harrison; two cows and their calves to Seith Anderson, the daughter of Jacob Henderson; and 1000 pounds tobacco to Seith Lucas, the wife of Henry Lucas. (27)

Is it only a coincidence that the three women who received bequests as friends, not immediate family members, shared the first name Seith (Seth), or were they related to West and to each other? This name for a woman is now forgotten and was uncommon even then. In fact, other than these three ladies the only women known to have the name were a daughter and three granddaughters of Captain Harrison and a Seth Linton, the daughter of Moses Linton.

This last was surely a godchild of the Harrisons and may have been their niece. The 1729 will of her father Moses Linton included a bequest to her of one hundred acres adjoining a "tract given her by Capt. Thomas Harrison on Morrumpsco Creek." (See Chapter XVIII.)

Seth Lucas had another more tenuous connection to the Harrisons. In 1723 Thomas Harrison, denoted as of the "Retirement," leased one hundred acres, part of the West–Pearson–Harrison–Harrison patent, to Seth's second husband, John Summers, for the "natural lives" of himself, herself, and their son John. Such a "lease–for–lives" was a common form of long–term lease throughout the eighteenth century. (28)

We wonder why Harrison called his residence the Retirement, the name assigned by "old Captain Brent" to his home at Aquia Creek, some miles south of the Chopawamsic. Perhaps the whole area claimed by Brent running from the Aquia to north of the Chopawamsic came to be known by that name. It included part of the Harrison plantation.

It was not only John West who wrote a will entrusting his family to the care of Captain Thomas. Fifteen years after West's death, Captain Simon Pearson, son of the member of the consortium, bequeathed "all that tract of land bought of Captain Thomas Harrison on branches of Great Hunting Creek" to his daughter Margaret. After other bequests he named his son Thomas executor and asked him to pursue and follow the "advise" and directions of "his very good and trusty friend, Captain Thomas Harrison," in the management of the estate and the care of his two underage daughters. Pearson left his friend Harrison twenty shillings to buy a mourning ring and offered to pay for the requested assistance, but Harrison did not charge for it. (29)

Margaret Pearson later married William Terret. She and her husband sued Harrison over the Great Hunting Creek land, after the heirs of the lawyer William Fitzhugh had proved that the 1707 survey had overlapped part of their 1690 Ravensworth tract. Since Captain Thomas had guaranteed the title to the area under contention, as was the custom in all land sales, he agreed to replace the lost land with the adjoining part he still held. Conflicting surveys of early grants occasioned many such law suits in later years.

It is a pity that all we know for certain about Mrs. Seth Harrison is that lone mention in John West's will. She was said to have been born Sithia Elizabeth Short by the same source that gave a maiden name for her husband's mother, i.e., a lost journal kept by a great-grandson. (30) She and Captain Harrison had at least five children. The three sons were Burr, Thomas Jr., and Cuthbert. One known daughter, Seth, married John McMillion. (31) Elizabeth wed Benjamin Bullitt, and his first wife, Sarah, was possibly her older sister. (See Appendix B-Bullitt.)

Captain Harrison was the first of his family to reach the social status of "gentry." He was in the right place at the right time for such a move "upward" in a society generally dominated by class distinctions. In Prince William County of his day there were few representatives of the ranking Tidewater families and fewer still upper-class English immigrants. The Fitzhughs, Masons, Alexanders, Washingtons, and other sons and grandsons of the region's leading citizens in the seventeenth century, mostly resided in the area that remained Stafford in 1731 or the portion that became Fairfax in 1742. The Scottish merchants who supplied many of the area's leaders in the second half of the eighteenth century were just beginning to arrive in Virginia.

His unusually long life was a factor in his advancement; seniority gave privileges even then. Physical characteristics, personal popularity, as well as leadership capabilities, could make him a militia captain in his early thirties, an age about equal to that of his fellow officers of the rank. Yet it took the passage of about twenty more years to gain him appointment to the commission of peace, membership in which signified acceptance into the ruling class. Once on the commission his age as well as his competence moved him up the ladder to the first justice post very quickly.

By no means do these considerations minimize Captain Harrison's achievements. He must have been an excellent farm manager, since his wealth was gained from growing tobacco. If measured by landholdings, his riches were appreciable, but less than that of some twenty others on the 1723 quitrent list. Even more responsible for his success, in our opinion, was his trustworthiness. Not only do we see this in the West and Pearson wills, but it is apparent in his treatment of the Terrett land suit in which he immediately agreed to arbitration and to a result that left the Terretts with more acres than they had had originally.

Thomas Harrison built on the foundation set by his immigrant father and left his children and grandchildren a secure base on which they could construct their own careers as Virginia advanced toward statehood.

Notes:

1. St Records, 1686-94, p.20. William Green, the seller, was the brother of Lettice (Green) Smith, the first wife of Burr Harrison Jr. Thomas Harrison, the buyer, resold it to Major John West.
2. St Records, 1689-93, p.111. Sarah Matheny, the widow of Daniel Matheny, was a neighbor of the Harrisons.
3. Ibid., p.137 (Gibson) and p.167 (Brent).
4. *Calendar of State Papers* 1-69.
5. Des Cognets, *Lost Records*, p.269. George Mason II, William Fitzhugh II, and Rice Hooe were at various times burgesses for Stafford.
6. St Z-47, 1700.
7. St Z 84, 1701. Gibson sold to Abraham Farrow, millwright, land at head of Quantico on S side.
8. Des Cognets, *Lost Records* p.252, 1702.
9. St Z-313, 1705/6.
10. N.N.3:92, 1705. 112 a. on Occoquan and Morumsco.
11. N.N.3:153, 9/23/1706.
12. Mitchell, *Beginning at a White Oak*, p.280. Unfortunately the deed from Harrison to Pearson was registered in one of the Stafford lost books. It would have shown whether Mrs. Harrison was alive to give her consent.
13. Virginia Historical Society, Mss. 11:3 W5205:1. The division was recorded in 1714. The plat shows that one of Thomas Pearson's two parts had been sold to a man named Ragan. "Spanish oak" is now an alternate name for the Southern Red Oak. The "red oaks" of the plat were the Northern Red Oak, whose range overlaps that of the southern species in northern Virginia.
14. N.N.3:170, 1707.
15. N.N.3:198, 1708. 800 a. on Chopawamsic, Quantico, and Little Creeks. Thomas "Harris's" perhaps should read Thomas "Harrison's," although there was a Thomas Harris in St a few years earlier.
16. N.N.4:8, 1710. 938 a. on S side of Cedar Run and E side of

Dorrills Run.

17. Harrison's parts of the Cedar Run tract remained in the family until well after the Revolution.

18. King, *Register of Overwharton Parish, 1723-1758.* Quitrent roll of Stafford Co. for 1723 returned by James Carter.

19. Ibid, Section IV. The names of the white employees were Nat Jacobs and Thomas Quinn and the boys Wm. Kelly and Jacob White. The blacks, who would have had only a first name, were not identified.

20. Des Cognets, *Lost Records* has the appointments to the Stafford commissions of peace for 1702, 1714, and 1726.

21. *Executive Journals,* 4/27/1731. The members of the commission of the peace for the newly organized PW were Thomas Harrison, Dennis McCarty, Wm. Linton, Francis Awbry, Robt. Jones, Burr Harrison (son of the Captain), and Moses Quarles of the quorum and Leonard Barker, Wm. Harrison (son of William of the West et al grant), Valentine Barker, John Wright, John Allen, Wm. Hackney, and Joseph Hudnall.

22. PW W C-274. Ann Hancock's bond to Dennis McCarty, "the first justice," as administratrix of her late husband Scarlett, who was the son of Katherine (Smith) Hancock, the adopted daughter of Burr Harrison Jr. (See Chapter XVIII.)

23. *Executive Journals,* 10/29/1742. Of the commission named in 1731 only Thomas Harrison, Robert Jones, Joseph Hudnall, and John Wright remained. There were twenty-four others on the PW commission and fourteen on that of FX headed by William Fairfax. None of the FX justices were on the 1731 commission.

24. Ibid C-443, 1743/4. Sibell Farrow's bond for administration of husband Abram's estate.

25. *Executive Journals,* 3/26/1732. According to Groome, *Fauquier during the Proprietorship,* the ringleaders of the uprising were Thomas Furr, Thomas Furr the Younger, James Bland, and Henry Filkins. They were required to appear before the General Court at Williamsburg.

26. Ibid. 5/3/1737 and 6/16/1737.

27. Fx Land Records of Long Standing, 1742-1770, p.166. West's will was dated 11/16 1716, proved 2/13 1716/17.

28. St D J-36, 1723. Henry Lucas died in 1716; his widow married Summers the following year. The lease allowed the substitution of another child of Summers, if the named son should die, on the payment of a one-time double rent. The witnesses were Burr Harrison (eldest son of the Captain), Elizabeth Colon, and John Harrison. We think it unlikely that John was a son, because he signed with his

53

mark and he was not among the tenders of tobacco for Cap
tain Harrison. Nevertheless he may have been one suffer-
ing from a physical handicap. (See Chapter XX.)

29. St M-101, 1733. Peàrson's will was made in 1731.

30. Although the reputed journal said Mrs. Seth Harrison was a
Short from Maryland, we have so far been unable to find a
man there who might have been her father. On the other
hand, a John Short was on the list of transportees for a 1666
patent of Major John Weire for 3000 a. on the S side of the
Rappahannock. Also the will of a John Short was indexed
on lost St W K-22, ca. 1722. We believe that the maiden
name of Mrs. Harrison very likely was Seth Short. However, we wonder where the "Sithia Elizabeth" came from, be
cause we are under the impression that middle names for
women were unusual in the seventeenth century.

31. John McMillion was a neighbor of the Harrisons on the
Chopawamsic. He was the son of Peter and Elizabeth
McM. of Maryland. He and his wife Seth had two sons John
and Cuthbert, neither of whom ever married. There were
probably other children who either died in infancy or were
girls whose marriage records were lost. John (Jr.) was a
vestryman, justice, and sheriff of PW. St Z-313, 1705/6.
Daniel McMillion? power to John Waugh to ratify, confirm,
and acknowledge to Elizabeth McM., the widow of Peter
McM., 449 a. on Burgesses Creek in St to be enjoyed during
her life, then by her sons George and John. Signed: Daniel
Woolens and Susannah Woolens?

   PW Bond Book p.55, 1762. John McMillion (Jr.) with
securities Burr Harrison and William Bennett bond as
executor of John McMillion.

   Ibid. p.97, 1771. John McMillion executor of Cuthbert
McMillion dec'd.

   PW D X-189, 1788. Seth McMillion deed of trust for
son John, land on Chopawamsic inherited from her father,
Thomas Harrison.

   PW W K-126, 1811. John McMillion wills all his
estate to Sarah Keich for natural love and affection and
services rendered.

Chapter IV

Burr Harrison (1699–1775)
(Burr 3, Thomas 2, Burr 1)

The first grandson of the immigrant Burr Harrison was his namesake born in the last year of the seventeenth century, May 21, 1699. (1) In 1722 he married Ann, the daughter of Matthew Barnes, at the bride's home at Portobaco, Maryland. (2) The groom, only twenty-three years old, was considerably below the average age for a male to marry at the time. Apprentices and indentured servants were not allowed to marry without their master's consent. Sons of small farmers or tradesmen often had to wait until they were financially capable of obtaining land or tools of their own. But even in well-off families the sons usually married when they were twenty-five to thirty years old.

On the other hand, because of the distinct shortage of eligible females, girls married early, often before they were sixteen. We wonder how young Harrison happened to go across the Potomac to find his bride; usually marriages took place between neighbors. His mother was said to have come from a Maryland family. Had young Burr been visiting relatives when he first encountered Ann?

The newlyweds began their married life on two hundred acres belonging to Burr's father, Captain Thomas Harrison. (3) Presumably this small plantation had been part of his grandfather's holdings on the Chopawamsic.

The first child of the young couple, a son named Thomas for his paternal grandfather, was born in 1723. From then on for over twenty-five years a steady parade of new babies arrived every two to three years. Ten lived to adulthood, namely:

Thomas (1723–1756) m. Anne Peyton.
Jane (1726–1759) m. John Linton.
Seth (1729– ?) m. John Peyton.

55

Elizabeth (1731-1781) m. Joseph Combs.
Burr (1734-1790) m. Mary Anne Barnes.
Anne (1736- ?) m. Craven Peyton.
Matthew (1738-1798) m. four times.
Sarah (1740-1815) m. Leven Powell.
George (1745-1805) m. Elizabeth Beale.
Cuthbert (1749-1822) m. three times.

Most of these data are taken from the "Kentucky Bible," which belonged to the youngest son Cuthbert. Although other secondary sources differ in birth-dates and names of spouses, we have found no case in which this Bible record was incorrect.

Some of its names and dates are corroborated in an old prayerbook in the possession of a twentieth century Burr Harrison. It adds the information that Burr raised a total of eight grandchildren, including four sons of Thomas and four Lintons named William, John, Anne, and Sarah. (4) The Linton children were the orphans of John and Jane (Harrison) Linton, both of whom died in 1759. Burr Harrison was the administrator of the estate of his son-in-law. (See Chapter XVIII.)

In addition, according to the prayerbook, Harrison adopted and raised five "olphns": Alexander Ballenger, John Wilson, John Cotter, Mary Pritchet, and Susan Pritchet. The Kentucky Bible noted that:

> *Marey Pritchitt was born April 9th 1735. Sarah Pritchitt was born Augst 30th 1744. The above was taken out of a prare book of Chris'r Pritchitt [their father] del'd to me by his wife that was ---- [signed] B. Harrison. Marey & Susan Pritchett was boun to me the 27th of March 1749 [1750] by order of Cort.*

The Harrison household must have been a lively one. Happily, the mistress of the house would have had plenty of help in caring for all those children.

To provide for such a large and growing family, Harrison needed other income to supplement that afforded by his annual tobacco crop. He obtained appointment to well-paying positions in the county. When Prince William was partitioned from Stafford in 1731, Burr Harrison, at the age of thirty-two, was appointed to its first commission of peace. (5) Although the justices received no pay for their services, noblesse oblige being the order of the day, membership on the commission was proof of acceptance into the ruling class and readiness to share the privileges that accompanied its responsibilities.

In this initial commission for Prince William, Burr's father, as the first justice named in the executive decree, presided over the court when present; otherwise the sitting justice next in the ranking took over. Burr Harrison was fourth in rank out of a total of fifteen appointees. The first seven named were "of the quorum"; at least one of this designation plus any three other justices were needed in attendance for a court session to be legal. The ranking of the justices made no difference in deciding a suit, at least in theory. Few dissents were recorded in the minutes. As we have seen, the county courts seem to have provided an even-handed administration of the law without attention to social rank or personal friendships.

About this time Harrison was commissioned as a captain in the county militia commanded by his father. From then on he was usually termed Captain Burr Harrison. Again, militia officers and men were paid only when on active military service.

Nevertheless, Burr did participate monetarily in the perquisites due the Virginian equivalent of an English country squire. We know of them through an unfortunate scandal that broke about the head of the young man. In November, 1733 the Governor's Council ordered that "Burr Harrison late inspector at Quantico Warehouse be removed from his office for his misbehavior and Mr. John Diskin take his place." Then in June, 1734 the Council further resolved:

> *whereas it appears to this board that Burr Harrison collector of the levies and other public dues in the county of Prince William hath exacted from divers of the inhabitants the 20 percent allowed them by law for paying the said levies and dues by inspector's notes under pretence that the same were paid after the tenth day of April. It is ordered that the said Burr Harrison do forthwith repay to the several aggrieved persons the tobacco he hath exacted of them on pain of being prosecuted for his said offence. (6)*

Inspectors of the public warehouses used to control weight and quality of export products, primarily tobacco, were appointed by the government at Williamsburg. The positions were lucrative ones, often held within a family for years. So was the post of tax collector; he received ten per cent of the amount collected.

Of course, we shall never know Harrison's side of the story, but in a new commission of peace named in November 1734

Burr was replaced by his brother Thomas. It was not until about 1760 that he was once more made a justice of the county.

However, Harrison was appointed clerk of the Dettingen vestry at its first meeting, after the Parish had been set off from Hamilton in 1745; he had been the clerk of the Hamilton vestry. The post, that of a secretary-treasurer, was paid 500 pounds tobacco annually. In contrast, the Rev. James Scott received a salary of 16,000 pounds tobacco plus the use of the glebe farm of two hundred acres and a parsonage, as prescribed by law. In Dettingen the rector served two churches, one at Quantico and the other on Broad Run. The two lay readers, one for each church, who conducted services at the church on the alternate Sundays that the rector was preaching at the other, received 1200 pounds each. The sexton of each church got 500 pounds per year for his work. For many years John Peyton Jr., Harrison's son-in-law, was a reader. (7)

The new glebe house built for Mr. Scott measured 40 x 20 feet. It had a barn of the same size with a 10-foot-wide stable shed attached, a dairy and a smokehouse each 10 foot square, a 100-foot-square garden, plus a hen house, a "settle house," and a corn house. The cost of constructing these buildings totalled 38,500 pounds of tobacco.

The boundaries of the new parish fixed by the Assembly at Williamsburg coincided roughly with those of modern Prince William County. Truro Parish had already been set off from Hamilton in 1732, and its territory later became Fairfax County. The remainder of Hamilton constituted Fauquier, when that county was formed from Prince William in 1759.

The original vestry of a new parish was elected by its freeholders, but later in most cases it became a self-perpetuating body. It chose two of its members to be churchwardens, usually for a term of two years. In addition to the duties of modern Episcopalian vestrymen of overseeing and managing the business and finances of the parish, the vestry had other responsibilities. They included providing for the poor with funds received by levies on the inhabitants; apprenticing poor orphans or bastard children, whose fathers could not or would not support them; and "processioning." The latter task was to step off the boundaries of every property to insure the affected landowners agreed on their locations.

A minute of a Truro vestry meeting read: "upon motion of Edward Barry on behalf of Mr. Burr Harrison, clerk of the vestry of Hamilton Parish, for an allowance for copies of the oaths for this parish, this vestry of opinion the said Harrison did but his duty and therefore will allow him nothing." (8)

References to Burr Harrison in the Dettingen vestry minutes

include the following:

6/1/1745   named clerk of the vestry.
12/21/1756 paid for curing Adam Rains.
10/8/1757   still clerk of the vestry.
12/15/1760 for attending and burying John Cotter.

Thus, this third Burr Harrison remained an important citizen of the county. He showed up frequently in the records as a witness to wills and deeds and as an appraiser of estates. In one such instance Burr and his cousin, Thomas Whitledge Jr., witnessed an agreement among John Fishback, John Hoffman, and Jacob Holtzclaw that none would exercise his right of survivorship respecting the land patent they held jointly, but that the heirs of each would inherit his share in the tract. The three men were Germans representing ten families who had been brought over by Governor Spotswood in 1714 to work his mine at Germanna on the banks of the Rapidan River. The deed was to the settlement at Germantown to which all the families had moved in 1724. Since foreigners could not own land, the three leaders of the community had had to be naturalized, for which they had qualified by completing their terms of servitude and by anglicizing their names. (9)

Harrison did not even get completely out of politics. In 1736 he made a deposition in behalf of Peter Hedgman, who claimed foul in his defeat for burgess from Prince William by Thomas Osborne. Harrison's stance was taken even though Osborne was married to Mrs. Harrison's sister.

Such challenges to elections made to the House, the final arbiter of its own rules, were not uncommon. Most often the charge was that the candidate had bought the election by offering excessive quantities of hard liquor to the voters, a practice that was against the rules, but more honored in exception than in compliance. The voting took place at the courthouse in front of everyone, the very antithesis of the modern secret ballot. In this case, Osborne was expelled from the House, which ordered a new election won by Hedgman and Valentine Peyton.

Like his father and grandfather before him, Harrison engaged in various land transactions. In 1734 he bought from cousin Thomas Whitledge Jr. 200 acres of land on the south side of the Chopawamsic that had belonged to their grandfather, the immigrant. In 1739 he got a patent from the Proprietor for 195 acres more on the south banks of that creek. (10) The rent rolls of the Hamilton Parish of Prince William for 1736 showed Capt. Burr Harrison with 712 acres while his father owned 1317 and his brother, Thomas Jr., held 663. These lands were not

59

necessarily all in the parish, as the quitrents were collected for all the land a person owned within the Northern Neck Proprietorship. The Harrisons were by no means the largest landowners living in Prince William. For example, the "Widow Lynton" (Mrs. William Linton) paid on 1889 acres; she was acting as administrator of the estates of her two first husbands and was about to marry her third spouse. Scarlett Hancock, the son of Katherine Smith, the stepdaughter of Burr Harrison Jr., held 4075 acres. (11)

When his father died in 1746, Burr inherited a major part of the Chopawamsic land, enough to take him out of the market for some years evidently. In 1762 he sold the 200 acres on Great Hunting Creek that his grandfather had bought from the Nixons. He had probably lived there as a child and the plantation had been the home of his oldest son, Thomas, before the latter's death in 1756. (12)

Harrison's namesake son had gotten an appointment as assistant surveyor in Augusta County in the Shenandoah Valley in 1754. No better position could be imagined for uncovering open ungranted land, (unless perhaps he had been an assistant to George Washington, the county surveyor in neighboring Frederick.) From 1754 through 1768 father and son took up several grants totalling about 1500 acres from the Proprietor, Lord Fairfax, in what is now Shenandoah County. (13)

Nevertheless, real estate ventures were not his main interest. That continued to be farming. Harrison wrote his son-in-law Leven Powell a letter in August of 1775. He had promised to send Powell hemp. When he couldn't get it "down" as soon as wanted, he had asked an acquaintance who had a "tun" of the fiber for sale to deliver Powell the quantity wanted. On his return from the "Convention" he had discovered that the hemp had not yet been sent off.

After this matter of business, the letter continues with some news. Apparently one of Powell's apprentices had been discovered in Gloucester "wanting to ship himself to England or some of the Islands" (the West Indies) according to a mutual friend whom Burr had met at the "Boling Green." The friend promised to secure the run-away. The letter is signed:

I am with esteem
your affectionate kinsman
B. Harrison

At the bottom the note was addressed "to Leven Powell Esqr., Loudon, hand by Mrs. Combs." (Daughter Elizabeth Combs lived near Powell, fifty miles from the Chopawamsic.

60

She must have been visiting her parents.) (14)

The Convention to which Harrison alluded was held July 17, 1775 in Richmond for the purpose of defending the colony from an invasion. Presumably Captain Harrison had also attended the previous conventions called in 1774 and in March 1775. As the first action of the third one, approval was given to the raising of two regiments of troops to be paid for by the "publick." The first regiment was to muster eight companies of forty-eight privates each and the second seven companies of that strength. Each company would be officered by a captain, two lieutenants, and one ensign. It would have three sergeants, a drummer, and a fifer. The regiment would be commanded by a colonel, lieutenant colonel, and major and would have a chaplain, paymaster, adjutant, quartermaster, surgeon, two surgeon's mates, and a sergeant major. The men were not to be compelled to serve more than one year provided they gave three month's notice that they wished to be discharged at the end of that period.

Each of sixteen "Districts" were to raise one company. Culpeper, Orange, and Fauquier made up one district; Prince William, Fairfax, and Loudoun another. Companies from the western districts including the one to which Fauquier belonged were to be riflemen, i.e., light infantry. The frontier counties of West Augusta, Botetourt, and Fincastle were to provide one company each to be stationed in its own territory at Fort Fincastle (Wheeling), Point Pleasant (Charleston), and "where needed." In addition, two rifle companies were to be sent to Pittsburg.

The convention fixed the pay scales, which ranged from a colonel's twenty-five shillings per day to a private's shilling and fourpence. Majors and chaplains, and surgeons got ten shillings; captains, adjutants, and quartermasters, six; sergeants, two; corporals, drummers, and fifers, one shilling, eightpence. Each officer was to be supplied a tent; two non-commissioned officers or six soldiers would share a tent. The riflemen were to furnish their own arms, but the other soldiers would be provided a musket and bayonet. Many of these provisions were never practiced.

A long list of Articles of War was drawn up to govern the conduct of the army. The convention then turned its attention to the county militias, requiring all white males over sixteen and under fifty to serve, including servants and apprentices. Exception was made for Quakers and "the people called Menonists" (Mennonites).

Finally, it was decided that delegates to subsequent conventions would be elected under the same regulations as for burgesses. (Three more conventions were held before the Commonwealth of Virginia was established in July, 1776.)

After attending the Convention, Burr Harrison lived only three more months. Even though the letter to Powell said nothing about its writer's health, he "departed this life on Wednesday the 18th of October at 2 o'clock in the morning in 1775." (15) His will that might have cleared up any uncertainties about his children and grandchildren has been lost. The first of the immigrant's grandchildren to be born became the next to the last of the third generation of Harrison men to pass on. (16) (A cousin who called himself Burr Harris was the last.)

Perhaps his early mistakes, if such they really were, had been due to his father's pushing him into positions for which he was not well prepared. Whatever had happened, he had overcome the disgrace and reached the status of respected elder citizen entrusted with the representation of his county in the defense of the homeland. Looking at his career may help us understand how Virginia gentlemen the age of his sons could become the leaders of a revolution.

Notes:

1. *Records of Dettingen Parish* p.124; op. cit.
2. *Kentucky Bible Records*, op. cit. Letter J. Frederick Dorman to G.H.S. King in King papers. Capt. Mathew Barnes died in Charles Co., Md. in 1746 at age 76. (Md. Proprietary Wills 24-308). He was seventy-two in 1742 (Court Proceedings 1741-3, p.321). His widow, Mary, died in 1751 (W AC#4-349).
3. King, *Overwharton Parish Register*; op. cit.
4. The original of the prayerbook belonged to Burr Powell Harrison of Winchester, Va. Copies are in the National DAR Library and the King papers.
5. *Executive Journals*, IV-239.
6. Ibid., IV-310 and 317.
7. *Records of Dettingen Parish.*
8. *Minutes of Vestry of Truro Parish.*
9. St D L-275. Germanna was in Orange County and Germantown in Fauquier. Near his Germanna iron works, Governor Spotswood built his "Enchanted Castle" mansion, currently site of archaeological exploration.
10. NN E-120. 195 a. adjoining land of Cary Broadhurst.
11. Undated Manuscript, misc. PW Papers, Huntington Library. Copies in Manassas, Va. and Va. State Libraries.
12. Fx D E-186.

13. NN K–289, 1761. 400 a. Stoney Creek. O–139, 1768. 200 a. Stoney Creek. O–141, 1768. 234 a. Stoney Creek.
14. Leven Powell Papers, Manuscript Collections, Library of Congress. The signature differs from that of other later letters in the collection written by son, Burr Harrison, (1734–1790). PW W G–392, 1787. Will of William Powell leaves son Leven only twenty shillings sterling, but names him an exector. Other children are sons William, son Peyton, daughters Frances Eliot, Margaret Bristoe, Sarah Powell and Elizabeth Powell. His wife Eleanor (nee Peyton) is also an executor. L W I–250, 1811. Will of Leven Powell names wife Sarah; dau. Sarah Harrison Chilton; sons Burr, Cuthbert, Alfred, Leven dec'd, and William dec'd., and several grandchildren.
15. *Kentucky Bible Record*, op. cit.
16. St Index (lost) Liber N, 1767–1783, shows "Will [of] Burr Harrison, p. 315." This would be a copy of the original filed in PW and lost there also. The St index shows the will of John Alexander, p.303 and of William Mountjoy, p. 343. Copies of those two wills proved in 1775 and 1777, respectively, have been preserved elsewhere.

Chapter V

Thomas Harrison (ca. 1704–1774) of Fauquier
(Thomas 3, Thomas 2, Burr 1)

The descendant of the immigrant Burr Harrison who gained greatest prominence in northern Virginia prior to the Revolution was his grandson, Thomas Harrison Jr., the second son of Captain Thomas Harrison. Although his birth-date is not known, he was younger than his brother Burr, who had been born in 1699, and was older than sixteen in 1723. Thus he must have been born between 1700 and 1707, probably while his father was living in the area of Great Hunting Creek, in what is now Fairfax County. Unlike his older brother, he was not mentioned in the 1716 will of his father's friend, Major John West. Perhaps this was because he had been only a baby when his father and Major West had been neighbors.

In fact the first record of this third-generation Thomas Harrison is in the 1723 census of tobacco plantings, which shows that he was still living with his parents. (1) He does not appear next until 1731, when he received a grant from the Proprietor of 271 acres on Holmes Run. Two other deeds recorded in 1743 and 1744 in Fairfax County referred to a tract of 392 acres on "Homes Run." This land originally granted in 1726 to James Robertson was sold by him in October, 1730 to Ann Quarles. First, Thomas Harrison Jr. and Ann Harrison, his wife, formerly Ann Quarles, sold the tract to John Hamilton for fifty pounds sterling. Nine months later Hamilton sold it back to Harrison for the same price. Title to the property remained in the hands of the Harrisons until it was sold in 1767. (2)

Harrison must have married Ann, the widow of John Quarles, in 1731 or soon after. She was the daughter of John Grayson, originally of Lancaster County and later of Spotsylvania. (3) Her brother Ambrose was a leading citizen of the latter county and her brother Benjamin a wealthy merchant in

Prince William County. His son, William Grayson, became one of Virginia's first two United States senators.

Ann had married her first husband, John Quarles, in 1722. He died in 1729 leaving her with three small children: Moses, John, and Betty. All were raised by their mother and stepfather (father-in-law in the terminology of the day). (4)

In 1767 both tracts on Holmes Run were sold to John Carlyle, an Alexandria merchant. Signing the deed for the parcel of 392 acres, besides Harrison, were John Quarles Jr. and his wife, Ann Quarles, and John Quarles. (5) The last was the son of Ann (Grayson) Quarles Harrison, and John Jr. was her grandson. Clearly, Ann Harrison herself had died. Maybe she had requested that if the property were sold, all or part of the proceeds should go to her Quarles heirs. These properties on Holmes Run are now the site of the Five Corners shopping mall, one of the first to be built in the Washington metropolitan area. It is likely that after their marriage, Thomas and Ann lived there or nearby on a part of the 1706 West-Pearson-Harrison-Harrison grant still retained by his father.

In 1740 Thomas Harrison Jr. "bought" from his father part of the parcel that the latter had been granted in 1707 in partnership with Thomas Whitledge located where the present Prince William, Stafford, and Fauquier counties intersect. (6) Harrison and his family lived on this plantation (enlarged later) for the rest of his life. The family home was located on Dorrill's Run in the southeastern corner of Fauquier.

Harrison's career as a public servant began in 1733 when Governor Gooch appointed him sheriff of Prince William. This office and that of county clerk were the two most lucrative ones in the county administration. Unlike the county clerk who usually served until he died, the sheriff held his office only for two years before it passed to another of the county's gentlemen. Harrison succeeded Robert Jones in the position and was followed in 1735 by Jeremiah Bronaugh. To insure the performance of his duties, Harrison together with his father and John Farrow signed a bond for one thousand pounds sterling. His two deputies also posted bonds; Samuel Smith served "from Occoquan and upwards," i.e., the area that became Fairfax County, and John Quinn was responsible in the rest of the county. (7)

In November, 1734 Thomas Harrison Jr. was named to the new commission of peace for Prince William replacing his brother on the list. Since a sheriff was not permitted to sit as a justice of the county court, Harrison began that service in 1735 and continued until 1759 when Fauquier County was set off from Prince William. (8) He acted as head justice from

1744 until 1759, when he took the position in the new Fauquier court. (9) He faithfully attended the monthly sessions in Fauquier through 1771.

As we have noted, the first-named man on the commission of peace chaired the court, whenever he was in attendance. However, there was an exception. Thomas Lord Fairfax, the Proprietor, was ex-officio a justice of all the courts in his Proprietorship and out-ranked all other members of the bench. Although he attended regularly only the Frederick County court, at any other court he chose to visit he became the presiding judge. For example, His Lordship rather than Harrison presided over one day's session of the Fauquier court in September, 1762 and again in July, 1763. (10)

When a new commission of the peace was appointed, the first justice took the oath of loyalty to the king and subscribed to the "test" of conformity to the creed of the established Anglican church. He then swore the other justices. In February, 1761 Harrison administered a special oath to the other justices "in favor of the heirs of Princess Sophia, being Protestant, and for extinguishing the hopes of the pretended Prince of Wales." King George II had died, and there had been a question as to who should succeed him. The choice was his Protestant grandson, George III, who reigned during the Revolution.

Usually the first justice was the one authorized to receive and disburse money for the court. For example, in Prince William Harrison employed and paid an attorney to defend the justices in the General Court at Williamsburg in a suit brought against them. With others he contracted for a bridge to be built over Cedar Run. He and Henry Peyton negotiated with George Mason over the fees for operating the ferry over the Occoquan. Mason had refused "to keep the same for 1500 pounds of tobacco as usual." On another occasion the sheriff was ordered "to take into his possession sundry goods now in the hands of Col. Thomas Harrison, which were delivered to him by persons who took up sundry slaves, which said goods are imagined to be stolen and that he advertise the same." Slaves were becoming common in northern Virginia, and some were running away.

On May 24, 1759, at the opening session of the court of the new Fauquier County, the justices present were Thomas Harrison, William Eustace, William Grant, Thomas Marshall, William Blackwell, John Churchill, Yelverton Peyton, and George Lamkin. Those not present (some because of a dispute over where a courthouse should be built) were Joseph Blackwell, John Wright, John Frogg, Wharton Randall, Elias Edmonds, John Bell, John Crump, Duff Greene, Thomas

McClanihan, and Richard Foote. At about fifty-five, Harrison was the oldest. Yelverton Peyton, only twenty-five, was the youngest. Harrison was appointed to get weights and measures for the county and to provide a seal for it. As late as 1771, he was still a keeper of "publick money" transferring seventy-one pounds to Martin Pickett.

The controversy over the location of the courthouse was probably engendered as much by the opposing parties' real estate interests as by their desires to reduce their travel time in getting to the monthly three-day court sessions. Almost without exception, a courthouse became the setting for a burgeoning village. In the end, the accepted compromise fixed the place on the big Turkey Run tract of non-resident Richard Henry Lee, later a signer of the Declaration of Independence. (Lee had done a little lobbying with the governor and gotten him to turn down the recommendation of the court's majority.) Fauquier Courthouse later changed its name to Warrenton, but the successors to the original building have remained there.

Harrison, like most of the other justices, lived too far away, seventeen miles in his case, to travel daily to and from court. Undoubtedly, he stayed at the house of his long-standing friend and colleague, Joseph Blackwell. The house was built especially for the purpose on a lot near the courthouse. Blackwell and his friends would have spent the evenings socializing and no doubt playing cards. Lesser lights were happy to attend court as witnesses and jurors, because court days were the monthly chance to meet friends, do business, drink, and gamble at cock fights, card games, dice, or whatever other chance presented itself. The only difference in gambling tastes between them and their "betters," the justices and lawyers, was in the stakes they played for. Such court attenders, unless they lived nearby, would stay with friends or at the local tavern, or "ordinary" as it was called in colonial times.

The extent of the gambling mania to which Virginians of the day were addicted is indicated by a suit brought in 1765 by Sampson Turley against Benjamin Grayson (Jr.) and his brother William (later to become U.S. senator). The bill of complaint reads:

> To the worshipful court of Loudoun County
> ---- your Orator Sampson Turley ---- having
> gamed with a certain Benjamin Grayson at divers
> games and sundry times --- and very fairly won
> ---- in whole the sum of seventysix pounds ----
> and your Orator had an open account with ----
> Grayson for goods, wares, & merchandizes that was

unsettled. [When Turley and Grayson agreed to submit the merchandise account to arbitration, Turley] charged Grayson with the money he had won of him, but as it was for gaming, the arbitrators would not allow [the claim and ruled] in favor of Grayson for a very considerable sum of money. ---- Subsequently ---- your Orator gamed with Grayson again and Grayson's luck proving fortunate, he won of your Orator the sum of twenty pounds and your Orator being greatly and mightily intoxicated with the innebriatiting [sic] fumes of liquor which your Orator always well liked and Grayson taking advantage of your Orator ---- did actually prevail on your Orator to give him his note for the said sum of money which Grayson afterwards for the sum of fifteen pounds transferred to William Grayson. ---- William Grayson has actually commenced suit agt. your Orator tho your Orator told [him] before the suit was brought that the note was unjust as Benjamin Grayson was largely indebted to your Orator.

Turley asked for an injunction to prevent the Graysons from collecting on the note and the arbitrers' award. The Graysons' reply admitted the gambling, stating that both had often won or lost substantial sums to Turley, but denying that they had ever taken advantage of the latter's liking for liquor and claiming they had always settled their gambling debts promptly. Nevertheless, Turley got his injunction.

Benjamin Grayson lost the fortune left him by his father and ended up confined within the Loudoun prison bounds for debt. How much his propensity for gambling contributed to his financial disaster was not disclosed in the records.

The "high-living" habits of some of the Virginia gentry began at a young age. For instance, in December 1774 16-year old Chandler Fowke did "by his mother's consent and the approbation of the county court of Fauquier bind himself for five years an apprentice" to Wharton Ransdell, a house carpenter. He promised to keep his master's secrets and willingly obey all his lawful commands and not to "frequent any tippling houses nor taverns, nor play at cards, dice, or any unlawful game." Ransdell was to do his "utmost to learn [Chandler] all the art, trade, and mistery of a house joiner and to provide him with sufficient meat, drink, washing, and lodging."

The youthful delinquent was either the son of Colonel Harrison's daughter Mary, or more likely her nephew by marriage. Just as has happened many times since in such cases, Chandler was later allowed to enlist in the army. Gwathmey noted he was a sergeant in the Third Virginia Regiment, the one recruited in the district that included Fauquier.

Returning to Thomas Harrison, we may assume his court duties did not include many cases the like of Turley vs. Grayson.

In addition to his magisterial office, Thomas Harrison Jr. was a militia officer. In 1740 he was called "Captain"; by 1744 he was "Major"; and in 1746 after the death of his father, he became "Colonel." Although the record of his appointment has been lost, it is apparent that he succeeded his father as commander of the Prince William militia. He remained so until the formation of Fauquier. Then Henry Churchill, a young aristocrat who probably had served under Braddock, was named the first county lieutenant of the new county's militia. (11) When he died less than two years later, Harrison took the office and retained it for the rest of his life.

In 1741 Harrison was elected to a seat in the House of Burgesses for the first time. The results of the polling in Prince William as certified to the Assembly by Catesby Cocke, clerk of court, were William Fairfax 249, Thomas Harrison 234, Col. John Colville 175, Valentine Peyton 141, Maj. (Richard) Blackburn 29. (Each freeholder opted for two of the candidates.) There has been some question as to whether Harrison Jr. or his father was the one elected. In addition to other indirect evidence, a reading of the poll shows conclusively that it was the younger man. (12) Of the five candidates only Blackburn and Peyton voted. Neither voted for himself, and each clearly voted after conceding his defeat. For example, Peyton was sixth from the last name on the list of Fairfax's supporters. Evidently, the unwritten rules required a candidate abstain from voting until he had withdrawn from the race. Since Thomas Harrison Sr., recorded that way, did vote for his son and for Fairfax, he could not have been the Harrison elected.

As would be expected, Thomas Harrison Jr. was backed largely by men from the southern part of the county, who split their other vote between Fairfax and Peyton. Colville's adherents lived mainly in the northern sector, soon to become Fairfax County.

Harrison served as a burgess of Prince William through the Assembly of 1752-55. In the 1756 election it is not known whether he and Joseph Blackwell, the incumbents, did not run because both expected the early formation of Fauquier or whether they ran and were defeated. In 1759 Harrison and John

Bell were chosen as the first burgesses from Fauquier. Ten years later Harrison was defeated for reelection by Thomas Marshall and James Scott, the husband of his niece Elizabeth, daughter of Cuthbert Harrison. (13)

The record of Thomas Harrison's activity in the House of Burgesses is indicative of the work and procedures of that body. Even before Harrison became a member, he had been involved with four fellow justices of the Prince William court in a matter concerning the right of petition. The journal of the House of Burgesses recorded:

> *June 3, 1740*
> *Mr Conway reported that the committee had also under their consideration the ---- complaint against the justices of Prince William County ---- for refusing to receive and certify two propositions ---- at a court held the 12th of May 1740 for proof of public claims and receiving propositions and grievances, a propositon signed by several subscribers praying that the rents of the several public warehouses in that county might be raised and that a town might be erected at Occoquon Ferry ---- and another praying that a town might be erected at the Head of Quantico Creek ---- were presented in court by Richard Blackburn, one of the subscribers thereto and that a majority of the justices then present viz. Valentine Peyton, a member of this House, John Diskins, Anthony Seale, Thomas Strippling, and Thomas Harrison Jr., Gentlemen, did refuse to receive and certify same without giving any reasons for so doing ---- Resolved that the said [justices] ---- have acted illegally, arbitrarily, and contrary to the Rights of the People ----.*

This right of the people "to petition the government for a redress of grievances" is guaranteed for ourselves by the First Amendment, which in this particular derives directly from the liberty infringed by Harrison and the other Prince William justices.

The resolution called for Peyton, the burgess, to acknowledge his offense and ask the pardon of the House. After being censured by the Speaker, Peyton apologized saying "he was truly sensible of his error for which he was sorry and humbly asked" for pardon.

It was then ordered that the other four magistrates of Prince

William "be sent for in the custody of the Serjeant at Arms to answer for their misdemeanors." Ten days later the journal minuted :

> *A petition of John Diskins, Anthony Seale, Thomas Strippling, and Thomas Harrison was presented to this House acknowledging their offence in refusing to receive and certify certain propositions presented to them at court ---- but assuring the House that they proceeded from an error in their judgment and not from any view of gratifying private resentment or consideration of their own interest and expressing their sorrow and concern for having fallen under the displeasure of the House whereby they should not only suffer a lasting disgrace but had also been put to great trouble and expense in travelling two or three hundred miles and praying the House would take their case into consideration and discharge them out of custody. Ordered that the said offenders be discharged out of custody without paying fees.*

The first session of the General Assembly that Harrison attended as a burgess was held from May 10 to June 19, 1742. Another Harrison, Benjamin of Charles City, was also a burgess. So there is sometimes confusion as to which Mr. Harrison the journal refers. When that other Harrison died, he was succeeded by his son, also named Benjamin, and in the next Assembly there were even two Benjamin Harrisons in the House. The first unequivocal mention of Thomas Harrison in the journal came on March 26, 1746 when he, Mr. Colville of Fairfax, Mr. Hedgman and Mr. Waugh of Stafford were given leave to be absent from the House. (14) Perhaps a late winter storm had interfered with travel from northern Virginia.

In the organization of the Assembly of 1748-49 Harrison was appointed to the Committee for Courts of Justice. He served on this committee in all subsequent Assemblies of which he was a member. Two items of business of that Assembly illustrate the type of legislation in which Harrison was involved. In one, he and Messrs. Carter, Washington, Fitzhugh, Hedgman, and Fairfax were named to take a bill encouraging the shooting of crows and squirrels to the Council for concurrence. In another, he alone was charged with carrying to the Council a proposed act enabling the justices of Prince William County "to levy tobacco on said county to defray charges for clearing a road from Pignut to the Blue Ridge" (a distance of about twenty-four miles).

One of the first items of business for the Assembly of 1752-55 was a petition from Bertrand Ewell complaining of an "undue" election of Mr. Thomas Harrison and Mr. Joseph Blackwell. The committee in charge reported that a greater number of the freeholders voted for each of the sitting members than for the petitioner, that the sitting members were not guilty of any malpractice nor used any illegal methods to procure themselves to be elected; that the sheriff of the county "demeaned" himself fairly and impartially in the execution of his office during the election; but that "Abraham Farrow, Joseph Nevill, and Henry Peyton whilst the sheriff was taking the poll acted riotously and unlawfully and assaulted the said sheriff who was doing his duty and intimidated such of the freeholders as offered their votes for the sitting members and endeavored to oblige them to vote for the petitioner." It was resolved that Ewell's petition was "frivolous and vexatious." He was required to pay the costs of Harrison and Blackwell "occurred by the said petition." Farrow, Neville, and Peyton were reprimanded and then discharged out of custody "paying fees."

Another challenge to an election of burgesses in Prince William came in 1756 when the winners were Henry Lee and John Bell. Henry Peyton complained about Lee, who admitted having treated freeholders to quantities of whiskey. The election was declared void, and Peyton won the seat in a new poll. In 1759 John Bell complained about Peyton's win, but must have dropped the matter when he won election with Harrison to the seats belonging to the new Fauquier County.

In 1769 it was the defeated Thomas Harrison's turn to complain about the "undue" election of James Scott and Thomas Marshall (the father of Chief Justice John Marshall). The committee summed up the situation noting that Marshall had been appointed sheriff in October 1767, which disqualified him for retaining his seat as a burgess. In June 1769 (anticipating the end of his term as sheriff) he announced his candidacy for the post. Before resigning the well-paying county job, he appointed September 18 as the day for the polling. Then William Eustace took over as sheriff and conducted the poll. The results were Marshall 329, Scott 273, and Harrison 196.

Harrison's complaint was that Marshall had been informed that Harrison expected to get all of the votes of the freeholders with residences in adjacent counties. (Eligibility to vote depended on land ownership rather than residence.) To obviate this prospect, Marshall fixed the day for the election knowing that it would conflict with the poll to be held that day in neighboring Stafford County. The committee reported that Mr. Marshall acted improperly in appointing the Fauquier election on the same day as the Stafford one with the view of preventing the inhabitants of Stafford from voting in Fauquier, but that it did not appear that his conduct had affected the results. It was resolved that Marshall and Scott were duly elected. (15)

In all probability Harrison's defeat resulted from a change in demographics. Both Scott and Marshall were from the northern part of the county where most of the population growth was occurring. There the average freehold was smaller than in the older area. Presumably people still tended to vote for their neighbors, as they did when Harrison was first elected in 1741.

Colonel Thomas was also active in the affairs of his church. When Dettingen Parish was divided from Hamilton in 1745, his home was on the western edge of the new parish. Later when Fauquier County was formed, its boundaries coincided with those of Hamilton Parish except for a small piece including Harrison's home property put in Fauquier but left in Dettingen.

Although at the time of the division Harrison was on the Hamilton vestry, he was not one of the original group elected for Dettingen. However, in 1749 he was added to the Dettingen board and remained on it until his death. In fact, in November 1773 he and Henry Lee were named churchwardens for the ensuing year, but a minute in April of 1774 appointed Lewis Reno to the post "in the room of Col. Thomas Harrison deceased." (16)

One of the first minutes of the Dettingen vestry ordered that "Major" Thomas Harrison "have the liberty of building a Gallerie for the use of himself and family in Broad Run Chapple, not discommoding any of the pews of the Chapple." That church was about five miles from Harrison's home, well within the present boundaries of Prince William.

Like his father, Harrison was a tobacco grower; that activity plus his inherited wealth made possible his public service. Unlike many of his contemporaries, Harrison was never a buyer of land to sell soon after for profit. He did, however, purchase several tracts in addition to his grant on Holmes Run. For example, in January 1741/2 he was granted 409 acres between branches of Slaty Run. The survey refers to a corner to land now belonging to the said Harrison and others. A second grant obtained at the same time was for 221 acres on the west side of the main branch of Quantico Run. Again, a corner to land of Harrison is mentioned. The 395 acres on Quantico Run that he sold to the churchwardens of Dettingen in 1749 for use as the parish glebe included the 221 acres of the grant.

When and from whom Harrison obtained the tracts adjoining the two grants is not known, because some early deed books of Prince William are missing. Harrison made other purchases, for which no copy of the deed remains, as we know from his will and from a sale to his son Thomas in 1771 of 200 acres on Kettle Run described as part of land bought from Henry Harden.

In 1764 Harrison purchased from Elias Edmonds 400 acres in northern Fauquier County, some forty miles distant from his home plantation. The next year he bought from John Mercer 1000 adjoining acres described as lying on both sides of branches of Goose Creek near the Cobblers Mountains. Both tracts were crossed by the road from Pignut Mountain to the Blue Ridge that Harrison had helped get authorized by the General Assembly fifteen years earlier. (It appears that even in those days road construction preceded and promoted real estate development.) In 1768 he sold 520 acres of the larger piece to his son William. (17)

Colonel Thomas, like his father, was considered a trustworthy friend. For example, he cosigned the bond of Jane Farrow, required as administratrix of her husband's estate. (18) John Farrow had died less than two years after he had been surety for Harrison as sheriff. A few years later (1739) Edward Sute died having asked his "trusty and beloved friends," Thomas Harrison Jr. and Benjamin Bullitt, to be his executors and guardians of two young daughters "until they arrive at the age of fourteen." (19) When Harrison's brother-in-law, Benjamin Grayson, died in 1759, he made Harrison the principal executor of his estate. (20) Similarly, Benjamin Bullitt, at least one of whose wives was a sister of Harrison, chose him as executor of his will in 1761. (21)

In September, 1773 Colonel Thomas must have had a serious illness, for he too made a will. Apparently, he got past the first crisis, because only a month later he received a commission from Governor Dunmore to be sheriff of Fauquier. At the November session of the county court, he presented the commission, posted the requisite bonds with his son William and son-in-law, Jonathan Gibson, as co-signers, and took the oath of office. (22) Forty years had passed since he had been the young sheriff of Prince William. It was just a few days later that the Dettingen vestry appointed him churchwarden.

Probably both appointments were made in part to honor the Colonel for his long service to state and church. His friends may have wished to encourage him in his recovery. If this was the case, it did not help. Sometime in December 1773 his illness must have recurred, for in January 1774 William

74

Edmonds produced his commission as the new sheriff "dated the seventh day of this instant." The last will and testament of Thomas Harrison, Gentleman, deceased, was presented to the same court.

The will was a long one. (23) It was witnessed by Original Young, John Peters, John Shumate Sen., and John Copage, all neighbors. As usual the signature was "Thos. Harrison" with the first "s" made with an upward flourish of the pen and the second being the old long version of the letter. However, the signature is so shaky compared to one six years before as to make one think that he was being helped to hold the pen.

Named as executors were his sons William and Benjamin and his son-in-law Jonathan Gibson. The following bequests were made:

Son William: five slaves.

Sons William and Burr ---- to be divided equally between them the land bought from Elias Edmonds, "wheron I now have a quarter" and a small part of the land purchased from Mr. Mercer.

Son Thomas: two slaves; several hundred acres, except that he was to complete sales of parts of these tracts as agreed to previously; the money from these sales plus ten pounds sterling money of Great Britain [Virginia currency was crossed out]; and "all my wareing bodily cloaths."

Son Burr: Four Negroes and 408 acres bought of John Mercer with the plantation thereon. Also a slave that he was to sell to pay his debts.

Daughter Susannah Gibson: five slaves, 200 pounds Virginia currency, and furniture.

Daughter Mary Fowkes: five slaves and 150 pounds Virginia currency.

Daughter Ann Gillison: two slaves, 150 pounds, and furniture. The money was to be left in the hands of Jonathan Gibson, who was to pay Mrs. Gillison annually the interest for the support of her and her children. Obviously, Ann's husband, James Gillison, had fallen out of the good graces of his father-in-law.

Grandson Thomas Gibson: the plantation where son Benjamin was living and one "negroe boy."

Grandson John Gibson: two Negro boys.

Son-in-law Jonathan Gibson: cancellation of debt of 79 pounds, 2 shillings, five pence.

Son-in-law Chandler Fowke: cancellation of loans totalling about seventy pounds.

Grandsons Benjamin Harrison, son of Burr; Thomas Harrison Fowke; John Gillison; Burr Harrison, son of William; and

Jonathan Catlett Gibson: each a Negro boy.

Granddaughters Ann Harrison Fowkes; Lucy Harrison, daughter of William; and Ann Grayson Gibson: each one Negro girl.

Son Benjamin Harrison: "the old plantation, mill and land ____ purchased of my father," the adjoining tracts purchased of Thomas Whitledge, John Orear, and Bertrand Ewell (except for the part bequeathed to Thomas Gibson), and "the plantation and land wheron I now live, formerly the Glebe of Hamilton Parish adjoining the aforesaid land." Also, seventeen slaves plus rights to one whose ownership was in dispute with the Garners, and all his household furniture "except before given," all his "several stocks both horse, cattle, sheep and hoggs (those excepted at my quarter in the mountains, and fifty head sheep)," all his several head of oxen, and all his residual estate. Benjamin was the youngest child of Thomas Harrison, twenty-nine years old, married three years previously. In case he left no "bodily heirs" his share of the estate was to be divided among grandsons Thomas Gibson, Burr Harrison, and Thomas Harrison Fowke.

Friend and nephew Cuthbert Harrison and nieces Seth, Frances, Ann, and Sarah Harrison (children of brother Cuthbert): twenty shillings each to buy "morning" rings.

Sons William, Thomas, and Burr: all the horses, cattle, and hogs at the plantation at the mountains with fifty head of sheep to be divided equally among them. Also twelve slaves to be divided among them.

In the inventory presented to the court by the executors there were seventy-six slaves, considerably more than the number mentioned in the will. It is strange that no bequest was made to his oldest Harrison grandson, William B., or any other child of his son Thomas.

One wonders what the elderly Colonel Thomas may have thought of the brewing storm that in just a year after his death would erupt into the Revolution. There are only a few clues to his opinions. In 1769 the governor, fearing loss of control because of the uproar over the quartering of British troops in Boston and the Townshend Acts, had dissolved the Assembly, the last one to which Harrison was a delegate. (The Townshend Acts of Parliament in replacement of the Stamp Act of 1765 had prohibited trade by the colonies with foreign countries and imposed customs duties on imports from Britain.) Most burgesses including Harrison adjourned to a private house and formed an association to boycott British goods. He was one of the signers of the Association, along with Washington, Jefferson, and Patrick Henry. Thus it is unlikely that his views had anything to do with his defeat for reelection. Governor Dunmore, who had appointed Harrison sheriff of Fauquier, became a hated figure in 1775, so much so that the county in the valley named in his honor changed itself to Shenandoah. However, in 1773 he was still respected and liked. Of course, the oath that Harrison took in late 1773 was to His Brittanic Majesty, King George, who had succeeded to the throne in 1760, but undoubtedly Washington, Jefferson, and many other Virginian patriots took the same oath then.

One thing is certain; none of the Colonel's children or close relatives were Tories. His sons, Burr and Benjamin, were both officers in the Fauquier militia and saw active duty in the war.

It is somewhat surprising that Colonel Thomas Harrison Jr. is not remembered in Fauquier County, where he was so prominent a citizen during its first years. There is no plaque or portrait in the courthouse and no district or street bears his name. Two reasons are apparent. First, the most famous son of the county is Chief Justice John Marshall, who in 1773 was an 18-year-old growing up on his father's farm adjacent to Harrison's "plantation at the mountains."

Second, by 1800, or soon thereafter, only one family of Harrison's descendants remained in the county, and the last Harrison of this line residing in Fauquier died in 1899.

Notes:

1. G.H.S. King, *Records of Overwharton Parish*.
2. NN D-38, 1731. Lord Fairfax to Thomas Harrison Jr. 271 a. joining to Capt. Simon Pearson's Red Oak land and to land of James Robertson in possession of Quarles. NN B-2, 1726. Grant to Robertson confirming sale to him by Pearson; Robertson sold to Ann Quarles in 1730. Fx D A-68 and A-150. Sales by Harrison to Hamilton and Hamilton to Harrison.
3. The genealogy of the Grayson family has been treated in: T V-195-208 and 261-68, (1923-4) by Frederick W. Grayson, *The Grayson Family*. T XII-181, (1930) by James D. Evans, *Grayson Family Addenda* that corrects errors in the earlier reference. V 92-423, (1984) by Joseph Horrell, *New Light on William Grayson,* which reports on Benjamin Grayson's (Benjamin 3, Benjamin 2, John 1) guardian account for his brother William. The data summarized below is derived primarily from those sources, which have been checked with original records in Sp, R, KG, PW, Fx, and L counties.

John 1 (? - 1735/6) m. Susanna ---- .
Thomas 2, John 1. Moved to Deal, Kent, England.
Ambrose 2, John 1, (ca. 1701-1743/4).
   m. Alice (----) James. She m. (3) James Stevens.
   Children: John, Ambrose, Benjamin, Thomas, Alice, Susanna, Ann, and Reuben.
John 2, John 1, m. Barbara Cullom.
   Children: Ambrose, William, John m. Sally Cater, Susan
   m. ---- Thompson, Nancy, Mollie m. Wm. Hall, Elizabeth
   m. (1) John Gordon, (2) Joseph Davis.
William 3, John 2 (1732-1829), m. Rachel Cowley.
Benjamin 2, John 1, (----1758).
   m. 1734 (1) Susanna (Monroe) Tyler Linton (1693-1752).
   1752 (2) Sarah (Ball) Ewell.
Benjamin 3, Benj. 2, (ca. 1735-1768), m. 1759 Elizabeth
   Osborne, dau. of Capt. Robert Osborne.
Spence 3, Benj. 2, (ca. 1740-1798).
William 3, Benj. 2, (ca. 1742-1790).
Peter 2, ? (Known only from 1740 purchase of land on Great
   Hunting Creek from Thomas Harrison.)
Ann 2, John 1, m. 1722 (1) John Quarles.
              m. ca. 1731 (2) Thomas Harrison.
Mary 2, John 1, m. 1726 John Catlett.
Elizabeth 2, John 1, m. 1731 (1) Thomas Hill.
              m. 1744 (2) William Cowne.
Susanna 2, John 1, m. 1731 ---- Linton.

    Peter Coldham, *The Complete Book of Emigrants*, 1607-1660, p. 162. 10 August 1635 William Grasson, age twenty, embarked on ship *Safety* (for Virginia). Possibly this man was the emigrant ancestor of the Graysons.
4. Spotsylvania Marriage Book 1. The first license issued on 10/2/1722 is to John Quarles, but the name of the bride is not given on the first few licenses. Quarles moved from Spotsylvania to Stafford about 1724.
5. Fx Liber G-167, 1767. Ann (Grayson) Harrison died before 1767 and after 1749, the year of the birth of Ann, her youngest child.
6. Joyner, *Northern Neck Warrants* Vol. III, abstracts following surveys: 1731. Thos. Harrison Jr., 271 a. on Four Mile Run adj. Capt. Simon Pearson's Red Oak land and James Robinson (now Quarles). 1741. Capt. Thomas Harrison Jr., 221 a. on Quantico. 1741. Capt. Thomas Harrison, 409 a. on Kettle Run and Slaty Run adj. James McDaniel, now said Harrison's, and Brenttown line. 1744. Major Thomas Harrison owns land adjacent to survey for Francis Jackson

on main run of Quantico. 1755. Col. Thomas Harrison, 344 a. on Slaty Run and branch of Cedar Run. PW Deeds involving Thomas Harrison include: D-147, 1738. Lease for lives to Thomas Harmer, 150 acres in Truro Parish on main road from Great Hunting Creek to Goose Creek. D-158, 1738. Sale to David Thomas of 150 acres in Truro Parish. E-156, 1740. Purchase from father, Thomas Harrison Sr., 238 acres, one fourth part of the grant from the Proprietors to Thomas Harrison Sr. and Thomas Whitledge, late of Stafford County, in the lifetime of the said Thomas Whitledge divided into four lots. Survey begins at the mouth of Dorril's Run. E-185, 741. Sale to Wm. Davy land on Great Hunting Creek. M-31, 1749. Sale to Richard Blackburn, Benjamin Grayson, and Louis Reno of 395 acres on Quantico Run to be used for the glebe of Dettingen Parish. The site is near present-day Independent Hill. R-354, 1770. Sale to Edmund Homes Jr. Description of the property is missing from the court copy. Probably it is the proceeds of this sale that are bequeathed to son Thomas. R-250, 1771. Sale to son, Thomas Harrison Jr. of Prince William, 200 acres on S. side of Kettle Run.

7. PW D B-40, 1733. Harrison's bond to King George II. B-365, 1734. Bond of deputy Samuel Smith to Harrison.

8. PW 1752-57: p.58. Harrison attended as evidence for Timothy Reading for thirty days, to be paid 750 pounds tobacco. p.91. Suit for trespass against Ann Apple Butler is agreed. Trespass was the term for dispute over a property boundary. The defendant was the mother-in-law of Harrison's son Thomas. p.160. To employ attorney for court. p.180. Negotiate for George Mason's ferry. p.281. Sheriff to sell sundry goods. p.293. Bridge over Cedar Run. p.304. In behalf of William Pickett, obtains certificate for a runaway slave belonging to James Duncan.

9. F M-1, May 1759-Dec. 1762. p.2. Appointed to obtain set of weights and measures for the county. p.67. John Harrison admits debt of 53 pounds to John Quarles. "Plaintiff agrees to take a subscription in the hands of Thomas Harrison, Gent. for 17 pounds in part (payment) of this judgment." The relation, if any, of John Harrison to Colonel Thomas is unknown. p.115. The county levy for 1761 includes payments to John Bell of more than 8 pounds sterling plus 1800 pounds tobacco and to Harrison of over 5 pounds as expenses for attending the Assembly as burgesses. This seems to be the only time that Fauquier paid expenses of its representatives to Williamsburg. Burgesses did not receive a salary. p.125. Administration of oath

favoring the heirs of Princess Sophia. p.155. Harrison takes oath as county lieutenant, John Bell as colonel, and Wm. Eustace as major. p.191. To provide a seal for the county. p.242. To pay county funds in his possession to Bertrand Ewell for running the "county line" with Prince William. Ewell's survey shows the location of Harrison's mill, which was still standing in 1967. Book 3, Nov. 1764–July, 1768. p.272. Harrison to receive money levied for the county's arms. Book 4, Aug. 1768–Mar., 1773. p.161. Harrison presides over Court of Oyer and Terminer trying a slave named Jack for stealing a cow worth 3 pounds. Jack was found guilty and branded on his left hand. p.368. The grand jury presents Thomas Harrison, Gent., for not declaring his chair carriage in his list of tithables. p.392. His account for money given for arms is settled. Book 5, Apr. 1773–Sept. 1779. p.103. Appointed collector of the county levy. p.104. Presents commission from governor as sheriff. Bond to King George III recorded. p.133. Wm. Edmonds presents commission as sheriff. p.135, 1/24/1774. Last will and testament proved. Ordered that Nicholas George, Original Young, John Orear of Prince William, and Charles Waller divide the Negroes devised by Thomas Harrison, Gent., dcd., between his three sons, William, Thomas, and Burr according to his will and that Thomas Marshall, John Moffet, and Thomas Nelson divide the lands devised to William and Burr between them and the stock between William, Thomas, and Burr. The first four dividers were neighbors of the deceased in the southern part of the county. The other three lived in the vicinity of the Colonel's lands in northern Fauquier.

10. Lord Fairfax was present and presided at PW court in August, 1755. Fairfax lived at his Greenway Court estate in Clarke County (then part of Frederick) from about 1749 till his death in 1781.

11. Henry Churchill, born ca. 1735, died of pleurisy December, 1760.

12. PW D E-524. The complete poll for burgesses taken in November 1741 gives the names of the 414 voters. William Fairfax of Belvoir, a relative of Lord Fairfax, was agent for the Proprietor from 1732 to 1747. When Fairfax County was set off in 1742, he became one of the two burgesses from that county.

13. Joseph Blackwell Sr., like Harrison, lived in the part of Prince William that became Fauquier. He died in Fauquier in 1787. John Bell resigned as burgess to become the second sheriff of Fauquier replacing Blackwell. Colonel

Thomas Marshall moved to Shenandoah County in 1772 to become its first county clerk. He had been an assistant surveyor of Frederick County under Washington and served as a colonel in the Revolution. After the war he moved to Kentucky and became the owner of thousands of acres there. James Scott, son of the Rev. James Scott, was an officer in the Revolution. He died in 1781.

14. *Journals of House of Burgesses.* References to Harrison include: 10/27/1748. On Committee for Courts of Justice. 2/27/1752. Again named to Courts Committee. 2/29/1752. Ewell's complaint on election. 11/24/1769. Harrison's complaint on election of Marshall and Scott.

15. Burgesses for Prince William and Fauquier from 1741 to 1769. The standard sources, namely the *Journals of the House of Burgesses* and Stannard's *Colonial Register* have one or two inaccuracies corrected below. Prince William: 1741-47. William Fairfax and Thomas Harrison Jr. but in 1742 Fairfax was elected in newly formed Fairfax Co. and Richard Blackburn took his seat. 1748-55. Harrison and Joseph Blackwell. 1756-58. Henry Lee and John Bell elected, but Henry Peyton complained successfully about Lee's election and won seat in new election. 1759-61. Henry Lee and Henry Peyton. Fauquier: 1759-61. Harrison and John Bell. 1766-69. Harrison and Thomas Marshall elected. In 1767, Marshall resigned to become sheriff, and James Scott took his place. Nov. 1769. Thomas Marshall and James Scott.

16. King, *Records of Dettingen Parish*, 7/11/1745. Harrison authorized to build gallery. 11/4/1749. First noted as present at vestry meeting. 11/19/1750. Paid 400 lbs. tobacco for keeping "pore" man. 8/28/1756. "Decents" to accept new church as completed. 11/27/1773. Named churchwarden. 4/19/1774. Deceased. Lewis Reno becomes churchwarden.

17. Fauquier deeds involving Harrison include: 2-104, 1764. Purchase from Elias Edmonds of 400 a. near what is now Marshall, Va. Part of a grant of 2003 acres to Major James Ball in 1732. 2-338, 1765. Purchase of 1000 acres from John Mercer, an original grant to Mercer in 1730 on branches of Goose Creek near the Cobblers Mountains adjoining the tract bought from Edmonds. 3-167, 1768. Sale to son William Harrison of 520 acres, part of the land purchased from Mercer.

18. John Farrow was the son of Abraham Farrow, partner of Thomas Harrison (1665-1746) in 1708 land grant.

19. PW W C-176, 1741. Will of Edward Sute, planter.

20. PW D Q-508, 1760. A receipt by Benjamin Grayson (Jr.) to Thomas Harrison on account of Col. Benjamin Grayson's estate.
21. See Appendix-Bullitt.
22. F D 5-454, 1773. Three bonds: 500 pounds for collection of quitrents, fines and forfeitures; 100 pounds for collecting, receiving, and paying officer's fees and dues; 1000 pounds for collection of taxes.
23. F W 1-231. Will dated 9/23/1773, pr. 1/25/1774.

Chapter VI

Cuthbert Harrison (ca.1712–1768)
(Cuthbert 3, Thomas 2, Burr 1)

Captain Thomas Harrison and his wife, Seth, had three sons who survived to maturity. They named the eldest of these Burr for the Captain's father; the second, Thomas for the captain himself or possibly for Seth's father; the third, Cuthbert, for the Captain's paternal grandfather.

Cuthbert was probably born between 1710 and 1715. Since he was not named as a helper on his father's tobacco plantation in 1723, he may have been less than ten years old that year. The first known mention of him came in November 1738 when he married Frances (Barnes) Osborne, the widow of Thomas Osborne, who had died the previous year. (1)   Frances, the daughter of Mathew Barnes, was the sister of Ann (Barnes) Harrison, the wife of Cuthbert's oldest brother. Both sisters were named in their father's will.

Osborne had had four daughters: Ann, Mary, Margaret, and Prudence. John Kincheloe gave bond as guardian of the three older orphans in 1739. Harrison did not become the official guardian of Prudence until 1744. (2)   It would appear that Frances may not have been the mother of the older Osborne girls, but that Prudence was her daughter.

What happened to the Osborne girls was described in a deed in 1777 from Cuthbert Harrison (Jr.) to Henry Lee for 100 acres on Neabsco Creek. The land had been sold by Richard Cropes (Crupps) the Younger to Thomas Osborne in 1732 and later "vested" in Osborne's daughters. Prudence Osborne died "soon after, a minor without issue." Ann married John Randolph, Mary married William Hendly, and Margaret married John Bland; these couples had sold their interests to Cuthbert Harrison, the father of the seller, in 1750 and 1751. (3)

83

Trying to find more about Cuthbert Harrison himself, we came across a note that a man of that name was indicted in 1744 by a grand jury in Frederick County in the Shenandoah Valley for selling liquor at his home without a license. Altogether there are at least eight notations about Cuthbert Harrison in the first two order books of Frederick, which cover the years 1743 to 1748. Six of these are for suits that he brought to collect debts. (4)

In one such, the defendant pleaded he owed nothing; the "parties put themselves upon the court who, after hearing the evidence and arguments," awarded Harrison three pounds "current money" and costs plus seven shillings sixpence, the standard amount for an attorney's fee in such cases. The lawyer collected enough to buy himself a half gallon of rum at the ordinary, one of which was certain to be located near the courthouse. Still, his earnings were at a rate five or six times the "minimum wage," taken as the allowance for a day's attendance as a witness at court. No doubt his charges were higher for any services not regulated by law.

Yet the Prince William wills and deeds named "our" Cuthbert Harrison in 1741, 1742, 1744, and 1746. In the last of these he was called a freeholder of Hamilton Parish. At first we thought the Frederick citations could not refer to the son of Captain Thomas, but eventually we discovered there was no need to invent another individual having the name. Harrison had moved from Prince William to the northern Shenandoah Valley probably before his marriage. When he returned is uncertain, but he was definitely back in Prince William by the end of 1745.

The proof that only one Cuthbert was involved was an order by the Frederick court in December of 1745 that "John Madden pay Cuthbert Harrison "285 pounds tobacco for attending three days as evidence for him ---- and for coming and going seventy miles." Seventy miles is about the distance from the southern part of Prince William to Winchester, then and now the county seat of Frederick. Harrison's value as a witness for Madden obviously derived from a period of residence in Frederick. But he would not have been paid for his travel to the court if he had still lived within the county.

At any rate, looking to obtain a grant of 164 acres on Lucky Run adjoining the land patented by his father with Thomas Whitledge in 1710 in Prince William, he had a survey made for him in 1740. Then a couple of years later he received a grant for 481 acres on branches of the Chopawamsic. Neighboring landowners there included John McMillion, his brother-in-law. (5) Harrison was not listed on the 1737 quitrent roll, but in the next roll still in existence, that of 1752, he was charged with 1086 acres.

Once "back home" near his brothers and sisters and their growing families, the trail of records on Cuthbert widens. For example, the Dettingen Parish vestry minuted a payment to him for "keeping a bastard child" and then "bound" the baby girl, "the issue of Hannah Murfey" to him in 1747. Since the child was white, the term of the indenture was until she was twenty-one, ten years less than if she had been a mulatto.

Additional references to Cuthbert Harrison were entered in the order books of the Prince William court; those for 1752–1757 have been preserved. Obviously, most were about suits before the court, but one recognized a deed to James Homes and two noted payments due for attendance at court as a witness. One of these was for six days on behalf of Thomas Botts against William Whitledge, Harrison's cousin and neighbor. Another citation mentioned a road to his house from Whitledge's mill.

Yet another order granted "Cuthbert Harrison, Gent.," a license to keep an "ordinary" at his house. (6) Equivalent to a modern liquor license, it was what Cuthbert had lacked when indicted in Frederick. Nowadays it would be strange for a "gentleman" to have a tavern at his residence, but in those times it was common for persons living close to a highway to have one on their property. ("Southern hospitality" might have required that a travelling stranger be given shelter. The ordinary license was perhaps a means of controlling such visitors.)

Rather than one large house, many wealthier individuals had several buildings, perhaps to reduce damage in case of fire. Some of these would have served as sleeping quarters for children and guests. A tutor might have lived over his school, an overseer and his family in another, and there would have been a kitchen for the main house, slave quarters, stables, and other farm buildings. Probably Harrison's ordinary was in one of the outbuildings.

Following in the footsteps of his father and older brothers, Cuthbert became a captain in the county militia and a justice of the county court of Prince William. From 1750 on he was usually referred to by the military title. He was named a justice in 1749. Appointments as a magistrate in the colonial system were for life or good behavior, unless the gentleman moved out of the county. In 1770 in a renewal of the commission of peace by the Governor's Council, Harrison's name was removed, because his death had been certified. (7)

Cuthbert, the youngest of the three Harrison brothers, was the first to die. The bond for the administration of his estate was registered in October 1768 by his son Cuthbert with nephews Cuthbert Bullitt and John McMillion as securities. (8) His personal estate was divided among his heirs by his nephews Thomas Harrison, John McMillion, and John Whitledge, appointed by the court for the task. (9) Harrison was survived by his widow; his son; and five daughters, the Misses Seth, Ann, Sarah, and Frances Harrison and Mrs. Elizabeth Scott.

Little is known of Cuthbert Harrison (Jr.). Apparently he was about thirty when his father died. He and his mother and unmarried sisters continued to live on the family residence, close to that of his uncle, Colonel Thomas Harrison.

The younger Cuthbert purchased a grant of 1350 acres on Summerduck Run in Fauquier County from the Proprietor's Office in 1775. (10) Very likely he was the Captain Cuthbert Harrison "of Prince William" identified by Gwathmey as serving in March 1776 under Colonel John Quarles and Major Leven Powell in the District Battalion. His cousin of the same name and almost the same age did not live in Prince William.

Cuthbert Harrison (Jr.) died in 1780. He may have been in poor health for some time, because he had written his will a year and a half earlier. He left all the land "I now live on" on the south side of Cedar Run adjoining the tract "taken up by my grandfather Thomas Harrison" to his sister Seth; other lands in that neighborhood were to be divided equally between his sisters Ann and Frances. He ordered that the lands on the head branches of the Chopawamsic be sold to pay debts. His married sisters, Elizabeth Scott and Sarah Harrison, were bequeathed one hundred pounds each. Seth Harrison and William Alexander were named the executors. (11)

The inventory of his estate listed fourteen slaves including "one old wench" of no value and two unnamed children. Their values ranged between fifteen hundred and two thousand pounds current money, as compared to a maximum of seventy pounds for the slaves of Cuthbert's cousin, William Harrison, just five years earlier. The annual rate of increase averaged over the period was almost one hundred percent, evidence of the inflation rampant in Virginia during the Revolution. As usual in such appraisals, slaves accounted for about seventy-five percent of the total worth of Cuthbert's personal property.

In October 1783 Ann Harrison died. She left all the land received from her brother Cuthbert to Seth and made smaller bequests to Elizabeth Scott; Frances Short; her mother; nephews Thomas Harrison and James Scott; Mary Ann Harrison, the daughter of Colonel Burr; and Mary Stuart Alexander, the daughter of Colonel William, with anything left to be divided between James and Nancy Scott. Thomas Short, who had married

Frances Harrison, was a witness. (12)

Seth died unmarried and intestate in 1786 or 1787. That meant that the eventual heirs of the elder Cuthbert Harrison were his three married daughters. Elizabeth was married to James Scott, Frances to Thomas Short, and Sarah to her second cousin, the Reverend Thomas Harrison.

In considering the career of the Cuthbert Harrison (Sr.), the importance of slavery to him and to other "gentlemen" of the time stands out. Already by the middle of the eighteenth century the social and economic status of the gentry of northern Virginia depended on slave ownership, as the list of titheables in Fairfax County compiled by the Reverend Charles Green for the year 1749 demonstrates. Excluding nonresidents, the 626 heads of households or establishments owned 613 male and female slaves over the age of sixteen. 468 households (75%) had none of these slaves. Only 24 of them (less than 4%) owned more than six slaves, but these 24 held 61% of the total number. Fourteen of the 19 justices of the county were among the twenty-four. No justice owned less than 4 slaves. In 1749 there was not a single free black in the county. (See Appendix A-Statistics for more details of this analysis of the Fairfax titheables.) Similar statistics for Prince William are not available, but surely there too the wealthiest 5% of the citizens owned more than half of the slaves.

Cuthbert (Sr.), a youngest son, may not have been among that "top" five percent before his father's death. Probably that was why he had to go off to Frederick where he set up a shop or store and where he had to institute suits to recover the debts of delinquent customers. But his life must have changed greatly after he returned "home" and inherited land and slaves from his father. At the end of his life he must have owned at least as many slaves as the fourteen on his son's inventory and probably several more.

In one sense, slavery facilitated the Revolution and the Constitution, because wealth and position based on ownership of slaves allowed Cuthbert and his brothers and others of his class to accept the responsibility for local government. Such schooling in the county courts contributed greatly to the formation of Washington, Jefferson, Mason, Henry, and the other Virginian patriots. Without indentured servants and then black slaves the English country squire system could not have been transplanted to an unpopulated wilderness where ordinary white people could get land of their own to work.

This is not to say that slavery was essential to our democracy. New Englanders developed the town meeting. The opening of the lands west of the Appalachians, where the great majority owned few or no slaves (as in the frontier section of Fairfax in 1749), brought Jacksonian democracy to the fore.

Notwithstanding the terrible injustice of their slave-owning, we can be grateful to Cuthbert Harrison, his brothers, and their ilk for their conscientious participation in the affairs of their communities and their even-handed administration of the laws.

Notes:

1. V-23/24 Harrison genealogy states: Cuthbert Harrison m. 11/19/1738 Frances Osborne, dau. of Mathew and Frances Barnes. Their Children: Elizabeth (1740-1823) m. 1760 James Scott; Seth (1742-1783) unmarried; John (1744- ?) no other information; Cuthbert (1747-1780); Frances (1749- ?) m. (Thomas) Short; Ann (1752-1783) unmarried; Sarah (1754-1842) m. Dec. 1775, Thomas Harrison.

2. PW W C-131, 1737. Thomas Osborne's inventory. PW W C-174, 1739. John Kincheloe's bond for guardianship of the three Osborne girls. PW W C-428, 1743. Estate Account of Thomas Osborne submitted by Cuthbert Harrison. PW W C-525, 1744. Cuthbert Harrison guardian bond for Prudence Osborne.

3. PW D T-70, 1777. Cuthbert Harrison to Henry Lee 100 a. PW D M-117, 1750. John Randolph and wife Ann, "one of the daughters and coheirs of Thomas Osborne," to Cuthbert Harrison. PW D M-218, 1750. William Hendley and wife Mary, a daughter and heir of Thomas Osborne, to Cuthbert Harrison.

4. Fk O 1, 1743-45, pp. 44, 236, 250. Fk O 2, 1745-1748, pp. 19, 22, 61, 466, 485. The formation of Frederick County out of Orange was authorized in 1738, but it was not organized until 1743. We have not searched the early Orange records.

5. NN E-416, 1742. 164 a. on Lucky Run near Cedar Run. NN E-417, 1742. 481 a. on branches of Chopawamsic and Beaver Dam Run of Aquia. PW D I-57, 1746. 99-year lease to Andrew Beard of 113 acres purchased of Christopher Holmes.

6. PW O 1754-55, p.12.

7. *Executive Journals*, Vol II, p. 375, 1770. Cuthbert Harrison, member of PW commission of peace, certified as deceased.

8. PW Bond Book, 1753-82, 10/3/1768.

9. PW O 1769-1771, p.215, 1770. On petition of James Scott Jr., Cuthbert Harrison, Seth H., and Frances H., Ann H., and Sarah H. by their guardian, sd. Cuthbert H. ordered John

McMillion, Cuthbert McMillion and Thomas Harrison to set apart and divide estate of Cuthbert Harrison (Sr.). When Cuthbert McMillion died early in 1771 he was replaced by John Whitledge. PW D R-334, 1771. Division of the es tate.

10. NN I-266, 4/12/1775. Cuthbert Harrison (Jr.) 1350 a. in Fauquier on branches of Summerduck Run. In 1796 this land was the subject of a suit by his heirs named as Elizabeth Scott, Thomas and Frances Short, and Thomas and Sarah Harrison.

11. PW W G-70, dated 1778, pr. Feb. 1780. Will of Cuthbert Harrison. PW W G-81, 1780. Inventory.

12. PW W G-261, pr. Oct. 1783. Will of Ann Harrison.

Chapter VII

Thomas Harrison Jr. (1724-1756) of Fairfax
(Thomas 4, Burr 3, Thomas 2, Burr 1)

The English habit of naming the eldest son after his paternal grandfather and the second or third after the maternal one can be the boon or the bane of genealogists. If the name is an uncommon one, such as Burr, it may aid in determining a relationship between men of different generations, particularly if they have different surnames. On the other hand, if the name is John or William or Thomas, it is little help and is often the source of confusion and error. Establishing the minimum data of birth, marriage, and death dates; places of residence; and names of parents, wives, and children can be a challenging task when several contemporaries share names. It may be next to impossible to determine which of two such men is referred to in an eighteenth-century record.

In the case at point, the Fairfax record books from 1750 to 1756 failed to distinguish consistently between two Thomas Harrisons. One of these was a great-grandson of Burr the immigrant and the eldest son of Burr (1699-1775). He was named for his paternal grandfather, Captain Thomas Harrison (1665-1746). The Dettingen Parish register stated he was born on March 3, 1723/4. He married Ann Waye Peyton, the daughter of John and Ann (Waye) Peyton, on July 2, 1747. (1) He died in February or March of 1756, when several suits in which he was involved "abated" because of his death. Ann Harrison and Yelverton Peyton, her brother, gave bond in Fairfax County for her administration of his estate in April. He was survived by four sons: Burr, John Peyton, Valentine, and Thomas. He had no daughters. These bare bones are well documented. (2)

The problem arises in attempting to flesh out this skeleton by searching the Fairfax documents. Although the county was formed in 1742, its earliest surviving order book begins in May,

1749. The first pertinent citation came the following September when "Cate a negro girl belonging to Thomas Harrison is adjudged to be nine years old." On the same date Thomas Harrison Jr. reported that his servant, John Campbel, ran away for ten days, and the court ordered Campbel to pay the cost of his retrieval (probably by serving extra time at the end of his contract). At the court session the next day John West Jr. and Thomas Harrison were appointed inspectors of pork, beef, flour, tar, and turpentine for the county. From then until 1756 a Thomas Harrison appeared occasionally, sometimes with the identifying appendage but usually without it. Never was there any "Sr." Mostly these were brief notices of suits, but in September, 1753 and again a year later Harrison was recommended (tantamount to being appointed) for the lucrative and responsible position of Inspector at the Hunting Creek tobacco warehouse. (3)

At the same time, in between these notices, Thomas Harrison, with no word or phrase distinguishing identity, was declared an insolvent debtor and released from custody after he declared an inventory of his goods, which were ordered to be sold at public auction to pay his debt to Benjamin Grayson. The full pathetic list named: "about three bushels of corn, a hh. [hogshead] of tobacco to pick [up?] at Pohick warehouse, four small middlings and one jamon of bacon, one mare colt, an old rug, a debt due me from Charles Wright - 70 pounds tobacco, from James Orchard - 20 pounds tobacco, materials for a jacket and breeches which I bought from Mr. Ramsay, two razors and two knives." The clerk copied his signature as Thomas Harrison with no Jr. A few months later, the man failed to make a court-ordered payment, and James Roberts was allowed to foreclose on his mortgage.

While these misfortunes were occurring, Thomas Harrison was three times an appraiser of the estate of a deceased neighbor, each of the neighbors living between Four Mile Run and Hunting Creek. Although all the appointments named him without the addendum, he signed each inventory "Thomas Harrison Jr." In the same period he was one of four citizens selected by the vestry of Truro Parish to "procession" land in the area circumscribed by Hunting Creek, the Potomac River, the road from Awbrey's ferry to the upper church, and the road from Cameron to that church. Only two months after the foreclosure, the court recorded deeds to Thomas Harrison of two lots in the Town of Alexandria. (4)

The up-and-down pattern of finances would be incredible, if it had not pertained to a melange of two individuals, whom their contemporaries had no difficulty in separating, but we

91

have a struggle to tell apart after the passage of nearly 250 years. One Thomas Harrison, the descendant of the first Burr, was well-to-do; the other, probably unrelated, was impoverished and in debt.

The Fairfax County list of titheables in 1749 showed only one Thomas Harrison, who had no slaves aged sixteen or older and no male white servants. He must have been the poor person never called Junior. Evidently, when the census was taken, the other Thomas Harrison, who always signed as Jr. and was sometimes but not always designated thus in court records, had not yet moved to the county with his slaves and his titheable white servant John Campbell.

The minutes by which the court named the administrator and the appraisers of the estate of the husband of Ann called him Thomas Harrison, but the bond itself specified Thomas Harrison Jr. He was indeed comfortably off; bond for the administratrix was set at 1000 pounds, nearly the maximum amount required for any estate at the time. According to the inventory taken in June 1756 but for some reason not presented to the court until June 1757, he owned seven slaves, one of whom was "Cate." His property also included a bay horse, two colts, and one "fleabitten" horse. Two-thirds of the total value of 226 pounds was in the slaves. (5)

The deceased Thomas Harrison Jr. may have gotten his start with a small inheritance in 1746 from his grandfather, for he was the oldest grandchild as well as the namesake of Captain Thomas. More important may have been the help he got from his family connections in gaining the profitable positions he held in the county. In addition to the post of inspector, he was sworn in as under-sheriff of the county a few months before he died. Inspectors and sheriffs garnered handsome fees for their work.

As far as is known, he did not own much land. Besides the lots in the town of Alexandria, the only other real estate to which he held title was a 1750 grant of forty-one acres of "waste" (previously unassigned) land and marsh on Great Hunting Creek "joining land whereon he now lives." He resided on two hundred acres owned by his father, the plot which the immigrant Burr had bought from the Nixons in 1688. The tract including his grant was sold by the Harrisons some years after his death. (6) Most likely its fields would have long since become unusable for tobacco cultivation, but there is no record that Thomas rented farm land elsewhere.

A deposition given in 1785 by John Sommers, who was "upwards of ninety two years of age" at the time, compounds the conundrum. He recalled that "in 1715 he had moved from

92

Dogues Neck to a place near the church (Christ Church) not far from the (present) Town of Alexandria where he lived until 1723 when he moved into the forrest about eight miles from Alexandria." He further noted that "when he came up, he found Henry Lucas living on the plantation where Thomas Harrison late of Fairfax County lived since." Lucas was "claiming under old Thomas Harrison, who was grand-uncle to the same Thomas Harrison that resided upon it many years since." (7)

Sommers's testimony related to the location of the corner of a Brent patent to land of the Alexanders at the mouth of Hunting Creek. To aid in fixing the point, Sommers remembered long ago having helped to drive rockfish up the creek with bushes and to have caught about four hundred of them stranded when the tide went out.

The plaintiff in the suit for trespass was the grandson of the Robert Alexander who had refused to allow the immigrant Burr Harrison have the land he had bought from the Nixons surveyed. Therefore, Sommers referred unquestionably to the 200-acre tract where Thomas Harrison Jr. had lived nearly forty years before.

What puzzles us in his testimony is that "old" Thomas Harrison, the son of the immigrant, was the grandfather, not the great-uncle, of that Thomas Harrison Jr. The easy explanation would be that the ancient Sommers had been mistaken about the relationship between Captain Thomas Harrison (1665-1746) and Thomas Harrison (1724-1756). Still part of the place "in the forrest" to which Sommers had moved in 1723 was leased to him by Captain Thomas, and so Sommers should have known the Harrisons well. The deposition itself demonstrated that the aged man was still in good physical condition, for the day before it was taken he had walked the bounds of a large disputed tract with a surveyor. Furthermore, none of the other witnesses impugned his memory or contradicted his testimony. Sommers lived three more years after making the affidavit.

This brings us back to a consideration of the identity of the Thomas Harrison of straitened finances. One candidate is the Thomas Harrison, planter, of the Parish of Truro who in 1734 sold land on the south branch of Pohick Creek. The tract was his share of a 1730 grant to Andrew Smarr, Burditt Harrison, and himself. The deed was signed with his mark; it had no release of a wife's rights. (8) No definite later record of the man has been found. It may be pertinent that the forfeited tobacco of the unfortunate debtor was stored in the Pohick warehouse in Truro Parish, not in the Hunting Creek warehouse where Thomas Harrison Jr. was an inspector. On the other hand the copy of the inventory included in the court order declaring the bankruptcy did not show that its signer was illiterate. If not the planter himself, perhaps the unidentified Thomas Harrison was his son or the son of Burditt Harrison.

Possibly old John Sommers had confused the poor Thomas Harrison with the better-off one. For that hypothesis, the only known Harrison grandnephews of Captain Thomas would be sons of Burr and Thomas Calvert alias Harrison. These Calvert/Harrisons may even have been the Harrisons of the Pohick grant. (See Chapter XV.) Favoring this conjecture is the fact that Burr Calvert alias Harrison Jr. secured a lease for lives in Fairfax County in 1756. The court minute acknowledging the lease called him Burr Harrison and indicated he was already living in the county. The Calvert-Harrisons also were called Harrises at times; in November, 1752 a Burr Harris was paid for appearing in Fairfax court as a witness, and the next month a Thomas Harris was sued there for debt. Both men were customers of the Colchester (Fairfax) store of John Glassford & Company in 1760. (9)

Further fuel for puzzlement is provided by a separate inventory of the goods of a Thomas Harrison taken in December 1756, six months after the one of the estate of the great-grandson of the immigrant. It was recorded in July 1757, one month after the other one. The two sets of appraisals were entirely different. Entitled "An Inventory," but not otherwise designated as a supplement to the earlier one, it listed only one slave, a few animals, a number of tools, and some corn. The report says the appraisal was ordered by the court, but no minute has been found for that action or for recording its submittal by the executor of the estate. (10) However, two of the three signatories were ordered in June 1757 to view work performed by George Nevill for "Ann Harrison, adm. of Thomas Harrison dcd."

Still more confusion is engendered by a court minute in November 1759 ordering the churchwardens of Truro Parish to bind Thomas and Burr Harrison, sons of Thomas Harrison dec'd, to Burr Harrison to learn the trade of carpenter and joiner and to read. A year later Burr Harrison posted bond with John West Jr. for his guardianship of John Peyton Harrison and Valentine Harrison. Then in February 1761, Burr Harrison again was bonded as guardian of Thomas and Burr, sons of Thomas Harrison deceased, this time with Hugh West as co-signer. Without any doubt the guardian bonds were for the orphans of Thomas Harrison Jr., as the four boys are listed in the Powell prayerbook among those raised by their grandfather, Burr Harrison (1699-1775). But what about the orphans apprenticed in 1759? Could they have been the children of the poor

Thomas Harrison? Why would Grandfather Burr have used the legal form of an indenture for two grandchildren, aged nine (Thomas) and eleven or twelve (Burr)? Were the specifications about teaching the boys a trade and to read just a standard formality? Once holding the indenture contract, why would Grandfather later change to a guardianship? The fact that John Peyton, the maternal grandfather, made bequests on his death in 1760 to the two boys with Peyton family names and none to the two with Harrison names could be explained by an agreement among the two men and the mother of the children.

Nevertheless, to have two Thomas Harrisons die in the same year, both leaving sons named Thomas and Burr, and all four of these orphans coming under the tutelage of a Burr Harrison, seems much too great a coincidence to be true.

With all this uncertainty we may never know who the other Thomas Harrison of Fairfax was or what happened to him after November 1754. If he had sons named Burr and Thomas, their fate has also been lost in the jumble of men with these names who came of age at about the time of the Revolution.

In contrast, the careers of the four sons of Thomas Harrison Jr. can be traced with considerable certainty. The eldest one, Burr, was living near the present town of Middleburg, Virginia, by 1771. In that year as guardian and "best friend," in the legal terminology of the day, he instituted a suit in the Fauquier court in behalf of his brother, John Peyton, who was not yet of age. In 1773 he acted for his brothers John Peyton and Valentine against Yelverton Peyton and Elizabeth Strother, an uncle and an aunt who were executors of the estate of the young men's grandfather, John Peyton. (11) About the same time Burr and John Peyton witnessed the Loudoun County will of Elijah Chinn, one of whose executors was their uncle, Leven Powell. (12)

Most likely this man was the Burr Harrison fatally wounded in an Indian attack on Logan's Fort, Kentucky, in May 1776. (13) At that time Kentucky was part of Fincastle County. There were only three settlements in the area: Harrodsburg, Boonesborough, and Logan's Station. Each was defended by its nearby stockaded fort, in which the inhabitants took refuge in times of danger from the Indians, much as their ancestors had done a century before in northern Virginia. Burr was not a militia officer; he was a citizen taking part in the defense of the fort. He was about twenty-eight years old when killed.

John Peyton Harrison received a bequest in the 1760 will of his maternal grandfather, for whom he was named. He was born after 1750, probably the third son. As noted previously, he was put under the guardianship of his Harrison grandfather in

1761 after the death of his Peyton grandfather. (14) Then in 1766 when he was about sixteen, he was apprenticed to Leven Powell, his uncle by marriage; he was included in the household of Powell in the Loudoun list of titheables for 1771. (15) In a note written about 1860 by a great-grandson of Powell, John Peyton and his brother Valentine were said to have been relatives and employees of Powell with whose approbation they enlisted in the Revolutionary army. (16)

The two brothers were commissioned as ensigns in the Second Virginia Regiment, became lieutenants in its Company Four, were promoted to captain in 1777, and served until 1780. John Peyton as captain of Company One was at Valley Forge in February, 1778. After the war the Commonwealth awarded each of them four thousand acres in the military district of Kentucky. (17)

How the brothers converted their military warrants into Kentucky land was delineated in powers of attorney they gave to Burr Powell (Leven's son) in 1790. That from John Peyton stated the purpose was for his cousin, a lawyer, to lay off and convey to Isaac Hite and two associates or their legal representative one-fourth of "3000 acres which Leven Powell on 1 May 1780 did on my behalf engage them for locating and securing the same in the then county of Kentucky." The power from Valentine used the same wording except that it was for 1000 acres and added "to transact & negotiate any kind of business which I may have in Kentucky."

In the case of John Peyton a mix-up ensued. He issued a new authorization to Burr Powell in 1795 explaining that Hite, to whom his associates had "relinquished their part," had been assigned and deeded 162 acres, part of a 1000-acre tract on the waters of Simpson's Creek. Hite had transferred this parcel to Leven Powell. "It now appearing that I had sold the whole of that tract to [blank] Chinn and neglected to make any reserve," Harrison authorized the selection of 184 acres out of another tract that had been surveyed by Hite "on the waters of Floyds Fork." This other parcel had originally contained 1000 acres, but one-fourth had already been conveyed to Leven Powell. The 184 acres were to be laid out as was most convenient to Powell in full compensation for the 162 acres that had been sold twice. (18)

Isaac Hite "found" land, surveyed it, and did the paper work necessary to secure a title. Much of his work was done in association with Colonel Powell, who was in effect Hite's sales agent in northern Virginia and probably provided financing. The services of Hite and Powell were evidently paid for with a quarter share of the land granted to the client. It looks as if Harrison did not entirely understand the procedure or he "plumb forgot" about it.

In 1779 Harrison married his doubly related cousin, Frances Peyton, the daughter of John and Seth (Harrison) Peyton. In 1784 he bought two tracts that had been devised to two sons of Elijah Chinn in the will he had witnessed before the war. One of the parcels adjoined land he already owned. After his first wife died in 1795, he married another cousin, Elizabeth, the daughter of Yelverton Peyton. There were reportedly seven children by the first marriage and one more from the second. (19)   About the time of his second marriage he moved from Fauquier to Stafford. In 1798 he and Elizabeth sold 305 acres on the north side of Bull Run Mountain (near Middleburg) in Fauquier, undoubtedly his previous residence. The deed did not recite the previous ownership of the parcel, and this has not been traced. (20)

Openly recognized class distinctions endured in Virginia for a long time after the Revolution. All men may have been created equal, but they did not remain so in economic or social status. In 1787 John Peyton Harrison, "Gent.," took the oath as a magistrate of Fauquier County, following in the footsteps of his Harrison and Peyton forebears. (21) In the Fauquier census of titheables taken the same year "Peyton Harrison" was entered as having no white males under age sixteen, five blacks below that age and six over it, eleven horses, and fifteen head of cattle. Soon afterwards he was appointed commissioner of the "turnpike road leading to Alexandria." This was one of the first toll roads. It is now Route 50 and still is the main street of Middleburg. Harrison lived near it in the northeast corner of Fauquier. (22)

Valentine Harrison was the youngest of the four brothers. After the war he made large investments in land in Jefferson County, Kentucky, but he remained a resident of Loudoun. (23)

The Reverend Thomas Harrison (1750-1814) was the second son. He was ordained in the Church of England in 1774 by the Bishop of London, whose diocese included the colonies of Virginia and Maryland. Since the bishop never came to America, the young man studied in England. Soon after his return he married his second cousin, Sarah Harrison, the daughter of his grandfather's brother, Cuthbert. The good opinion held of him among his relatives and friends was suggested in a postscript to a letter from Leven Powell to his wife written in December 1775. "I forgot in my last letter to inform you that Parson Tom was married to Miss Sally Harrison last Fryday." Mrs. Powell was the aunt of the groom, but only 4 years older than he. (24)

97

Bishop Meade writing in 1845 said he did not know what rectorships the Reverend Mr. Harrison held in Virginia, but apparently he first served Trinity Parish in Maryland and then Bloomfield in Culpeper County.

Hayden noted that he succeeded Rev. Spence Grayson as rector of Dettingen Parish in 1792. This was seven years after the disestablishment of the Anglican church in Virginia. For some time, however, it remained the church of the people whom we would now call The Establishment. Although the vestry book of the parish continues until 1802, no record appears to have been made of Harrison being its rector. It did mention him as an overseer of the poor in 1792.

From the beginning the established church had had responsibility for the poor. Its role in apprenticing poor orphan children has already been noted; in a few cases the vestry actually took children away from an irresponsible father. In addition it looked after poor adults. The annual vestry levies often included payments for such items as "caring for a poor man." Furthermore, as was done in England, small cash gifts were made to the poor annually. For example, William Bennet in 1763 deposed that he believed Thomas Snow was dead, "for Snow was one of the poor of this parish and at the three last times of laying the parish levy, there was nothing levied for him and nobody appeared to ask any allowance for him."

By about 1790 Harrison was living on part of the original plantation of his great-great-grandfather, the immigrant Burr Harrison. Harrison also owned other property in Prince William in the Cedar Run area where his father-in-law (and great-uncle) Cuthbert Harrison had resided. Some of that acreage may have been a legacy to his wife from her father; some was purchased. Like his brothers he also invested in Kentucky land. In 1810 he sold property on Harrison's Creek on the waters of Hanging Fork in Lincoln County; other land in that vicinity was sold by his executors. (25)

Manifestly, the extended Harrison family held their clerical relative in high esteem. On at least two occasions he served as trustee for older family members who wished to secure property for their heirs. In 1788 his great-aunt Seth, the widow of John McMillion, made the Reverend Harrison trustee for land on the main branch of the Chopawamsic in Stafford County. The tract had been willed to Seth by her father, Thomas Harrison (1665-1746) in entail, that is, limited to her and her descendants and not legally transferable to anyone else. It was to be held for her son John McMillion. However, the English law of entail had been revoked by the State Assembly, and even if it had been in effect still, her son was an eligible heir. So it is not clear why she took the step of putting it into a trust. Maybe she was afraid that otherwise her creditors or those of her late husband would lay claim to the land.

Another instance of such trusteeship had a sequel in 1840. In 1802 Beverly Robinson Wagener had made Harrison his trustee for land to be passed after his death to his wife, Margaret Short Wagener. (She was the daughter of Benjamin Harrison and granddaughter of Colonel Thomas of Fauquier). Although Mr. Wagener died in 1809, the Reverend Thomas never conveyed the land to the widow. In 1840, when she wanted to sell it, she had to get the Fauquier court to appoint a commissioner to make the conveyance to her. (26)

Thomas Harrison "of Fairview" dated his will on the last day of 1810, adding codicils later. He died June 21, 1814. The will named seven children: Philip, Burr, James, John, Walter, Betsy, and Sally. Other children not named in the will because they had died before it was written or had been taken care of previously were Cuthbert, Thomas, Frances, Ann Barnes, and Seth. Harrison instructed that his Kentucky lands be sold, but he did not want his property in Virginia divided, because he felt that would be injurious to his widow and children. (27)

It was the Reverend Mr. Harrison to whom the diary giving the names of Sarah Francis (Burdette) Harrison and Sythia Elizabeth (Short) Harrison was attributed. We hope someday to find that journal. In addition to confirming genealogical data, it would surely provide much historical information of wide interest.

Notes:

1. The date of birth was probably placed in the Dettingen register by Thomas's father, the clerk of the vestry. The source for the marriage record is G.H.S. King, *Overwharton Parish Register*.
2. Fx. Bond Book, p.29, 4/20/1756.
3. Fx. Minute Book references include: p. 33, 9/26/1749. Cate adjudged to be nine years old. John Campbel a runaway servant. p.36, 9/27/1749. Appointed inspector of Pork, etc. p.46, 12/26/1749. Sworn as inspector. p. 71, 3/31/1750. To pay John Pagan 950 lbs. tobacco. p. 131, 3/27/1751. To appraise estate of John Jones. p. 154, 4/3/1751. Defendant on petition of Thos. and Wm. Gilpin. Suit dismissed---statute of limitations. p.189, 4/1/1752. With Wm. King to pay Gerrard Alexander 1000 lbs. tobacco. p. 343. Road surveyor in room of Wm. Ramsey. p. 366, 5/18/1753. To appraise estate of Joseph Boling. p.

447, 9/18/1753. Inspector at Hunting Creek with Richard Sanford, Robert Sanford, and John Moss. p. 470, 11/20/1753. Defendant in trespass, assault, and battery on Robert and Jane Highsted. p. 71, 4/16/1754. Insolvent debtor to Benjamin Grayson, goods sold by sheriff. p. 150, 9/17/1754. Inspector at Hunting Creek with Sanford brothers and Presley Cox. p.155, 9/18/1754. To inventory estate of Edward Masterson. p.171, 11/21/1754. James Roberts forecloses. p.204, 1/21/1755. Deeds of Alexandria lots acknowledged. p. 408, 9/17/1755. Sworn as under-sheriff. p.478, 2/19/1756. Three suits abate; plaintiff dead. p.492, 3/17/1756. Two more suits abate. p. 500, 4/20/1756. Administration of estate of Thomas Harrison, dcd. granted Ann Harrison who with Yelverton Peyton acknowledged bond. John Dalton, Richard Sanford, and Robert Sanford to appraise estate of Thomas Harrison. 3/23/1757. Suit of Highsteds abates. p.123, June, 1757. George Nevill ag. Ann Harrison, admx. of Thomas Harrison. Wharton Randall, Duff Green, and Richard Hampton to view work plaintiff performed for defendant. p.425, 11/22/1759. Churchwardens of Truro Parish bind Thomas and Burr Harrison, sons of Thomas Harrison deceased., apprentices to Burr Harrison to learn the trade of carpenter and joiner and to read. p.524, 10/21/1760. Burr Harrison guardian of Valentine and John Peyton Harrison. p. 553, 2/16/1761. Burr Harrison guardian of Thomas and Burr Harrison, sons of Thomas Harrison, deceased.
4. The deeds, although listed in the general index, have been lost.
5. Fx W B-1-164. Inventory of Thomas Harrison dec'd taken 6/22/1756 by John Dalton, Richard Sanford, and Robert Sanford; recorded 6/21/1757.
6. NN F-359, 1750. Also Fx E-186, 1762. Burr Harrison of PW and Ann, his wife, to John West Jr. of Fx., 250 a. on Great Hunting Creek. Willed by John Alexander to Elizabeth Holmes who m. Richard Nixon. The Nixons sold to Burr Harrison who willed it to son Thomas. John West Jr. was the son of Hugh West and the great-grandson of Major John West of the West-Harrison-Pearson-Harrison patent.
7. PW Land Causes, Oct. 1790, pp. 286-293.
8. PW D B-471.
9. Fx M Sept. 1756, p.30. Fx D D-334, 8/13/1755.
10. Fx W B-1-165. Inventory of Thomas Harrison taken Dec. 1756 by Duff Green, Wharton Randall, and Joseph Minter; recorded July, 1757. Total value was 57 pounds. According to the will book the court ordered both the taking of the

inventory and the recording of it, but neither minute can be found. They may have been entered on one of several missing pages of the pertinent order book.

11. F M Aug. 1771, p.325. John Peyton Harrison by Burr Harrison Jr., his guardian, ag. Charles Rector. Ibid, Mar. 1773, p.489. Burr Harrison vs. Peyton's Executors.
12. L W A-290, 1/22/1771. Elijah Chinn of Shelburne Parish.
13. Illinois Hist. Collections, Vol. 8-22, George Rogers Clark papers, 1771-1781. "May 30 (1776), Indians attacked Logans Fort, killed and scalped Wm. Hudson wounded Burr Harrison & Jno. Kennedy. June 13, Burr Harrison died of his wounds."
14. See Appendix-Peyton.
15. L O C-279. Harrison bound to Powell.
16. Leven Powell Papers, Library of Congress, op.cit.
17. V 23-332 summarizes military records. See also Gwathmey.
18. L D S-166, 1790. John Peyton Harrison, power of attorney to Burr Powell. Ibid S-167. Power from Valentine Harrison.
19. V 23/24 genealogy says John Peyton Harrison m. (1) 1/12/1779 Frances Peyton (1754-1795) and (2) Elizabeth Peyton (1761-1816). Children: Robert, Seth, John Peyton, Sarah Ann, Frances, Elizabeth, Jane Linton, and Daniel; all but last by first wife.
20. L D O-128, 1784. Rawleigh Chinn Jr. of Loudoun to John Peyton Harrison of Fauquier, tract in Loudoun willed by Elijah Chinn, "corner to Leven Powell." Ibid. O-138, 1784. Christopher Chinn to Harrison. Two tracts in Loudoun and Fauquier bequeathed by Elijah Chinn, bounded by ---- Leven Powell, John Peyton Harrison. F D 14-261, 1798. John P. Harrison and Elizabeth his wife of Stafford to Henry Downs of Loudoun.
21. F M Aug. 1787, p.355.
22. Ibid. Aug. 1788, p.503. Appointed commissioner. Ibid. Apr. 1798, p.530. Resigned as commissioner.
23. F D 13-323, 1790.
24. V 24-211.
25. P W D references to (Rev.) Thomas Harrison: Y-705, 1772. From Elizabeth Scott, widow of James Scott, half of land on Cedar Run of Seth Harrison dec'd.; adjoins Harrison. A. Harrison a witness. Z-412, 1799. For natural affection to Thomas Harrison of Thomas, 305 a. on Cedar Run purchased of John Whitledge. Z-454, 1799. Lease by Thomas and Sarah Harrison to Gavin Adams for life of him and wife. Land bought of Wm. Tyler dec'd by Burr Harri-

son Sr. late of Chopawamsic. 1-19, 1799. 54 a. to John Bridwell. 1-20, 1800. 330 a. from Beverley R. Wagener and wife Margaret and Mary Harrison, relict of Benjamin Harrison. 1-425, 1799. 200 a. from same sellers. 3-268. Seems to be same as Z-412. 4-176, 1810. To James Warren, tract on Harrison's Cr. on waters of Hanging Fork. 4-417. 350 acres in same location to Larkin Sandage. PW Land Causes, 1754-1811, p.512. Suit concerns sale by heirs of Thomas Harrison of land on Dick's Creek in Lincoln Co., Kentucky.

26. PW D X-189, op. cit. F D 40-275, 1840. Beverley R. Wagener by Seth Combs, commissioner, to Margaret Short Wagener.

27. PW W K-112, will; K-133, inventory; K-506, estate account.

Chapter VIII

Burr Harrison (1734-1790), Merchant
(Burr 4, Burr 3, Thomas 2, Burr 1)

Colonel Burr Harrison was born on June 16, 1734 in Prince William County, the second son of Burr and Ann Barnes Harrison. (1) During his career he reached the positions of presiding justice of the court of his county and of burgess representing it in the Assembly. He inherited the home plantation of his great-grandfather, the first Burr Harrison, on Chopawamsic Creek and passed it on to one of his sons.

The first notice of this fourth generation Burr Harrison contrasts sharply with his later accomplishments. As "Burr Harrison, the Younger" he celebrated his upcoming eighteenth birthday a bit too boisterously. On that anniversary in 1752 he and his brother-in-law, John Peyton, had to appear in the Fairfax Court. They had been arrested by William Ramsay, a justice of the peace, on the complaint of Anne Jennings. When their accuser failed to appear in court, the two were released, but each had to post bond of five hundred pounds sterling to guarantee his future good behavior. (2)

Still, only two years later, young Burr had left home on the Chopawamsic to work at the highly responsible position of assistant surveyor of Augusta County. Surveyors were licensed by the College of William and Mary, and their fees for a new survey and plat of up to 1000 acres were fixed at five hundred pounds of tobacco. A sixth of the fee went to the college.

Just where in that large frontier county his job took him is not known, but it kindled his interest in Shenandoah Valley land. (3) In fact, that same year in a grant that identified him as Burr Harrison Jr. of Augusta County, he obtained 250 acres on the drains of the North River. (4) He was to live for most of the next twenty years on that tract located on the east side of the North Fork of the Shenandoah near where the main road from Winchester to Staunton crossed the river. Today's maps place the spot in Shenandoah County just south of Mount Jackson off Route 11. (5)

After the 1754 patent the young man appeared next in a list of payments to the College of William and Mary in 1758. The payment may have been for his certification as a surveyor. Another possibility was that he hoped to become a lawyer, but if that was his goal, he did not achieve it. (6)

Just how long he attended the college, if at all, is not known. It could not have been for more than a year, for by the middle of 1759 Burr and his brother Mathew were in the merchandising business running one or more general stores in the Valley. The two, as Messrs. Burr Harrison Jun'r. & Mathew Harrison, gave a bond cosigned by their cousin, John McMillion, and brother-in-law, John Peyton, for a credit of 175 pounds sterling to John Glasford & Company. (7)

The parent Glasford Company was located in Glasgow, Scotland. It had stores in Norfolk and on both sides of the Potomac. In northern Virginia its outlets, which sold both wholesale and retail, were found at Dumfries, Colchester, and Alexandria. Complementing its sales of mainly imported items, Glassford and Company was an exporter of tobacco, generally in its own ships. It also acted as banker for its clients, receiving and disbursing tobacco or currency for the client's account. It was probably the biggest of the Scottish merchandizing businesses in the area. Many of its ledger books for the decade beginning in 1758 have survived.

As an example of the type of goods the Messrs. Harrison bought from Glasford for resale, the August 23, 1759 entry in their account will serve. The items purchased that day were:

                    1 pr. mens silk stockings
                    1 pr. black wosted Ditto
                    3 dozn flat pewter plates
                    2 dozn soop Ditto
                    1 1/2 dozn pewter dishes
                    3 pewter porringers
                    3 gallon pewter basons
                    3 3 quart Ditto
                    3 3 pint Ditto
                    1/2 barrel gun powder
                    1 pss blue shalloon
                    10 yards black Mantua silk
                    7 1/4 yards bearskin
                    10 yards blue duffle
                    1/2 pss shaloon ... 15 yards

```
6 yd spotted rugs
1 womans cloak blue
2 ... Ditto green and cloth colour
2 ps hempen rolls ... 70 ells
1 dozn mens felts (hats) ... No        3
1/2 dozn Ditto ...................        5
1/2 dozn Ditto ...................        6
1 dozn  mens castors .......        1
1 Sursingle
```

The total cost of these articles came to a little over 31 pounds sterling to which was added 75% for the conversion to "Virginia currency" making the billing 54/13/7 1/4. (Quarter pennies or farthings did not go out of use in Great Britain until well into the twentieth century.) No interest was charged on any of the retail customer accounts. We did not determine whether customers who paid cash received a discount. (8)

The clerk who kept the ledger book for Glasford's wrote with a fine hand, and his antique lettering is generally decipherable. However, some of the archaic terms and spelling sent us to our dictionaries. Webster's enlightened us. Shalloon is a woolen twill cloth used for dresses and coat linings, and duffel is a coarse woolen with a thick nap. The English ell of forty-five inches was usually a cloth measure; it may have been in this case, but we believe the "hempen rolls" were coils of rope because of their length. At 0/1/8 the "sursingle" was the least expensive item. It was probably a saddle girth, but may have been some other type of band. We assume pss meant pieces. Men's castors were beaver hats. We were surprised to find that hat sizes had already been standardized and that some items of ready-made clothing were available and in demand even on the frontier.

The partners made additional purchases in six days and again in four days more. These included a cask of "hunters pipes," sixteen penknives, two dozen clasp knives, eleven mouse traps, and a quantity of "Muscadadoe" sugar. Messrs. Harrison and Harrison was the biggest customer of the Dumfries store.

In addition to tending his general store, Harrison operated a mill on Smith Creek which ran through his property, did some surveying, and engaged in buying and occasionally selling land in the area. In 1761 he obtained a grant from the Proprietor's Office for 400 acres on Stoney Creek. Other grants were for 350 acres on Flint Run in 1763 and 20 acres on the SE side of the North River in 1766. (9) Between 1761 and 1781 a total of fifteen deeds were registered by Burr for purchases and sales.

These included the sale in 1768 of the land on Stoney Creek. (10)

However, with so much land available it is unlikely that Harrison considered his real estate ventures as a means to make a profit on resale of properties after developing them by clearing and fencing the land, building houses and barns, planting orchards, etc. He probably made such improvements, but his true motivation in his transactions was most likely to put "money in the bank," to sell later if necessary but otherwise to pass on to his large family of children. No doubt he thought his land would help him to keep grown sons nearby and to get suitable husbands for his daughters.

Once established in the valley, Harrison played an important role in community affairs. He was one of the founding trustees of Woodstock, now Shenandoah's county seat. (11) He was a vestryman of Frederick Parish, and after it was divided, he continued on the vestry of the new parish of Beckford, becoming one of its two churchwardens in 1773. (12)

When Dunmore County was formed out of the southern part of Frederick in 1772, Burr Harrison, as the first-named member of its commission of peace, took the oath of office and then administered it to the other justices. He signed the first minutes and continued to preside over the court whenever he was present. (13) He was one of the justices who received Abraham Brubaker's gift of two half-acre lots in the town of Woodstock on Main and Front Streets to be the site of a courthouse in 1774. At the same time he was one of the vestrymen who accepted two more lots from Brubaker, directly across Main Street, to be used to erect a church with a burying ground. Main and Front is still the center of Woodstock; the present courthouse is across Front from its original location. (14) (The county was renamed Shenandoah in 1776, after Governor Dunmore had failed in his attempts to put down the Revolution at its beginnings.)

The Harrison residence was some fourteen miles south of Woodstock and only a few miles north of the southern limit of the Fairfax Proprietorship. Because of its location, the property was involved in a dispute over land titles occasioned by the 1745 delineation of that border line. The matter came to a head in 1772, when a series of deeds were recorded from "George Mercer, late of the Colony of Virginia but now of the city of London, and James Mercer of Spotsylvania for himself and as executor of Mrs. Ann Mercer, late of Stafford," to seventeen grantees, the first of whom was Burr Harrison. The wording of each deed was identical except for the description of the tract involved, the name of the grantee, and the amount paid the Mercers. (15)

All the deeds explain that Benjamin Borden of Augusta County in 1735 had bought 3300 acres, part of 100,000 acres granted to Robert McKay and Joist Hite by the governor and Council. In 1745 part of this acreage fell in the domain of Lord Fairfax. Although the order of King George II defining the boundary specified that Lord Fairfax should confirm all grants made by "His Majesty's Council in Virginia" including the one to McKay-Hite, Fairfax not only failed to comply, but he subsequently made grants that conflicted directly with the earlier ones. Some of these were for parts of the Borden tract.

McKay-Hite and the persons claiming under them initiated court actions to enforce their rights. Borden appointed attorney John Mercer to represent him, and when the suits dragged on, he made over his rights to Mercer. In 1759 Mercer had sold to his sons, George and James, undivided shares with himself in the property. Then Mercer died in 1768 and willed his share to his widow, Ann, as "tenant in common" with her stepsons. Ann accepted a proposal that James negotiate settlements with the parties in actual possession of the tract. Burr Harrison, one of these, agreed to pay the Mercers half the value of his own land and to make a survey at their expense of all the subdivisions of their property. After the survey was carried out, Ann reneged on the deal. Then she died and by her will ordered her executors to sell any land she possessed. The sixteen deeds were a final settlement, with the sellers renouncing any further right to claim under McKay-Hite and to defend the buyers against any claims the McKay-Hite heirs might have against them.

Harrison's new deed covered 187 acres on the banks of Smith Creek in the line of George Harrison (his brother) down the mill race to a pile of stones near Harrison's mill. Mathew Harrison witnessed the deed. The survey plat signed by Burr Harrison showed a total of 2134 acres, including 127 belonging to George.

In April, 1775 Harrison gave a deed to Peter Hogg and Gabriel Jones as trustees to sell nine tracts in the County of Dunmore. Seven of these adding up to 798 acres were already recorded in Dunmore or Frederick; two more grants of 400 acres each had not yet issued from the Proprietor's Office. Proceeds were to be used to pay the following debts: a bond for 160 pounds Virginia current money for which Jones and James Keith had given security in a suit still pending; 716 pounds to James Ritchie & Co. of Glasgow, merchants; 353 pounds to John McCall & Co., merchants; and 243 pounds to John Glassford & Henderson of Glasgow, merchants. (16)

Probably the reason that Harrison was selling out his Valley properties was that his father had asked him to move back to Prince William. When Burr Sr. died the following October, he willed Burr Jr. the ancestral plantation on the Chopawamsic.

There Harrison continued active in public affairs. In fact, he was promptly elected one of the county's two representatives to the House of Delegates. (17) A letter to his brother-in-law, Leven Powell, in November of 1776 noted that he was just back from Williamsburg and might "say with trooth that the House had done nothing." Dilatory action or outright inaction by a legislature was a subject of complaint long before present times. The same letter advised that by an express from Fort Pitt he had learned that "all my provision houses on the Little Kanawha is burnt by the Indians." On a more personal basis he was "sorry to hear of Coll. [Henry] Peyton's prodigious loss [of slaves] by disease and of your own." (18)

According to Gwathmey, Harrison was a colonel in 1776/7 and a Continental paymaster in 1780-1 during the Revolution. Indeed, in July 1776 he was appointed paymaster to the Virginian troops at Wheeling, Little Kanawha (Parkersburg), and Great Kanawha (Charleston) and contracted to furnish rations to these stations. He was referred to as Colonel Harrison in contemporary documents. In 1783 his claim for five shillings for rope requisitioned by the Continentals was allowed as was a receipt for 18/1/7 for beef supplied the militia. (19)

Another letter addressed to Colonel Powell in Kentucky in March 1780 treated business only. Evidently the two men were allied in various ventures in the West. Harrison acknowledged receipt of the Juiland (?) certificates, thanked Powell "for the trouble you have had with my business at Fort Pitt," and regretted that he had been unable to get Mr. Brent of Richland to take any part in the "Mississippi Company." Since "his brother" had informed him "of your 60,000-acre purchase on the western waters," he was "stopt from offering to trouble you about my military claim" and had put it in the hands of John Farrow to get a survey made. (20) The award by Virginia for his military service included 2000 acres on Floyd's Fork south of Louisville. (21)

Businessman Harrison had other projects underway. He set up a partnership with his cousin, the lawyer Cuthbert Bullitt, and family friend, Richard Graham, to produce rope. The ropewalk for the manufacture was built at his home plantation with the sales made from Graham's store in Dumfries. Bullitt's responsibilities in the venture were not defined. (22)

The next year Harrison purchased a gristmill on the south

108

side of Quantico Creek near the main post road from Dumfries to Fredericksburg. The seller was John Graham (the father of Richard) who had retired as county clerk of Prince William after more than a quarter-century of service. Whether the ropewalk prospered is not known, but the flour mill was important enough for Harrison to give instructions in his will that it be sold. (23)

Harrison supported his friend Cuthbert Bullitt in two real estate ventures, neither of which really got off the ground. By 1787 the port of Dumfries on the Quantico had begun to silt up, and much of its trade had moved away to Alexandria and other places. Bullitt, who owned land on both sides of the mouth of the creek, obtained authorization of the Virginia Legislature to lay out a town that he called Newport on thirty acres on the north bank. A year later Carrborough was authorized on fifty acres on the opposite bank. Harrison was a trustee for both towns. Although warehouses were built at Newport and a ferry across the Potomac to Maryland was already operating from the locality, the ambitious plans failed. (24)

Colonel Harrison made his will early in 1789, but he did not die until the following year. This may indicate that he suffered ill health for the last year or so of his life. That there are few surviving records of his activities in this period may support the conjecture. In his will he made specific bequests to three sons and two daughters. Matthew received a tract of land on Jackson's River in Botetourt County. Cuthbert was given the military claim for two thousand acres on Floyds Fork and his tuition at William and Mary for a year plus two hundred pounds so that he might qualify as a lawyer. Thomas was left land "beyond Black Hill" plus the family plantation on the Chopawamsic, obtained "by deeds from my father." Ann Catherine and Mary Ann received slaves as did each of the sons. Wife Mary Ann was the residual legatee, but she formally renounced her rights under the will, preferring her dower rights to one-third of the estate. Probably, she was advised to do so by her eldest son, Mathew, who had previously given up all his "benefits" under the will in favor of his two sisters. (25)

The widow Mary Ann Harrison died in 1803. In her will she named her daughters, Mary Ann Dade and Ann Catherine Hereford; her son Mathew; and her granddaughters, Mary Ann Hereford and Maria Harrison (daughter of Mathew). (26)

Burr and Mary Ann Barnes, his cousin, had been married in September of 1760, a year after he had gone into the merchandising business. Mary Ann was the daughter of Matthew and Catherine Barnes, and the niece of Burr's mother, Ann (Barnes) Harrison. Bride and groom were both twenty-six.

Burr and Mary Ann had the following eight children:

Anne Catherine, b. 10/23/1761, d. 12/6/1839, m. Francis
    Hereford on 9/5/1793.
Mathew, b. 9/19/1763, d. 8/22/1807, m. Catherine Elzey.
Jane, b. 9/29/1765.
Burr, b. 3/25/1767.
Cuthbert, b. 12/28/1768, d. after 1797.
Anne Barnes, b. 2/20/1771
Thomas, b. 3/22/1774, d. after 1820.
Mary Anne, b. 5/1/1776, m. ---- Dade.

Of these Jane, Burr, and Anne Barnes must have died
before their father, since they are not named in his will. (27)
    Mathew was an attorney who resided in Dumfries. He had
qualified for the Fauquier bar in 1786 and in 1792 was appointed commonwealth attorney for Loudoun County. His wife was
the daughter of William Elzey. The couple had ten children of
whom at least eight lived to maturity. His will provided for the
"education of the children in the most liberal manner that their
geniuses and tempers and habits will justify." (28)
    Cuthbert, the second son, did fulfill his father's hope that
he would become a lawyer, for he was licensed to practice in
the Fauquier county court in December 1797. (29)
    Thomas, the inheritor of the Chopawamsic lands, became
known as "Big Chappawamsic Tom." As a magistrate in
Prince William, he took the oaths of several persons who had
moved to Virginia from other states. The standard wording was:

> *I,----, do swear that my removal to the State
> of Virginia was with no intention to evade the act
> for preventing the further importation of slaves
> within this Commonwealth nor have I brought any
> slaves with the intent of selling them nor have any
> of the slaves now in my possession been imported
> from Africa or any of the West India islands since
> the 1st day of November, 1778. (30)*

The Virginia law requiring this oath followed the U.S.
Congress action in 1808 (as soon as permitted by the Constitution) to prohibit further importation of slaves.
    Thomas almost lost the Chopawamsic estate. The problem
had arisen several years previously when an Edward Moore
brought a suit against Mathew Harrison, the sole surviving
administrator of the will of Colonel Burr Harrison and one of
his heirs, the widow Mary Ann Harrison, and Thomas Harrison,

an heir. Moore wished to collect from the heirs on a bond given in 1774 in payment for whiskey stills furnished to Colonel Burr. Before final judgment in the case, Moore and all the defendants except Thomas had died. The court ruled for the plaintiff in the original instance and on appeal. Then, since the assets of the estate had long since been distributed, it ordered the sale of the seven hundred acres on the Chopawamsic that Thomas had been bequeathed. Fortunately his bid of 755 pounds at the sheriff's auction was the highest offer. Moore's executors were paid 580 pounds from the sale. Thomas was hit by two other suits for debts incurred by his father and lost both. Finally, with everything settled he received a clear title in 1810 to the land handed down to him by his Harrison ancestors. (31)

In spite of the expense of the suits, Harrison was in no danger of bankruptcy. The census of 1810 showed him owning twenty-five slaves. His household numbered two males aged 26-45 (one an employee), two under 10, one female 26-45, one 16-26, one 10-16, and two under 10.

Notes:

1. Both H.T.Harrison's genealogy and the "Kentucky Bible" of Cuthbert Harrison agree on the date of birth.
2. Fx. M 6/16/1752. Burr, whose parents lived in Prince William, must have been visiting the home of his brother Thomas near Alexandria. John Peyton was married to Burr's sister Seth. He was also a first cousin of Mrs. Thomas Harrison. Daniel French co-signed Burr's bond and Henry Peyton that of his brother John. Burr was "the Younger" in relation to Burr Harris/Harrison Jr., a cousin of his father, Burr Sr.
3. Au W 2-81.
4. NN H-438, 1754. Apparently, he was not yet 21.
5. Several deeds point to the location. E.g., Fk D 6-314, 1761. John Clark to Burr Harrison Jr. 4 a., part of 200 a., on E side of North River, where sd. Harrison now lives.
6. T 2-132.
7. John Glasford & Company Ledgers, Library of Congress Manuscript Division, Dumfries Store 1758-9, Part 1, p.183.
8. Ibid., Part 2, p.102.
9. Northern Neck grants to Harrison include: K-289, 1761. 400 a. on Stoney Creek. M-146, 1763. 350 a. on Flint Run. N-96, 1766. 200 a. SE side of North River. T-124, 1788. 325 a. NW side of North River, adj. own land. T-156, 1788. 400 a. incl. 80 conveyed by William Clark, on North River.

10. Fk D 7-175. William Clark to Burr Harrison, merchant, 37 a. on Shenandoah River.

11. Henning, VII-406, March, 1761. Burr's brother Mathew was also a trustee.

12. J.W. Wayland, *Shenandoah Valley Pioneers*, p.181.

13. *Executive Journals*, VI-456.

14. Sh D B-8 and B-10, 1774.

15. Sh D A-171, 1772.

16. Sh D B-179, 1775. The nine tracts all lay "in the North Fork of the River Shenandoah in the county of Dunmore, beginning near where the main road crosses the river." The lots were 225 a. and 4 a. obtained from John and Sarah Clark, 37 and 80 a. from William and Suzannah Clark, 220 a. from Joseph White, 20 a. from William and Ann White, and 212 a. from Cornelius and Ingobe Ruddle plus two surveys for 400 a. each for which deeds had not yet issued.

17. V 8-200, 1778. Burr Harrison was discharged out of custody of the sergeant-at-arms of the House of Delegates after paying fine for non-attendance.

18. Leven Powell Papers, Library of Congress Manuscripts, Item 24, 11/12/1776. Powell, two years younger than Harrison, married the latter's sister Sarah in 1765. She was born in 1746, making her ten years younger than her husband.

19. Va. State Archives has records on Revolutionary War claims.

20. Leven Powell Papers, Library of Congress Manuscripts, Item 23, 3/21/1780. Mr. William Brent of Richland was the great-great grandson of Captain Giles Brent and his wife Maria, the Piscataway Indian Princess.

21. We have been unable to find the grant for the military land in Kentucky mentioned in the letter to Powell and in Harrison's will.

22. PW D U-57 records the partnership agreement.

23. PW D U-196. Dumfries was laid out on land belonging to John Graham (1711-1787) on the north side of the Quantico Creek. His wife, Elizabeth, who signed the release was the daughter of Catesby Cocke, the first county clerk of Prince William. Graham succeeded him and then was followed in the office by his son Robert. Having this remunerative position remain in one family for many years seems to have been the rule rather than the exception in eighteenth-century Virginia.

24. *Prince William, The Story of its People and Places*, Bicentennial edition, p.88. Dumfries, which had been chartered in 1748 and made the county seat in 1762, was a bustling

112

port until after the Revolution but then declined gradually. Through its second century it was only a tiny village.

25. PW W G-474 is the will, which named Cuthbert Bullitt executor; H-47 is the first of three pages of the inventory of the estate; H-201, the estate account signed by Matthew Harrison Jr., who had become administrator after the death of Bullitt, shows that John Marshall (later Chief Justice) had purchased Colonel Harrison's Shenandoah lands. PW D X-481 is the renunciation of rights by Matthew; PW D X-513 is the renunciation by Mrs. Mary Ann Harrison witnessed by Matthew Harrison, Thomas Harrison, and Matthew Harrison Jr. The first of the witnesses was her brother-in-law and the second and third her sons.

26. PW W I-8. Maria Harrison was given a pair of earrings and Mary Ann Hereford, a slave. William Barnes, one of the witnesses, was probably a nephew.

27. H.T. Harrison, *Brief History Harrisons*. This source of genealogical data on the family is mostly correct, but the dates it gives for the death of Mrs. Mary Ann Harrison and her son Cuthbert are wrong.

28. PW W I-358, 11/2/1818 is will of Mathew Harrison.

29. F M Dec. 1797, p.374.

30. E.g., PW D 2-61.

31. PW Land Causes, p.494, Moore's suit. PW D 4-75, Deed from commissioner after auction.

Chapter IX

Mathew Harrison (1738-1798)
(Mathew 4, Burr 3, Thomas 2, Burr 1)

Burr Harrison, grandson of the immigrant, had five sons: Thomas, Burr, Mathew, George, and Cuthbert.   Mathew, the third son, was born October 7, 1738 according to the *Virginia Magazine of History* genealogy of the Harrison family. (1)

Probably it was this Mathew who, when just twenty-one, was already selling merchandise and had to sue John Jones to collect on a debt. The Prince William court allowed the attachment of some of Jones's goods, to wit two silver watches, a parcel of silversmith's tools, two pair silver shoe buckles, a parcel of old silver, etc., and ordered the sheriff to sell these and pay Harrison his due. (It is possible, but less likely, that an unrelated Mathew Harrison may have been the plaintiff in this action.) (2)

At any rate, before he was twenty-three, Mathew had left the family home on the Chopawamsic to take up residence in the northern part of the Shenandoah Valley.   Already, in November of 1761 he was one of the trustees who received the founding charter for the town of Strasburg in Frederick County, (now Shenandoah). A year later he brought suit against Peter Stover. (3) At first he lived in Frederick; when he obtained land grants on Brush Creek in that county, one (dated New Year's Day of 1767) noted that the tract adjoined his own land. (4)   By now it often took one or two years after the initial application to secure a grant from the Proprietor's Office. Time was needed to run surveys, make searches to insure that no part of the tract had been granted previously, and complete the office and legal work.   Thus, by the time the grants were issured, Mathew may have already moved to Augusta, just below the southwestern boundary line of Lord Fairfax's land.

About 1765 or earlier Mathew had married Mary Wood, the

daughter of Colonel James and Mary (Rutherford) Wood. (5) Among the justices of Frederick, Colonel Wood was second only to Lord Fairfax himself. Such a liaison must have been a help to the young man's business endeavors. At this time he had joined his brother Burr in a retail business that bought from the Scottish merchant importers of Dumfries and Alexandria and sold to the residents on the new frontier of northern Virginia. Both brothers must have been liberal with their credit policies, and perhaps overly so; in Frederick, Shenandoah, and Augusta courts, one or the other of them was often a plaintiff suing to recover small debts.

The Mathew Harrisons had three daughters before Mary, his first wife, died. In October 1769 her widowed mother deeded a large property to two sons-in-law: Mathew Harrison, husband of her late daughter Mary, and Alexander White, married to daughter Elizabeth. The tract known as Great Plains was just south of the line dividing Frederick in Lord Fairfax's Proprietary from Augusta outside the Fairfax domain. It was on both sides of the North Fork of the Shenandoah River, near the main Valley road. (6) Both before and after this deed Harrison bought other adjoining parcels. Mathew was appointed a magistrate of Augusta in 1769. (7)

Harrison's business could not have been prospering, for he began to mortgage his properties in May of 1769 continuing until August of 1771. The loans secured by this method came from Richard and Peter Footman of Philadelphia, John Ashburner of Augusta, Benjamin Marshall of Philadelphia, and Thomas Carson of Fairfax and Henry Mitchell of Spotsylvania. In all, he mortgaged more than 3650 acres. Of these loans, he paid off only the one to Marshall on 420 acres, his undivided part of the tract shared with the Whites. When he was unable to repay Carson and Mitchell on a loan secured by 1668 acres in Frederick and Hampshire Counties, the court decided that the value of the land was insufficient. Rather than face a sheriff's sale of other properties, Harrison chose in August 1771 to give the two creditors title to 1190 additional acres including 210 of his residence in "Great Plains."

In November 1772 Harrison and the Whites sold the 840 acres that they jointly owned. The deed denominated him as "Mathew Harrison, late of Augusta, now of Dumfries." The final chapter of his valley lands was written in March 1776. The Footmans had instituted a suit against their debtor in 1773. The court ordered payment, and when Harrison did not comply, they declared foreclosure of the mortgage. Finally in 1776, 480 acres were sold at a sheriff's auction to John Ashburner and Thomas Place.

In the meantime Mathew had remarried. The bond for his wedding in 1770 with his second wife, Ann Slaughter of Fauquier, was co-signed and witnessed by Cuthbert Harrison. (8) The custom was for the groom and a relative or friend of the bride to be signatories of the document, in effect a marriage license. We should have asked to see the signatures on the original bond, not just the copy in the marriage book. Then we could have confirmed that Mathew's brother Cuthbert signed and not his cousin Cuthbert Harrison of Prince William. (Original bond books whether for marriages or executors of estates give one a chance to look at and compare signatures, and sometimes provide a means for distinguishing between two persons of the same name.)

Hayden said there was only one child of this second marriage, a son named Mathew who went to Bermuda, married, and died there.

Ann Slaughter Harrison died before 1774, for in that year Mathew married his third wife, Elizabeth Webb of Richmond County. Because the bride had a large number of slaves in her own right, a prenuptial contract specified that she would retain ownership and control of them. (9) According to Hayden the marriage produced two children, George and Fanny, both of whom as adults went to Kentucky.

As a consequence of the paucity of records covering the war years, little can be told of Harrison's activities during them. In 1777 he paid in cattle for five years' rent of his residence in Dumfries, evidencing the shortage of strong currency and the low esteem in which the state's paper money was held. In 1779 he leased another lot in Dumfries, perhaps to use as an office, but after three years he transferred his lease to William Linton. (10) It has been said he was a colonel during the Revolution; if true, he must have held the rank in a regiment of Prince William militia. After the war he was paid for three public service claims for supplies furnished the army.

In 1779 he and John Chancellor were the principal inspectors at the Dumfries warehouse; they may have held the posts earlier and they were named again in 1781 and 1784. (11) Reportedly, Mathew was a justice in Prince William in 1788 and 1790.

Harrison married for the fourth and last time late in 1782. Most likely, Elizabeth (Webb) Harrison had died only a few months before. The daughters by the first marriage were already teenagers; possibly the oldest was already married. These girls must have kept in close contact with their grandmother Wood, for the two who married chose men from west of the Blue Ridge. Mathew would have had the three small children from his second and third marriages needing a stepmother to help care for them. His new bride, Eleanor Tyler, like Elizabeth Webb before her, secured a marriage contract. She wished to insure the care of any children that the couple might have, if either spouse should die. (12) In sixteen years of married life Mathew and Eleanor had four boys and two girls.

In 1793 Mathew Harrison, described as "of Dumfries" in Prince William, gave five hundred pounds to his wife Eleanor. Two years afterwards Mathew Harrison, now "of Fauquier," obtained a lease on 325 acres in Fauquier on Little River for the "natural" lives of his children, George, Gustavus Adolphus, and Frederick. Little River runs through the northeast corner of Fauquier and into Goose Creek across the line in Loudoun. Evidently, Harrison had moved there from Dumfries. (13)

It may be that, having been burned once in real estate, Mathew became cautious about such ventures later or that his finances never recovered fully from the losses incurred in the Valley. Unlike his younger brothers, George and Cuthbert, he did not invest in Kentucky land.

The Harrison-Powell prayerbook provides the following detail: "Mathew Harrison son of Burr & Ann Harrison departed this life on Sunday morning at 2 o'clock February the 18th 1798." He may have been buried in the Harrison family grave-yard on the Chopawamsic or in the Middleburg cemetery. Apparently his widow stayed on with the children at the home in the northern part of Fauquier. She married Captain Minor Winn, a neighbor there, in 1803. (14)

Hayden's *Virginia Genealogies* names the children of Mathew Harrison, but except for George, Gustavus, and Frederic named in the Fauquier lease, their existence has not been confirmed. A summary of his data on the children follows:

Marriage to Mary Wood
    Dau. m. Obed White of Winchester.
    Dau. m. Col. Andrew Wood of Romney.
    Dau. d. unmarried.

Marriage to Ann Slaughter
    Mathew went to Bermuda, m. and d. there.

Marriage to Elizabeth Webb
    George went to Kentucky.
    Fanny m. Mr. Jones went to Kentucky.

Marriage to Eleanor Tyler
    Charles to sea early---last heard of 1815.

Gustavus Adolphus (1791–1848) m. Elizabeth Magruder.
Wm. Alexander b. 1795, m. 1828 Anna Mayberry, resided
  Clarksburg, West Virginia.
Eleanor m. Wm. Hale of Loudoun, moved to W. Va.
Nancy m. Dr. Elias Safford of Gallipolis, Ohio moved to
  Parkersburg, West Virginia.
Frederic Tyler d. unmarried. (15)

Notes:

1. V 23/24 Harrison genealogy. The original source of the birth date is not given, but it agrees with that in the "Kentucky Bible."
2. PW O p.116, 1760. The other Mathew lived in Loudoun County. He seems to have been the brother named in the will of a Jeremiah Harrison who died in Fairfax in 1750. See Chapter XX.
3. Fk D 7-294, July 1762. Peter Stover to Mathew H., both of Fk.
4. NN grants to Harrison include: 0-2, 400 a. adj. own land on Brush Creek in Frederick Co. O-3, 400 a. more on Brush creek. O-4, 218 a. also Brush Creek. All three dated 1/1/1767. O-189, 1768. Land in Hampshire Co., now in West Virginia.
5. Wayland, *Shenandoah Valley Pioneers*, p.290. "Mary Wood m. Col. Mathew Harrison, officer in Revolution." No contemporary confirmation of his rank or service has been found. Mary's father was on the first commission of peace for Frederick in 1743. The second Col. James Wood, Mary's brother, became a governor of the state of Virginia.
6. Au deeds to or from Mathew Harrison: 16-152, Oct. 1769. Great Plains deed from Mary Wood. 16-530, Aug. 1770. Mortgage to John Ashburne. 17-101, Mar. 1771. Mortgage to Benjamin Marshall. 17-330, Aug. 1771. Mortgage to Thomas Carson et al. 19-35, Nov. 1772. With Alexander and Elizabeth White sale to Frederick Haines. 21-255, Mar. 1776. Sheriff's sale for benefit of Richard and Peter Footman to John Ashburner et al.
7. Au O VII-222, 324, 368 in 1769 and 1770. Recommended as justice.
8. F Marr. Book 1, 10/3/1770. Thomas Slaughter gave consent.
9. R D 14-296.
10. PW D T-399, U-86, and U-294. Leases of lots in Dumfries.
11. Misc. PW manuscripts now in Huntington Library, Califor-

nia. Mathew Harrison, John Chancellor, Alston Keith, and John Linton are recommended as principal and asst. inspectors at Dumfries, Sept. 1784.

12. PW D U–383, 1785.

13. F D 15–217, 1795. James Dunlop of Maryland to Mathew Harrison of Fauquier. Probably Mathew already resided on the site. On the same day Dunlop made leases to John Sullivan and to John Walker, both witnessed by John Peyton Harrison.

14. F Marr. Book 2–309, 1803. Captain Minor Winn was the brother of James and Richard of South Carolina. (See Chapter XIII.)

15. Hayden has the order of Harrison's marriages to Mary Wood and Ann Slaughter reversed.

Chapter X

George Harrison (1745-1805)
(George 4, Burr 3, Thomas 2, Burr 1)
Cuthbert Harrison (1749-1824)
(Cuthbert 4, Burr 3, Thomas 2, Burr 1)

The careers of the two youngest sons of Burr and Ann (Barnes) Harrison were curiously parallel. Both followed their older brothers, Burr and Mathew, into the Shenandoah Valley. The two men married sisters. Both left the valley in the mid-1770s moving back eastward to Loudoun County. Both were captains in that county's militia during the Revolution. After Yorktown, both went to Kentucky where they engaged in buying and selling land in association with their brother-in-law, Leven Powell. Each of them raised families there. Their lives were so intertwined that they must be reviewed together to prevent constant repetition.

The Kentucky (Cuthbert) Harrison Bible shows George born March 22, 1744/5 and Cuthbert, the last child in the family, born "Aug. the 11th (1749) at 10 o'clock at night & baptised the 17th of September following by Revd. Jas. Keith." Both were raised on the Chopawamsic plantation that had originally belonged to their great-grandfather, the immigrant Burr Harrison.

In an autobiographical note Cuthbert recalled that:

> my imperfect education was early closed, and at 12 years old I left the paternal roof of my father, and went into the store of my oldest brother [Burr] on the frontier of Virginia. In my 13 year I went as a volunteer against a party of Indians who had committed depradations on the south branch of the Potomac, we followed to the Allegany mountains without overtaking them. I was so

120

small as to be indulged by the Commander to go on
horse-back the only indulgence granted. (1)

The store, as previously noted, was located near the southern border of Frederick County, (now Shenandoah).

About 1770 George married Elizabeth Beale. Cuthbert married Ann Beale "Jan. 15th 1773 by the Revd. Peter Muhlenberg, Minsr. of Dunmore Parish." Ann, the "daughter of Tavr. and Frances Beale of Orange born March 31st 1754," was a younger sister of Elizabeth. Taverner Beale, second to their husbands' brother Burr on the first Dunmore/Shenandoah commission of peace, was their brother. (2)

George and Elizabeth made their home near that of Burr on Smith's Creek. Late in 1775 after Burr and his wife Mary Ann had moved back to Chopawamsic. George bought some of their land including the mill, dam, and race. (3)

Cuthbert and Ann lived a few miles to the north on Stoney Creek, on which Burr Sr. and Burr Jr. had obtained grants. It would seem that Cuthbert had a branch store in what is now Edinburg. (4) In the first Order Book of Dunmore County, which had been split off from Frederick in May 1772, Cuthbert appeared as the sole plaintiff in several suits and jointly with Burr in others. (5) George was not involved in any court matter in this period, but he did obtain a grant for 300 acres on a branch of Stoney Creek. (6)

Mathew Harrison left the area in 1772 to return to Prince William and Burr Jr. did so in 1775. Cuthbert was the next to go back east of the Blue Ridge. He was recommended for the Shenandoah commission of peace in September, 1776, but the very next month the court certified to the governor that he had removed out of the county. He and Ann sold 434 acres they owned on Stoney Creek early the following year.

George and Elizabeth sold their 300 acres on Stoney Creek at the same time. However, they did not dispose of their Smith Creek property, in all 550 acres, for another two and a half years. They were the last of the family to leave the Valley. Very likely first the embargo and then the war had made it impossible to get sufficient merchandise to keep the stores going, and George had to give up trying to make ends meet with only the farm and the mill to support his family. Even if there had been goods to sell, few people had money to buy them. The economy was reduced almost to barter status.

Cuthbert's difficulties in closing down his business were evident in a record entered in Prince William in 1791 by his nephew Mathew Harrison Jr. acting as executor of the will of his father, Colonel Burr Harrison. Cuthbert had given his note for 628 pounds to Burr in 1776, because Burr had taken over a debt of 314 pounds owed by Cuthbert to a certain Neil McCoole. The note was to be cancelled when Cuthbert reimbursed his brother the amount paid by the latter without interest. However, Cuthbert had paid back only 236 pounds; Mathew was trying to collect the balance for the estate. (7)

Both families relocated in Loudoun County. On the last day of 1777 James Wheelock of Loudoun assigned Cuthbert Harrison Jr. of the same county a lease-for-lives obtained from John Carlyle and John Dalton. The location of the tract was not specified, but the witnesses were Joseph, Robert, and Elizabeth Combs. Elizabeth was an older sister of Cuthbert married to Joseph. Robert was her son. They lived near what would become the town of Middleburg, founded in 1788 by brother-in-law Leven Powell. The latter had married Sarah, the youngest Harrison sister, four years older than George. In all probability Cuthbert and Ann resided on the leased farm, close to the Combs and Powells. George and Elizabeth must also have rented a farm in the neighborhood, but their lease was never recorded. (8)

There the brothers threw in their lot with the wealthy and influential Powell. In 1775 he was a major in the Loudoun militia, later lieutenant colonel in the regiment that William Grayson attempted to raise in 1777, and at the end of that year on active duty at Washington's headquarters at Valley Forge as colonel of the Eighth Virginia Regiment. Three of his young protegees had enlisted in one of the Virginia regiments in 1776. So Powell needed the business assistance that his two experienced relatives could provide.

Although Cuthbert was called Captain Harrison by 1784 and so was surely a militia officer, the militia was only called out when Virginia was invaded, and its officers were not subject to the draft. Thus he was usually free to pursue personal business. He and Powell were associated in selling supplies to the Continental army and its men, as the letter reproduced below makes clear. It has been preserved in the collection of Powell's papers in the Library of Congress. Written from Valley Forge in late spring of 1778, the hardships of the preceding terrible winter seemed forgotten. Instead, the patriot rejoiced, because the British, worried about their supply lines after the French had entered the war, were evacuating Philadelphia and retreating to New York.

In the meadow of an old Dutch
Farmer of the name of Jacob Frick in
front of the old encampment.

122

Dear Sir

Here I am left in as loansome & solitary a situation as a poor lad need be. The whole of the army decampt but the sick, the lame & the lazey of which class am I. On the night of the 17th the enemy threw themselves over the Delaware & at 7 o'clock on the morning of the 18th Capt. McClane with his party took possession of the city [Philadelphia] & am told he was so close upon them as to make the whole of their rear guard prisoners, those came to headquarters about 12 o'clock & about two Gen'l Lee's division & two others crossed the Schulkill & took their rout[e] by way of Currell's Ferry on the Delaware. At 8 o'clock in the morning of the 19th the whole army moved pursuing the same rout taken by those who moved the day before, but expect they will separate after crossing the Delaware. The enemy I am informed were on the 20th at Mount Holly where they had halted. Whether our Gen'l intends an attack I cannot say but am apt to think he will as the Jersey militia have turned out in great numbers to obstruct their march. They with Gen'l Maxwell's brigade are in front, Morgan with his light core & McClane's detachment harassing them in their rear & our whole army must by this be upon one wing of theirs ...

At this point a bottom corner of the page has been torn off and lost. Of eleven incomplete lines the last five read:

----------I have a most disagreeable time of it here & wha-----it more so of late is a rascally practice and--------of horse stealing (tho they do not call it so) by which lost mine & am convinced I shall never recover---------fore be obliged to do as I am come by & steal or t---

The letter continues at the top of the reverse side:

This affair distresses me the more as I have now some prospect of setting out home in a fiew days, Mr. Beatty informing me that Col. Peyton is on his way out. I wish he had been sooner, as I think the farther we go north the lower will be the price of liquor. Whiskey sold in camp for some time before the army moved at a dollar p. quart & rum at 3 & 4 [3 sh./4p.]. I have been obliged to let Gen'l Scott have the shoes I brought down & wait his getting me hides which he promised shall be as soon as possible but am much afraid it will not be in time for our return wagons. The martial ardor & spirit of our army in general and officers in particular give me great hopes. Whether it is an increase of valour or peevishness that have actuated our officers lately I can't say but we have had I suppose as much duelling within the last six weeks as have happened before since the commencement of the war. You will please present my compliments to my sister and the family. Believe me to be with

>   *Esteem yr mo obt srvt*
>   *C Harrison*
>   *June 21st 1778*

The letter was addressed to Powell at his home in Loudoun. It looks as if Colonel (Henry) Peyton was also a business associate. Possibly, Cuthbert's brother Burr was also, since he was a partner of Powell in some later ventures. Some of the liquor that they sold came from a still owned by Powell that produced rye whiskey from grain grown on his farm and ground in his mill. (9)

Not quite thirty years old, Cuthbert overcame his "laziness" immediately according to his autobiographical sketch:

>   *In the campaign of 78 I left a darling wife and served as a volunteer aid to General Mulenburg [his former pastor], was with the Army at the Battle of Monmouth, and late in the season returned home. When Cornwallis invaded Virginia, I again volunteered and served the campaign as aid to Mulenburg, under the Marquis Fayet. Here I was in Wanes battle at the Green Springs.*

A few extracts from the order books of Loudoun in 1780 give us a feel for Cuthbert's activities before he went back to war. "Cuthbert Harrison, Gent., appointed to furnish Mary Burns with necessaries according to law." Mrs. Burns must have been the widow of a Continental soldier. A year later as Mary Burns alias Mathews she was indicted for retailing spirituous liquors without a license. To the same court Harrison "returned a list of hands to work on the road from the Run by Mr John Thornton to the mountain road." Early the next year his suit against George Hammett was "agreed." Then he was "appointed to purchase a waggon and team for the use of the state." By October, 1780 he was one of the sitting justices of the court, although we have been unable to find his appointment to the commission or as an officer of the county militia. His friend, Leven Powell, sworn as a justice in 1777, now presided over the court. As before in Dunmore/Shenandoah, George Harrison never appeared in the Loudoun order books. (10)

In 1780 Cuthbert, described as a resident of Shelburne Parish of Loudoun County, sold his brother Burr of Prince William 188 acres on the west (southwest) side of the Chopawamsic. The land had been left Cuthbert by his late father and was part of the "old patten of [the immigrant] Burr Harrison, dcd." The selling price was five hundred pounds. (11)

Even before the war ended, Leven Powell had become greatly interested in Kentucky, which was starting to open up for settlement. When he first visited the region, which had become Kentucky County in December 1776, is not known, but he was a founding trustee of Boonesborough and of Louisville. He was definitely out there in March of 1780 and, as we have seen, was operating in a large way in "western" lands with Isaac Hite. (12) As Powell's investments grew in importance, he apparently recognized a need for trustworthy personal representatives in the field. Henry Tazewell Harrison's genealogy put it that: "George Harrison and his brother Cuthbert were sent by their brother-in-law, Col. Leven Powell, to Kentucky to look after a grant of 6000 acres of land which he had received from the Continental Congress in recognition of his services to his country, and there they made their homes." The point of the quote, that the two men were sent out by Powell, is indubitably well taken, though Powell had much greater interests in Kentucky than caring for his 6000-acre military grant (really from the state of Virginia for service as colonel of a Virginia regiment of the Continental Line). Consider, for example, the letter to Powell from Burr Harrison (Chapter VIII) mentioning Powell's 60,000 acre purchase there.

After chronicling his Revolutionary War service, Cuthbert continued:

> In 85 I moved to Kentucky. I had served as a
> magistrate in Virginia 7 years without compensa-
> tion, was not allowed for my services in the Army
> two campaigns, I never demanded or received a

cent. My services to my country since moving to Kentucky are known. I went thro the Indians [campaign?] in 87 [apparently some phrases left out by the copier] a delagate for the district. I have served twice in Convention once on framing the constitution. I have served in the Assembly and twice as an elector. Many have served this Country with more noise none with a more disinterested devotion.

Harrison had travelled to Louisville in March, 1782. It may not have been his first trip. Indeed, he may have journeyed back and forth more than once a year. Another letter to Powell from Kentucky remarked on hearing of

your loss of 32 bus. of salt when a corpulent heavy-headed dull-looking African of Mr. Cuth. Harrison shared your sleeping embers of recollection & told me in a tone that spoke more than words that as he was disappointed in a load of salt he expected from a Mr. Lewis, he would if I pleased take on a few bushels for Col. Powell.

If a slave belonging to Harrison was in Kentucky in January 1783, presumably Harrison was there too.

A letter from Hite in early 1785 informed Powell that:

Capt. Harrison & his brother George has [sic] done reasonable well in the money as to the cash directly out of pocket. Their lands are nearly secured & I expect they will divide and settle with me when they come out this spring.

Whether Ann Harrison went "out" with her husband that spring has not been ascertained. She died in November.

The procedure followed by Powell and Hite and others taking advantage of the press of new settlers, mostly from Virginia but also from Pennsylvania and Maryland, was to survey sizeable parcels on rivers and their tributary creeks in the watershed of the Ohio. These surveys were then "entered" in the county office in the name of a large client, who would subdivide and sell rights to the parts of the tract, often before he had paid for the land warrant and obtained the grant from the state land office in Richmond.

George entered claims on at least 4000 acres in Jefferson County beginning in 1780. Cuthbert claimed 6000 acres near his brother in Jefferson in 1780; in 1784 and 1785 he got provisional title to 1200 in Lincoln and 4550 in Fayette. Jointly the two held a 1000-acre tract in Jefferson and 4000 acres in Fayette. Grants from the Land Office were obtained by the brothers for less than half of the county entries. (13)

The Washington County tax list for 1792 showed Thomas Liver owning 106 acres on Rolling Fork, "entered by George Harrison." (14) The 1787 will of Charles Chinn in Fauquier included a bequest of 500 acres in Nelson County, Kentucky, adjacent to Cuthbert Harrison. Both these tracts were pieces carved from grants made by the Virginia Land Office to the brothers.

George Harrison died in Kentucky in 1805 "from the shock of his son Matthew having been killed by a horse two days previous." He had not made a will; his estate was appraised in January 1806. After his widow Elizabeth was assigned her dower rights, the rest of his property was divided among his heirs: George Harrison, Nancy Hynes (a daughter), and Fanny Harrison, whose receipt was signed by her guardian, Thomas Hynes. (15)

Cuthbert's will dated December 1821 was proved in November 1824. It named his son Burr and Thomas Speed, executors; the estate was to be divided among Burr; a grandson, Cuthbert Sidney Brasheare; and seven daughters. Of these he named only Sally Harrison as having received a legacy from her grandmother, Mrs. Sarah Tannahill. The will was witnessed by nephews John Combs and George Harrison.

Cuthbert and Ann had the following children, whose births were recorded in the family Bible:

Taverner, b. 1774, d. 1789.
Burr, b. 1776 m. (2?) Catherine Camp. (16)
Ann Frances, b. 1778, d. just before her first birthday.
Elizabeth Beale, b. 1780, m. Robert Brasheare.
Nancy Barnes, b. 1782, m. Nathaniel Cox.
Frances Madison (1784-1860).

The first child was baptized by the Rev. Muhlenburg of Shenandoah; the second by Mr. Manning of Hampshire (now in West Virginia); the next by the Rever'd David Griffith of Loudoun; and the next two in Fauquier by Mr. John Scott and the Rev'd. Wm. Thompson respectively. No baptism of Frances Madison was posted in the Bible. (17)

Another page of the Bible has a list of "the age of Negros born the property of C & A Harrison": one in 1770, the next in 1780, three in 1783-4, four in the 1790s, eight in 1800-1809, and four from 1812 to 1822. The pattern of slave births growing from one in the 1770s to eight in the 1800s and then decreasing is probably a typical one. No deed for the purchase or sale of a slave by Cuthbert has been found. Most likely he received his first slaves as a gift or bequest. It may be that initially they were his wife's, if the phrase "property of C & A Harrison" has any special significance. Subsequent build-up of the holdings came from births to the black women servants. The decrease in the last period probably reflected wedding or other gifts to his children.

However, the widower's "Kentucky Bible" does not mention Cuthbert's two remarriages in Kentucky to Frances Holt, who died within a year, and then to Anne Tannehill, and it does not mention any of the children born there.

According to the genealogy in the *Virginia Magazine* they were:

Charlotte m. Blankenbauer [Blankenbaker]
Martha m. Jacob Colfres or Matilda m. 1825 Henry Kalfus.
Rebecca d. 1882, m. Thomas Cox
Sarah d. 1860, did not marry.

Nearly two centuries after the two brothers died, we have a distinct impression of a salient contrast between their personalities. George, the older of the two, must have been retiring, quiet, and steady. Cuthbert was clearly a risk-taker and an extrovert, and at the same time dependable and loyal. We have been glad to "know" both.

Notes:

1. Kentucky Bible Records, op. cit.
2. Hodges, *The Beale Family of Virginia*. According to this source, Taverner Beale, (1713-1756) m. 1741 Frances Madison. She m. (2) 1756 Jacob Hite and moved to South Carolina where the entire family was killed by Indians. Orange WB 2-238, will Taverner Beale 11/3/1754, pr. 10/29/1756, names children: Charles, Taverner, Frances, Elizabeth, Ann. Taverner II (1742-1810) was first Sheriff of Dunmore/ Shenandoah. Much additional detail is provided on the Beales with references to original documents, but all material on Harrisons is derived from unreliable secondary sources.
3. Sh D B-304, Dec. 1775. 194 a. on Smith Creek.
4. Smith Creek runs NW from the Massanutten Mountain into the North River near Mt. Jackson. Taverner Beale lived on

the creek also. Stoney Creek flows eastward into the North River at Edinburgh.

5. Dunmore O 1772-1774. This book was found in 1936 among private papers and returned to the county. The next two order books are still missing.

6. Other Shenandoah deeds include: B-240, Sept. 1775. Cuthbert Harrison and Ann his wife sell half-acre lots in Woodstock. George a witness. B-480, April, 1777. Cuthbert and Ann sell 200 a. on Stoney Creek. B-483, April, 1777. Cuthbert and Ann sell 234 a. on Stoney Creek. B-487, Mar. 1777. George and Elizabeth Harrison sell 300 a. on Stoney Creek. C-200, Aug. 1779. George and Elizabeth sell 132 a. C-286, 1779. George and Eliz. sell 300 a. on Smith Creek. C-313, Aug. 1779. George and Elizabeth sell 118 a.

7. PW D Y-515, 1795.

8. L D M-95, 1777. James Wheelock to Cuthbert Harrison Jr. The lease assigned was for the lives of Wheelock, his wife Frances, and Mary Buckley, dau. of James Buckley. Cuthbert was junior relative to his cousin, Cuthbert Harrison (1747-1780) of Prince William.

9. Manuscript Section, Library of Congress, Leven Powell Papers, 6/20/1778, C. Harrison to Powell. Also see 11/26/1777, Craven Peyton to Col. Leven Powell of the 8th Virginia Regiment. "Your miller seems to raise some cavil about taking your rye on the terms you have mentioned in Mr. Farrow's instructions." The miller claimed no price was discussed, only that he was to "still you so much." Craven Peyton was Powell's cousin and married to Anne Harrison, sister to George, Cuthbert, and Mrs. Powell.

10. L O G-243, 244, 302, 322.

11. PW D U-151.

12. The Powell papers include several letters written to him from Kentucky. One in 1782 from William Pope notes that the trustees of Louisville "have not met since you left this country" and that he had had "a letter [delivered] by Capt. Harrison." Another in 1783 from Thomas Davis included the tale of the "heavy-headed" slave.

13. Virginia Land Office Grants: T-596 Cuthbert Harrison, Jefferson Co. T-602 Cuthbert Harrison, Jefferson Co. Y-85 Cuthbert Harrison, Jefferson Co.; V-262 George Harrison, Jefferson Co. George Harrison, Nelson "upper end of his settlement"; 25-487 George Harrison; 25-290 George Harrison.

14. Washington County 1799 Tax List copied by Joseph E. Johnson.

15. Burns, *Wills in Nelson County Kentucky*, pp. 41 and 52. Abstracts of W A-927, 935, 936 for George and E-206 for Cuthbert.

16. Coleman, *Kentucky, A Pictorial History*, reproduces a hand bill posted in Bardstown in 1819. By it Burr Harrison proclaimed TO THE PUBLIC that Martin Hardin Wickliff was a "gasconading cowardly poltroon and lying scoundrel." The proof was supplied by a note from Harrison to Wickliff. "Sir – Our differences require an effectual termination; are you willing, for that purpose, to appeal to the mode settled and sanctioned by Gentlemen; or are you resolved to retreat for safety behind the municipal law." Below, Harrison's second, Major Nathaniel Rector, submitted that "the answer of Capt. M.H. Wickliff was 'I will have nothing to do with it, I told the Doctor [Harrison] so. --- I have taken several oaths against it and could not meet him in that way without confiscating my property'" &c. Rector continued: "My real opinion upon my honor is that Capt Wickliff is lacking in courage and must possess very feeble nerves indeed to swallow such a communication without replying to it, as an officer and soldier should." The parents of Harrison, Wickliff, and Rector were all born within a few miles of each other in Virginia.

17. The Rev. Peter Muhlenberg of Woodstock, Virginia, was brigadier general in the Continental Army under Nathaniel Green. The Rev. David Griffith was an aide to General Washington, possibly the chaplain at headquarters.

Chapter XI

Thomas Harrison (ca. 1736-1827) of Kentucky
(Thomas 4, Thomas 3, Thomas 2, Burr 1)

Several of the early Harrisons had genes for long life. For example, Thomas, son of the immigrant, was eighty-one when he died. At least two of Thomas's children reached the age of seventy or more; Burr was seventy-six and Seth (Harrison) McMillion may have passed her eightieth birthday. A granddaughter, Mary (Harrison) Fowke, the daughter of Colonel Thomas of Fauquier, was ninety when she died in South Carolina in 1831. (1)

Mary's brother, Thomas, died in 1827. In his will made that year he said he was "upwards of ninety." Assuming that he meant over ninety by not more than one or two years, he would have been born about the year 1736. If so, he was probably younger than his brother William and his sister Susannah. (2)

This Thomas Harrison, great-grandson of the immigrant Burr, was much less a public figure than his father, uncles, brothers, or most of his male cousins. References to him in the county records are few in number and tell little of his activities. However, we do know that after his marriage he lived in Prince William County near his father's plantation just over the county line in Fauquier. Probably the residence was on the two hundred acres sold him by his father in 1771, described as lying on the south side of Kettle Run. (3)

Thomas must have been in his early twenties when he married, for William Butler Harrison, his oldest child, was born in 1759. His wife was almost certainly Ann Butler, the daughter of William and Ann Butler; the Butler plantation adjoined that of the Harrisons. William Butler had voted for Colonel Thomas Harrison in the 1741 poll for burgess and had been on the Dettingen Parish vestry along with his neighbor.

So the two fathers had presumably been friends. (4) However, after Mr. Butler died in 1748, some dispute over the boundary between their properties led to a suit for trespass being brought in 1752 by Colonel Harrison against the widow Ann Apple Butler. Perhaps their differences were never smoothed out entirely, for there are indications that the Colonel was not fully content with his son's choice of a bride. (5) They might explain why the Colonel's will made no provision for any of Thomas's children, even though William Butler Harrison was his oldest Harrison grandchild, granddaughter Mary was six or seven years old, and Thomas Grayson Harrison, his namesake, was three or four years old when the will was written. (6)

Nevertheless, Thomas (Jr.) himself was devised five slaves, livestock, money, and land. Parts of the land were to be sold in accord with commitments made by the deceased, with Thomas to keep the proceeds. In compliance with these instructions Harrison sold Samuel Orgin 186 acres, part of 409 acres which had been "taken up" (in the words of the will) in 1741. The body of the deed refers to Thomas and Nancy Harrison, his wife, but it is signed Ann Harrison with a cross as her mark. To explain the discrepancy, one can guess that Nancy was the name used for Mrs. Harrison in the family to distinguish her from her mother and that the deed was written by a lawyer who knew her by it rather than the name she had been christened with. (7)

Four records in Fauquier County in 1779 involve Thomas Harrison and a Coppedge family. In the first of these John Coppedge of Fauquier sells Thomas Harrison of Prince William three Negroes, two horses, seven cattle, and four sheep. In the second, Harrison is to sell some unspecified land at the best price he can obtain for it and with the proceeds is to remove Coppedge and his family "to any place in the United States" he thinks best for them. Any balance left is to be held in trust for Coppedge and his wife Susanna. In the next, William and John Coppedge sell Harrison 150 acres of land on White Oak Branch in Fauquier. The last of the series is for the sale of that land by Thomas Harrison and Ann his wife to Elijah Thornkill. No deed of sale of Harrison's own Kettle Run land or other property in Prince William has been found, but that too must have been disposed of within a few years. (8)

Although the records provide no direct clue to what was going on, later events make clear that an exodus to Kentucky was planned by the Harrisons and the Coppedges. The move may have been suggested by Thomas Bullitt, who had made the first surveys in the region of the Falls of the Ohio (now Louisville) in 1772. (9) Surveyors often claimed land for themselves and their relatives and friends. The Harrisons and the Coppedges were among the the first to relocate from northern Virginia across the Appalachians. Just a year before they made their plans, Kentucky had had only three settlements: Harrodsburg, Boonesboro, and Logan's Station.

The Harrisons arrived at the Falls of the Ohio in the spring of 1780. (10) The war in the west had simmered down somewhat after George Rogers Clark's victories in Illinois two years previously, but the threat from the British headquartered at Detroit and especially from their Indian allies was constantly felt. Thus the family took a house inside or just outside the fort and lived there until the war was over.

During the winter of 1781-2 the wedding of daughter Mary to a soldier stationed at the fort was celebrated. She married Sergeant-Major Michael Miles of the Illinois Regiment. It must have been a festive occasion, for Mary was escorted from her home by a guard of soldiers to the house of Squire Hansbery where the ceremony took place. We wonder if the squire officiated or if the regiment had a chaplain who performed the nuptials.

Soon after the close of the war, the Harrisons moved to the neighborhood of Springfield in what became Washington County. There, 200 acres on the waters of Chaplin's Fork of the Salt River had been granted Thomas in May 1780. The tract was described as lying in "Kentucky County" adjacent to Nathaniel Grigsby. (11)

The 1799 tax list of Washington County showed Thomas Harrison as owning 218 acres on Beach Fork. He owned one slave and three horses. His son Benjamin had one slave but no land; son Cuthbert possessed neither slaves nor land; son Thomas G. held 110 acres on Cartwright Creek, no slave, but seven horses. Among the neighbors were James, Alec, and Moses Coppedge; Philemon Waters and Isaac Froman, both sons-in-law; and several Hardins and Grahams. Valentine Harrison was absentee owner of 1500 acres in the county between Cartwright and Hardin Creeks. Cuthbert Bullitt also owned land in the county. Thomas Whitledge, like Harrison a great-grandson of the immigrant Burr, had owned land there. The majority of the landowners had come from northern and northwestern Virginia. (12)

When the patriarch of the family wrote his will in November of 1827, he was able to state that he was still "in perfect mind and memory." He made nominal bequests to his sons William, Thomas, and Cuthbert and to his daughter Eleanor, identified as the wife of George Graham, while leaving essentially all his estate to his daughter Mary Miles, with whom he was living at the time. She had been a childless widow for about thirty-five years. He did not "wish my negroes parted" and instructed Mary, his executrix, not to "sell or convey" them. The will was witnessed by Thos. H. Waters, a grandson; Thos. G. Harrison, a son; and W. B. (William Burr) Harrison, the son of Thomas G. (13)

Thomas and Anne (Butler) Harrison had the following children:

William Butler - b. 2/11/1759, d. 3/8/1835, m. Penelope Russell, 6/12/1783.
Thomas Grayson - b. ca. 1770, d. after 1840.
Benjamin - d. after 1805.
Cuthbert - m. Mary Hardin, 1/12/1805.
Mary - b. ca. 1764, m. Michael Miles, 1780.
Sarah - m. Isaac Froman.
Elizabeth - m. Philemon Waters Jr.
Eleanor (Allie) - m. George Graham, 4/15/1801. (14)

William Butler Harrison served as a cornet in the cavalry troop of Light-Horse Harry Lee throughout the Revolution. For his military service he was granted warrants for 2666 2/3 acres in the "Kentucky Military District." One thousand acres of these were sold by William and Penelope Harrison to William Elzey in 1807. After the war he did not join his father in Kentucky but resided to the end of his life in Loudoun County, Virginia, where he was a prominent citizen, often referred to as "Major." The family Bible records show that his death came "after a protracted illness which he bore with the patience and firmness that characterized him through the Revolutionary War which tried the souls of those that engaged in it. He entered it at sixteen and fought and bled unshrinkingly till the victory was gained and his country freed." Mrs. Penelope Harrison, the youngest daughter of Col. Anthony Russell, was born Nov. 30, 1756 and died July 18, 1833. Their children, born between 1784 and 1796, were Harriot, Thomas Grayson, Juliet, William B. Jr., Sarah Ann Amelia, Benjamin, and Alfred. (15)

William's brother, Thomas Grayson Harrison, became a respected citizen of Washington County, representing it in the State Senate from 1817-21. He and his brother-in-law, George Graham, had been nominated as lieutenants in the county militia in 1807. In addition to his son, William Burr, he had at least one other child, Elizabeth, who married William Chandler in 1818. (16)

An 1823 deed from Thomas Harrison Sr. to Cuthbert Harrison of Hardin County appears to confirm an earlier conveyance of one hundred acres, part of the tract on which Thomas and "Nancy" lived. The second deed named Benjamin Harrison in a context of his being a deceased son of the "seller." (17)

Besides Mary and Allie there were two other daughters of Thomas and Nancy/Ann, both of whom died before their father. Sarah had married Isaac Froman; Elizabeth was the wife of Captain Philemon Waters. Captain Waters had been taken captive by Indians in 1782 in Washington County, an indication of how "wild" the area was when the Harrisons settled there. (18)

It is apparent that Thomas Harrison, the son of a wealthy Virginia aristocrat, was every bit as much a pioneer as his great-grandfather, the orphaned immigrant Burr Harrison. Why did he and Nancy/Ann leave their comfortable home where they had grown up together for a new, dangerous, and surely more strenuous venture far across the mountains? We can only surmise the answer. As far as is known, it was not for religious or family reasons, such as those which led his brother Burr to move to South Carolina. It is unlikely that their objective was to become rich speculating in Kentucky land. They could have accomplished that while remaining at home in Prince William.

Very likely their thinking paralleled that of a Prince William County farmer who in 1784 provided a night's lodging to Johann David Schoepf, a German naturalist travelling from Philadelphia to South Carolina. The visitor commented:

> Our host had a numerous family; in order to provide for them, he wished to find a purchaser for his land, which was in good order with much clean meadow. Hereabouts, an acre of land fetches from 25 to 60 shillings Virgin. Current; he would sell his for 40 shillings cash money, and with the proceeds remove over the mountains to Kentucky, where he could buy as much land as would give each of his children a sufficient portion. For the people throughout are set upon establishing their children in land-estates which is difficult to manage in the older parts, and hence the incessant migrations to the farther regions. (19)

If Thomas and his wife thought that their personal sacrifices would result in greater opportunity for their children, that indeed did happen. We can appreciate their courage and hard work in accomplishing that goal.

Notes:

1. See Appendix–Fowke.
2. Although H.T. Harrison had some original letters from Thomas Harrison to his son William Butler (they have been misplaced or lost), his genealogy incorrectly gave 1726 as the year of birth and called him the oldest son of Colonel Thomas.
3. PW D R-250, 1771.   Thomas Harrison Sr. of Fauquier, Gent., sold Thomas Harrison Jr. of Prince William 200 acres on the S side of Kettle Run, "being land bought of Henry Hardin, the lower part of 300 acres that Mark Hardin the father of Henry had purchased of James McDaniel." PW Bond Book, 1753-82, 1771.   Thomas Harrison Jr. and George Florence Jr. bond as executors of Normand Drummond's estate.
4. King, *Records of Dettingen Parish*, Oct. 1747, "Collo. Benja. Grayson and Mr. Wm. Butler be churchwardens for the ensuing year." Idem, April 1748, "Capt. Wm. Triplett be vestryman instead of Mr. Wm. Butler, dec'd."
5. PW O 1752-57, p.91.   Thomas Harrison vs. Ann Apple Butler, for trespass. Suit agreed. St W M-8, 1730. Estate account of William Mason and Ann "Ayle" Mason, the widow and executrix of George Mason of Aquia.   According to G.H.S. King, the widow Mason married William Butler. Her name has also been written as "Anaple." Her first husband was called planter with 150 acres in the 1723 quitrent roll. His contemporary in Stafford, Colonel George Mason, held 18,807 acres. St D P-351, 1762.   This badly torn record of a deed from James and Mary Butler concerns a sale of land on Aquia Creek inherited by James from his father William.   A reference to "Harrison Jun" is legible and evidences a tie between Thomas Harrison Jr., the son of Colonel Thomas, and the Butler family.
6. F W 1-231, op.cit.   "---- to my son Thomas Harrison----one tract, land I took up containing 409 acres [NN E-401] except what I have sold to Joseph Kelly and Edmond Homes. ---- one other tract, land which I took up adjoining the above mentioned, being 344 acres [NN I-12]. My will and desire is that my said son do sell the several parts of the said land to the persons I have already agreed with --- they first paying him the sum of 40 pounds per hundred. ---- also what money is due from Edmond Homes."
7. PW D W-2. The first page of the copy of this deed has been lost.   Page W-3 begins "date in the Proprietor's

office January the fifteenth day AD one thousand seven hundred forty one on the branches of Slaty and Kettle Run, the said one hundred and eighty six acres of land joining the lands formerly belonging to Burgesses and the land of Philemon Waters Ju'r." The price paid by Orgin of 74 pounds 8 shillings was the 40 pounds per hundred acres fixed by Colonel Thomas.

8. F D 7-143, 144, 155, 188, 1779. In the last deed the sellers are called Thomas Harrison of Hamilton Parish and Ann his wife. The will of William Coppedge written in 1803 noted that he would have made a bequest to his son John of Kentucky, if he had not already provided for John some years earlier. William Coppedge had been married twice and had had five children by each wife. There are still five persons named "Coppage" in the Fauquier County telephone directory.

9. See Appendix-Bullitt. Captain Thomas Bullitt was commissioned as surveyor in Botetourt County in 1760 and sometime later for a district on the Ohio. In 1772 he made the first surveys of the locations of Charleston, WV and of Louisville and Frankfort, KY. Bullitt County, Kentucky is named for him.

10. US Archives, Revolutionary War pension applications, W 8456 - Miles, Michael. Depositions were made in 1840 by Mary Miles and her brother Thomas G. Harrison. Mary stated her husband served as sergeant-major in the company of Capt. John Bailey in the Illinois Regiment of Virginia troops from May 1780 to the end of the war. (The muster roll of the Illinois Regiment confirms Miles's rank and enlistment date but places him in Captain Girault's company.) The Mileses moved after the war to live in the home near Bardstown of Captain Philemon Waters, Mary's brother-in-law. After Michael's death circa 1795, Mary returned to her parents' home. Her only child had lived just two months. Thomas G. Harrison, aged seventy in 1840, resided in Marion County.

11. Virginia Land office G-81, 1782. Also Jilson, *Old Kentucky Entries and Deeds.* Two hundred acres on the Salt River in Jefferson County, Book A-46, 1780.

12. Washington County Tax List 1799, copied by Joseph Johnson.

13. Wash. W D-309 dated 11/12/1827, proved 12/24/87.

14. H.T. Harrison, op. cit. States Thomas had children, William Butler, Benjamin, Thomas Grayson, Cuthbert, Anne, Allie, and Elizabeth; no mention of Mary or Sarah. No other record of a daughter Anne has been found. Perhaps

Sarah may have been Sarah Ann or Ann Sarah. A marriage bond in Washington County for George Grayham and Ally Harrison places the bride as the daughter of Thomas Harrison Sr.

15. The birth date of William Butler Harrison and other records of his family and descendants through 1898 are found in his family Bible now in the possession of Mr. Gary Young of Centerville, MD.

16. *Pioneer History of Washington County, Kentucky* as compiled from newspaper articles by Orval W. Baylor and others, edited by Michael and Bettie Anne Cook, is the source for much of the information on Harrison's sons and sons-in-law in Kentucky. The marriage bond of Cuthbert Harrison and Mary Hardin did not name Mary's father. However, a Martin Hardin owned 300 acres in Prince William in 1752. Mark Hardin Sr. and Martin Hardin Sr. were Kentucky pioneers who had visited the area that became Washington County as early as 1775. Martin had entered a land claim there for a Charles Wickliffe. The latter or his father was also on the 1752 quitrent list in Prince William.

17. Wash D 3-192, 1805. Ibid. H-367, 1823.

18. Sarah (Harrison) Froman is known to be a daughter of Thomas and Nancy/ Ann Harrison by letters from a grandson, who identified her as sister of "Ally" (Harrison) Graham and of "Tom" Harrison. (Per private communication from Mr. Gary Young.) Isaac Froman died in 1809/10, and Benjamin Harrison, Sarah's brother, was administrator of his estate. It is likely that her eldest brother, William B., named his daughter Sarah Ann for her. Elizabeth Harrison married Philemon Waters Jr. Both a Philemon Waters Jr. and a Philemon Waters, probably father and grandfather of her husband, were on the 1752 quitrent list. A Philemon Waters had a 1723 grant of 403 acres on the S. side of Cedar Run having a corner to Capt. Thomas Harrison and Thomas Whitledge. In the 1799 Washington tax list Philemon Waters was shown as owning 400 acres on Cartwright Creek and 130 on Hardin Creek.

19. Johann David Schoepf, *Travels in the Confederation*, translated by Alfred J. Morrison.

Chapter XII

William Harrison (ca. 1734–1775)
(William 4, Thomas 3, Thomas 2, Burr 1)

One day in 1914 a boy who lived with his widowed father at Glanville went visiting when his after-school chores were done. His destination was an adjoining farm which, like that of his family, had been owned by a William Harrison for a few years before the Revolution. The boy probably didn't know this bit of history, but he did know and like the two bachelor brothers who owned Monterey. He called them Uncle Tom and Uncle Will, although they were really something like his second cousins. They raised horses and dogs and hunted with both. They were also great story-tellers, as the boy himself became after growing up. Uncle Tom, in particular, always had a sugar-cube or two in his pockets for the horses and some hard candy there for children who came his way.

On this day in early spring the stories and the candy must have been especially good, for it was getting dark before the youngster realized that it was time he should be home. It was the better part of a mile between the two houses, but he took only a few minutes to reach the Winchester road. It was really dark there, for the road ran through a patch of woods. The boy was running now, almost at the corner of the woods formed by the road and the lane into Rutledge. This was where the huge old oak stood. From there a path across the fields provided a shortcut home.

The tree was a beautiful specimen; two persons the size of the boy could not come close to joining hands around it. But it had a dreadful history, for a long time ago a man had been hanged from its limbs. The hurrying boy had nearly reached the spot when he heard the noise, a distinct clanking of chains approaching from the direction of Rutledge. Almost immediately he caught a glimpse through the bare tree trunks of a

139

ghostly white form that seemed to glide down the lane. The boy did not wait for further particulars. With a burst of speed he reached the fence, vaulted its rails, and headed for home. Only when impelled from lack of breath did he stop and look back to see if the apparition was following. Nothing of the kind was in sight, and he bent over trying to get a second wind. From the main road through the stillness of dusk he again heard the rattle of chains and then a "Giddap, Daisy" reached his ears. It was a neighbor's voice urging his white horse on its way. The man and his horse must have been helping the spring planting at Rutledge. The boy realized now that the chains were part of the apparatus used to hitch a team to a disk harrow or other machine. But oh what a fright it had given him! Not only did the tale of his encounter with the ghost save him from a scolding or worse from his father for getting back so late, but he would remember it and tell it vividly to the end of his long, productive life. (1)

About fifteen years after the appearance of the "ghost," a small girl coming to Marshall from out-of-state to visit her great-aunt was warned by playmates to stay away from that tree because of what had once happened there. Although she did not realize then that the hanged man was one of her own ancestors, oral tradition had kept the tragedy partially remembered for over 150 years. (2)

The oak and the boy are gone. The tree went first, the victim of progress in the form of Interstate 66. The girl now owns the woods and knows a good deal more about what happened to William Harrison in January 1775, just three short months before the "embattled farmers" stood on their rude bridge and "fired the shot heard round the world."

The unfortunate William Harrison was most likely the eldest son and the second child of Colonel Thomas and Anne (Grayson) Quarles Harrison. He was born after 1731, the probable year of his parents' marriage, and before 1738, reliably said to be when a younger brother was born. 1734 would be about the right year.

William was named in the records for the first time in 1760, when he witnessed a receipt given to his father by his cousin Benjamin Grayson, oldest son of his mother's brother. The elder Benjamin Grayson had died in 1758, naming his brother-in-law, Thomas Harrison, first among four executors of his will. Benjamin Jr., one of the others, had obtained a ruling from the Prince William court that he administer the estate. There is no indication that the uncle protested; at any rate he handed over 330 pounds belonging to it, the occasion for the receipt. Benjamin's administration turned out to be disastrous,

140

and his difficulties were the reason William Harrison had to swear to the authenticity of the receipt in 1767. (3)

This is not the only instance when William seems to have been the confidant of his father, more so than any of his brothers. It may be only that his brother Thomas, already married, was fully occupied in supporting his growing family by 1760. Brother Burr was away in the Maryland army that year and later went off to South Carolina for an extended visit. Benjamin, the youngest brother, was only sixteen in 1760. He was obviously his father's favorite, eventually became a shrewd businessman, but was never the one the father asked to share any responsibility, as far as the record shows.

In 1763 Harrison for the first time brought a suit of his own in the Fauquier court. In that year he was involved in separate court cases as plaintiff against Leonard Helms, John Wood, and Original Young, all for debts, collecting only from Wood. In the same year William Lambert and his wife Christian sued him for trespass and assault and battery. The matter was agreed to by the parties, but the terms were not reported in the minute book. Also that year Levin Powell brought a case against him for an unspecified reason. Harrison was defended successfully by his cousin, the lawyer Cuthbert Bullitt. Two years afterwards Powell married Sarah Harrison, still another cousin of William. William had some forty first cousins living in northern Virginia in 1763. (So it is not surprising that members of an extended colonial family were sometimes found on opposite sides in the courts.) (4)

A case was brought against him in 1764 by James Douglass. After that it was not until 1773 that Harrison again became a party in a court suit. In that year he won his complaint against Jacob Forbes. A suit against John Watts was undecided when Harrison died. His case versus William Cosgrove that evidently never went to trial was "abated" by his death, as was one brought against him by his brother Burr. (5)

He appeared twice as a witness in the Prince William court in 1765. First, he testified for his uncle, Benjamin Bullitt, in a suit against Richard Dixon. The same matter was tried in the Fauquier court, probably to avoid a claim by the defendant that one of the counties did not have jurisdiction. Subsequently, William gave evidence for John Graham, clerk of court in Prince William and a friend of the Harrisons, in his case with Robert Marshall. (6)

The suits against Dixon and Marshall may indicate that Thomas Harrison had already sent his son to manage the plantation "at the mountains" purchased in 1764 and greatly enlarged the next year. Dixon and Marshall lived in its neighbor-

141

hood in the northern part of Fauquier County. William had been raised about thirty-five miles away in the county's southeastern corner, when it was part of Prince William.

At any rate he was definitely living in the northern area by 1769, when he was named surveyor of the five-mile section of the Winchester-Dumfries road that ran from Goose Creek to Barton's Tract. That meant he was to "survey" the condition of the road and keep it in good repair. Barton's Tract referred to land held by David Barton on a three-lives lease from Lord Fairfax. Harrison was relieved of this responsibility after three years, when William Hansbrough took over. (7)

The road ran along one side of a 520-acre tract William had bought from his father in 1768, part of 1000 acres the elder Harrison purchased of John Mercer in 1765. The original of William's title to the property has survived. The deed was witnessed by four women relatives: Betty Quarles, his half-sister; Anne Gillison, his youngest sister; Frances Harrison, daughter of his uncle Cuthbert Harrison; and Elizabeth Bullitt, another cousin, daughter of Benjamin Bullitt. All the women signed their names; none had to make her mark. (8)

William Harrison needed the land because he had married Jane Humston in February 1767. Jane was the daughter of Edward Humston, the third Edward in consecutive generations. The first one had arrived in Stafford County by 1667. Bride and groom were both of age, not needing a parent's consent on the marriage bond, which was co-signed by Jane's brother, the fourth Edward. (9)

After his marriage some of Harrison's activities are indicated in the Fauquier records. He was one of three appraisers of the estates of Francis Watts, Thomas Watts, and Frances Burgess. In 1771 his petition to build a water-mill on Watts Run was granted, since he had land on both sides of "said run and land of no other person" would be affected. If he used the permit, no trace of his construction remains. (10)

In January 1770 he was on a list of citizens who could serve as justices of oyer and terminer to conduct trials of slaves accused of crimes. If this meant he was in line to become a member of the county's commission of peace, when a new one was named by the next governor or because more justices were needed, he never got the appointment. (11)

In November 1773 William and Jonathan Gibson, husband of his sister Susannah, were security on the bond for the performance of his ailing father as incoming sheriff of the county. When Colonel Thomas died the next month, William was the first person named in the will and the first of the three executors. He was bequeathed a half-share with his brother Burr in two tracts totalling 512 acres located across the road from his own land. He bought Burr's interest before the end of 1774. Under the will he also received slaves, horses, cattle, hogs and sheep. (12)

He had less than a year to enjoy his new properties, since taking possession of them was delayed by the normal legalities of settling an estate. Tragedy struck in early January 1775, when he was found hanged on the giant oak in the corner of the woods, to which only the month before he had received full title from Burr.

An explanation of the murder was given in 1940 to a WPA chronicler by Mrs. Anna Bowersett, a three-greats grandaughter of the victim. She said that the slaves who hanged their master had been brought from Clarke County by his bride. They had been unhappy in their new situation and had believed that after William was dead, "Miss Jane" would take them back home with her.

This family tradition, garbled over the span of 165 years and six generations, has obvious errors. William and Jane had been married for nearly eight years at the time of his death. Thus the slaves could not have still been homesick for Clarke County, which incidentally was not established until 1837. Furthermore, "Miss Jane" came from the same southern end of Fauquier as her husband, not from the west side of the Blue Ridge.

Still, Mrs. Bowersett's story may have had some element of truth. Submittal of the county account for 1775 was delayed until October 1776 by the onset of the war, but when it was made available, it noted the following expenditures in pounds of tobacco:

To Humphrey Brooke [clerk of court] for attending a called court for the trial of Bristoe, a negroe man slave belonging to William Harrison	200
Ditto Sam	200
Ditto Dublin, Sylla, & Pat belonging to Do.	200
To Thomas Watts for guarding Harrison's negroes	75
To Thomas Marr for guarding Harrison's negroes 25 days	625
To James Headley do.	75
To George Cordell do.	400

No record of the trials remains, but evidently justice was swift. Forty-seven days after being taken into custody three of the five slaves were found guilty and executed. Bristoe and Sam, given separate trials, were evidently the ringleaders. (13)

The grain of truth in the family tradition shows itself in a reading of the will of Colonel Thomas. "Item I give and bequeath to my son William Harrison, four negroes viz. Roger, Bristoe, Sylla, & Cate ---Also one other Negroe called Dublin." Another item lists twelve more slaves that are to be divided equally amongst his sons William, Thomas, and Burr. Sam was among those given to his son, Benjamin. The slave Pat was one of several not named in the will, but included in the inventory of the Colonel. He should have gone to Benjamin, who was to receive the residue of the estate. The two brothers must have agreed that William take Sam and Pat in addition to the five specifically given to him and his one-third share of the twelve others.

In the inventory of William's estate submitted to the May 1775 court, two months after the trials, Bristoe, Sam, and Sylla were missing, but Dublin and Pat were among the fifteen slaves named. Nine of these had been tabulated the previous year as belonging to Colonel Thomas. Probably all five of the accused were found guilty, but the less culpable Dublin and Pat escaped the death penalty. After all, they were valuable, accounting between them for almost twelve percent of the worth of their deceased master's personal property. (14)

It is indeed likely that resentment of Bristoe and Sam at being torn from their home and friends in the more populous southern part of the county was directed against their new master and was the root cause of the tragedy. Sam may even have known that he originally had been expected to stay where he was. William had had only six slaves of his own; he was not nearly as wealthy as his father, and accomodations for his new people in the colder winter near the mountains may have been inadequate. Homesickness, as in the family tradition, could have played a part. Who knows if the poor blacks might not have felt that their act would result in "Miss Jane" going "home" with her children and taking them with her back to their old neighborhood.

Another descendant of William had a slightly different version of his murder. "Aunt Becc" had said that when the slaves decided on their plan, one of them came running to the house crying that there was a bear in the barn. When the master went to investigate, he was felled with a blow from an axe. To make this gibe with the hanging on the oak, we might suppose that was how the plotters were able to overcome their victim and get him to the tree to finish their work. (15)

We suspect the general conception is that the killing of a master by his slaves occurred fairly often in colonial Virginia; if so, the opinion is unfounded. The murder of Harrison is the only such incident that we have come across in the records of the five northern Virginia counties from 1664 to 1775. There may have been others, because many records are missing, and our searches have not had the crimes and punishments of slaves as a specific objective. Nevertheless, it was a rare fate that struck down William.

The widow Jane was left with three young children: Burr, about seven years old; Lucy, around five; and William, still a baby. In the immediate aftermath of the crime, Jane was appointed administratrix of her husband's estate and guardian of the children. (16) She must have stayed on and managed the farm, for in 1781 she received a certificate for beef supplied to the Revolutionary army. (17)

She did not marry again immediately, as so many widows did in those times, but waited until 1784 when she became the wife of Captain Philip Mallory, a Revolutionary veteran, old enough to have a son who had also been an officer in the war. Lucy married her stepbrother, William Mallory, the next year. (18)

Jane (Humston) Harrison Mallory suffered new tragedies, long before her own death in 1807. Her youngest child, William, died of some illness in 1790, when only sixteen. (19) Her oldest, Burr, promising son and heir of his father, was declared insane in 1795, when he was twenty-seven or twenty-eight years old. He never recovered his senses, although he lived for fifty more years.

This fifth-generation Burr had married Lucy Pickett, the daughter of William and Lucy (Blackwell) Pickett in 1789, when both were only twenty-one or twenty-two. The officiating minister was Lucy's uncle, the Baptist John Pickett. (20)

It was not until eight months after the wedding that Burr signed a receipt for termination of his guardian's management of his estate. "I this day received full satisfaction of Captain Philip Mallory for my estate during the time he was guardian for me. Witness my hand this fifth day of April 1790. Signed Burr Harrison. Teste William Harrison." (21)

Nevertheless Burr was involved for some time in a lawsuit with his stepfather about his estate. In 1791 he and Lucy had deeded 107 acres, part of the "Monterey" tract, to Mallory in part settlement of his mother's dower. But the next year a jury ruled in his favor ordering Mallory to release to him five slaves; a man, a woman, and her three children. The slaves were valued from eighty pounds for the man to twenty for the youngest child, and eighty pounds was awarded as "damages for the detention of said slaves." However, a subsequent court minute noted that by consent of Harrison and Mallory, three arbitrators were appointed to allot Jane Mallory her dower in the Negroes recovered by Harrison and to determine if the damages were excessive. "If so, Harrison agrees to release such excess." We wonder why the two men didn't go to arbitration in the first place. (22)

In connection with this suit Mallory had requested depositions from Ann Southard, Mark Hardin, and Thomas Marshall Sr. and his wife Mary, all of the District of Kentucky—an indication of the magnitude of the exodus from northern Virginia to the "West."

In spite of the family quarrel, the youthful Burr must have been liked and respected in the community, for in 1793, at the age of twenty-six or thereabouts, he took the oath as a justice of the peace. (23) True, his links to the leading families of the county were impeccable. Both his grandfather Harrison and his wife's grandfather, William Blackwell, had been on the first commission of peace of Fauquier; his uncle Ben Harrison had been a magistrate; and his wife's uncle, Martin Pickett, was the current presiding justice. Furthermore, the Marshalls lived just down the road from the Harrisons. Although Colonel Thomas Marshall had moved to Kentucky and his son, the future chief justice, was now practicing law in Richmond, the family still had a "big say" in the county. They must have known Burr from his childhood and liked what they saw in him.

So the illness or accident that struck Burr down was all the more a great pity. In the October 1795 session of the Fauquier court the following action was taken:

> *It appearing to the court that Burr Harrison (son of William) is a lunatick and now of unsound mind and therefore incapable of conducting his own affairs --- ordered that John T. Chinn, Laurence Ashton, Alexander Scott, Joseph Chilton, and Joseph Smith, Gentlemen, take the custody and management of the estate both real and personal of the said Burr Harrison ----. (24)*

In those days no thought whatsoever would have been given to having Lucy Harrison take charge. As a woman, her place was in the home raising the children. She may have been consulted by the commissioners about her wishes in some decision they had to make, but she certainly had no veto power over their judgments.

Lucy had three small sons to look after: William, George Pickett, and Thomas Grayson Harrison. The oldest was probably five, and the youngest at most two years old.

We have not found the cause of Burr's insanity. Possibly, it was a severe depression, incurable by the treatments available at the time. Yet one would think such a disability would have displayed signs of an approaching crisis, significant enough to prevent his being named a magistrate. Instead, the indications are that it struck quickly. We can only speculate about encephalitis, meningitis, or some other fever, a blow to his head--perhaps from a fall from his horse, or other accident which robbed his brain of oxygen. Whether or to what extent speech and cognitive ability ("unsound mind"?) were damaged, we cannot tell. Nothing was said about any paralysis or loss of motor control. (25) It could not have been a degenerative disease. Thirty years after its onset when his sons obtained an Act of Assembly allowing them to take possession of his estate and divide it as if he had died, the act provided for its return to him when he regained his faculties. Even if that was only a legal formality, it gave some indication that his condition had not changed greatly for the better or worse.

Burr owned two houses. He had been born at the one, afterwards called Monterey, on the land obtained by his father from his grandfather in 1768. After his marriage he had moved to the other, later known as Glanville, located on the tract bought by his grandfather in 1763. The Mallorys lived at Monterey. Lucy and the children continued to live at Glanville. No record was made of where Burr was lodged on his return from the hospital, now Eastern State Hospital in Williamsburg, but in later years the commissioners' accounts show he was kept by William Eustace and then by John Casey. Casey was paid $120 annually at first and later was rented Monterey on the condition that he take care of Burr. (26)

The original commissioners served at least for the first two and a half years; afterwards many other persons acted in the capacity. Not until 1825 did his two older sons serve on the Comite. It was only terminated when the sons obtained relief from the Assembly in 1832.

Somehow a reasonable job of management had been done. At least there was never need to sell any of the land, slaves, or other property. On the other hand there was no surplus income to build up the estate for Lucy and her children, as there might have been, if Burr had been able to remain in charge.

This unfortunate Burr Harrison was the one referred to at the start of this history as being buried on our farm, Monterey.

147

He died in 1842, having outlived his wife and two of his three sons.

Probably Lucy is also buried in the family cemetery, but her name was not in the family Bible kept by a great-grand-daughter and therefore is not on the monument. What a struggle she must have had to raise her family. Our last piece of knowledge about her is that she owed the local pharmacist-doctor for a remedy supplied in 1823. How much we wish that we could know more about her and her predecessors among the Harrison womenfolk.

Notes:

1. Glanville was part of the tract left by Colonel Thomas Harrison jointly to his sons William and Burr. Monterey was essentially the farm purchased by William from his father in 1768 less his widow's dower portion. William was living on Monterey when he was murdered. The "uncles" Thomas and William Hume were his great-great-great-grandsons.
2. Mrs. Anna Hume Bowersett (1864-1947) was the sister of the Hume brothers.
3. PW D Q-508, 7/15/1760. The other executors were James Nesbitt and Spence Grayson, brother of Benjamin Jr.
4. F M (1762-1764): p. 92, Helms; 95-171, Powell; 109, Wood; 140-263, Young; 140, Lambert; 318, Douglass. Page numbers are those of the beginning and end of a case.
5. F M (1768-1773): p.474, Forbes. (1773-1780): 17, Forbes; 93, Watts; 372, Cosgrove; 372, Burr Harrison. The reason for the suit entered by Burr Harrison is not given. After their marriages, William and Burr lived near each other from about 1769 until William died. William's oldest son was named for Burr. Surely, their father would not have left property to them jointly if he had thought they were not agreeable to this disposition.
6. PW M 1765, p.82 Bullitt and p.111 Graham.
7. F M (1768-1773), p.102. David Barton was the holder of a lease for three lives in Lord Fairfax's Leeds Manor granted in 1759. See Chapter XVII.
8. F D 3-167, 6/23/1768. We have the original deed.
9. F Marriage Book 1-23, 2/23/1767. Jane's brother, Edward, married Susannah Quarles in January 1769. She was the daughter of William's half-brother, Moses Quarles, who had died.
10. F M (1768-1773), p.368, 1771. Petition to build mill.
11. Idem, p.161, 1770.

12. F D 6-170, 1774 and 6-172, 1774. Witnesses were Thomas Harrison Sr. (brother of William and Burr), Thomas Nelson, William Cosgrove, and Price Hansbruck.
13. F M (1773-1780), p.271, 1776.
14. F W 1-296, 1775.
15. "Aunt Becc" was Rebecca (Harrison) Luckett, great-great-granddaughter of William, born in 1851. She was the great-aunt of the person to whom she told her account.
16. F M (1773-1780), pp.223-224, 2/24/1775. Jane Harrison is confirmed as administratrix of William Harrison deceased and appointed guardian of his children. The month of William's death is given in F M (10/1795-10/1796), p.70. Boyle Somerville & Co. ag. Philip Mallory and Jane, his wife, "late Jane Harrison, adm. of estate of William Harrison, d'ced, who departed this life in January 1775." The claim is made that Mallory said that Jane had acknowledged Harrison's debt. All the principals of the company lived in Great Britain except Gavin Lawson. The court found for the defendants by reason of the statute of limitations and lack of proof. Plaintiff appealed to the district court at Dumfries.
17. Public Service Claims----Fauquier County, 1781. John Blackwell certified that he received 250 pounds of beef from Jane Harrison for "publick use." She was paid 3/8/6.
18. F Marriage Book, 1-136, 1/12/1785. Marriage of William Mallory and Lucy Harrison.
19. F W 2-183 proved 1/24/1791. William left two Negroes each to his mother, Jane Mallory; his brother Burr; and his sister, Lucy Mallory. 2-186 is the account presented by his stepfather and guardian, Philip Mallory.
20. F Marriage Book 1-268, 8/24/1789. Bond for marriage of Burr Harrison and Lucy Pickett, William Pickett cosigner of bond, no consent needed. Idem. 1-445. Certificate of marriage on 8/26/1789 returned by John Pickett, the officiating minister.
21. F D 12-89, 1790.
22. F D 10-534, 1791. Burr Harrison and Lucy, his wife, sell Philip Mallory 107 acres, part of Jane Mallory's dower. F M August, 1792, p.182. Burr Harrison against Philip Mallory over retention of slaves. F M May, 1793, p.393. Burr Harrison summoned to show why his mother's dower in land should not be reallotted to her. (Jane Mallory did not get more land.)
23. F M 1793-95, p.44. Burr Harrison, Gent. took prescribed oath to be justice of the peace.
24. F M Oct. 1795, p.23.

25. The early records of Eastern State Hospital that might have told more about Harrison's condition were taken to Richmond for safekeeping during the Peninsula Campaign in 1862 and lost in the fire that destroyed much of the city at the end of the War in 1865.
26. F M Oct. 1796, p.346. Charles Marshall gives bond of 60 pounds "to be void on condition that Burr Harrison who is a lunatic and now confined in the public hospital be kept secure and restrained from going at large until he be restored to his sences, the said Burr Harrison being released from said hospital."

Chapter XIII

Burr Harrison (1738–1822) of South Carolina
(Burr 4, Thomas 3, Burr 2, Burr 1)

One of the three great-grandchildren who shared the name of the immigrant Burr Harrison was born on September 20, 1738, the third son of Colonel Thomas and Ann (Grayson) Quarles Harrison. (1)

While this Burr Harrison was still a small child, his family moved from Fairfax County to what is now Fauquier. It was a large family with four sons, three daughters, and three children of the mother's first marriage. The siblings ranged in age from about twelve years older than Burr to eleven years younger. Since the family was wealthy, there was undoubtedly a tutor living on the plantation to teach the boys and girls, but who the instructor might have been is not known.

In 1756 service of God, King, and Country fighting the French and Indians must have appeared attractive to an 18-year-old Southerner whose father was the commander of the county militia. Just a year earlier, Braddock had been routed in his attempt to take Fort Duquesne. The vanquished army had included regiments from Virginia (commanded by Lt. Colonel George Washington) and Maryland. Burr's cousin, Captain Thomas Bullitt, was an officer of the Virginia regiment. The Bullitt plantation adjoined that of the Harrisons, but they also had land and connections in Maryland. So Cousin Thomas may have had something to do with Burr obtaining a commission as ensign (third lieutenant) in a company of the Maryland regiment raised by Alexander Beall. (2)

Captain Beall was left at Fort Frederick in April 1757 with 250 effectives when most of the Marylanders were brought back "east." The following November a report made to the Maryland Assembly included "Ensign Burr Harrison" among officers entrusted with money to use on recruiting service to pay to

151

volunteers who would enlist. He was given fifty pounds, enough for ten recruits. (3) The next February Ensign Harrison attended a parley with a group of Indians at Fort Frederick. On that occasion Thomas Bullitt chaired and reported on the meeting and Captain Beall was present. (4)

Ensign Harrison was listed as wounded in September of 1758 in the successful campaign to take Fort Duquesne. (5) No doubt his performance in that action resulted in a promotion granted by a new commission:

> *Frederick, Absolute Lord and Proprietary of the Provinces of Maryland & Avalon, Lord Baron of Baltimore, to our trusty Burr Harrison greeting. Reposing great trust & confidence in your fidelity, conduct & loyalty to His Most Sacred Majesty King George the Second & your good affection to me & my government, I have thought fit & do by these presents commissionate & appoint you, the said Burr Harrison, second lieutenant in the company of soldiers commanded by Captain Alexander Beall, willing & requiring you to take the said company into your charge & duly to exercise the men in arms & to keep them in good order and discipline, which I do hereby require the persons under your command to pay due obedience to you as second lieutenant of the said company, and you are to follow such commands & instructions from time to time as you shall receive from my Lieutenant General & Chief Governor or any other your superior officer or officers, hereby granting unto you to hold & enjoy this my commission during pleasure. Witness our trusty & well-beloved Horatio Sharpe, Esquire, Lieutenant General & Chief Governor of our said Province of Maryland, this 13th day of October in the eighth year of our Dominion, Anno Domini one thousand seven hundred & fifty eight.*

In the left hand margin of the parchment is the signature and seal of Horatio Sharpe. (6)

Harrison appears to have remained on duty until 1762, for in July of that year he is recorded as appearing in the court of Anne Arundel County to make his oath on "the Holy Evangels of God Almighty" for an accounting of his administration of the estate of John Terrill. The account notes receipt of a small sum of cash received from Col. John Dagworthy of the Maryland troops, indicating that Terril had been one of the soldiers under Harrison's command. (7)

Captain Bullitt served under Colonel Byrd of Virginia in the 1761 Cherokee expedition to Fort Loudoun, Tennessee (then North Carolina). Possibly Burr accompanied him. That may have contributed to his decision to visit South Carolina in 1764. In Charleston he had a tailor make him a pair of "breeches" from 2 1/2 yards of "crimson shag" (a cloth with a long rough nap) and 2 yards of Irish linen. A couple of weeks later the tailor produced for him a suit of clothes using 4 yards of cloth, 4 1/2 yards of shalloon, (a wool twill lining material) and 5 yards of white fustian (a cotton or cotton-linen corduroy). Apparently the young dandy did not accept the work; at least he did not pay for it. After thirty months had passed, the tailor sued for payment of his bill of 76 pounds, 16 shillings, three pence. He had charged only 1 pound 10 shillings for his work on the knickers, plus 9 pounds for the suit. The shag cost almost 17 pounds and the suit cloth 33 pounds. The balance was for other materials. One may compare this outlay with the bond of 20 pounds Burr had had to sign for the administration of poor Terril's estate. The marshal was unable to find and serve the summons on Harrison, who was reported to be living at the "Congarees," the back-country of the province in the area of what is now Columbia. So he was adjudged in default, and a jury awarded the tailor 160 pounds to which were added 55 pounds of court costs. (8) We wonder if the tailor ever collected.

Burr had gone up-country to visit friends. They included brothers John and Richard Winn, from his home neighborhood in Virginia who had moved south some years before. (9) The Winns would have introduced him to William and Catherine (Dargan) Strother, other Virginians who had gone to live in that part of South Carolina, if Burr did not already know the couple. (10) Presumably it was at the home of the Strothers that the 24-year-old Harrison met Elizabeth Dargan, the younger sister of Mrs. Strother. The wedding of Burr and Elizabeth took place in 1766. (11)

Elizabeth and Catherine were two of the eight children of Timothy and Catherine Dargan who had taken their family from Prince William to South Carolina early in the 1750s. Timothy's will was proved in South Carolina in 1762. Elizabeth was one of the younger children, if not the youngest. She was apparently born between 1745 and 1750 in Prince William County, Virginia.

Timothy Dargan, called a "planter of Stafford County," had purchased 156 acres on Accokeek Run in 1727. In 1730 he bought 253 acres on the south side of Cedar Run, near Thomas Harrison (1665-1746) and Thomas Whitledge, but he sold this tract after two years. His wife Catherine appeared in "open court" to give her consent to the sale. In 1736 he was paid by the estate of Edward Markham for a cow and calf sold to the deceased. Another estate account, that of Valentine Barton (probably a grandson of the first Burr Harrison), showed a payment received from Dargan. The account also credited Colonel Carter for his share of a crop on his quarter (plantation). Dargan's property on Accokeek Run adjoined land of Colonel Carter.

Other Virginia records concerning the Dargans include a 1749 deed from Owen and Mary Lord who transferred "all our goods and chattels, household stuff, and all other our sub-stance" to Timothy Dargan in return for "a sufficient dwelling house, good clothing----with such necessary attendance." Dargan gave a bond for 100 pounds to insure his compliance with the agreement. No relationship between the parties was spelled out in either document; a guess would place the Lords as the parents of Catherine Dargan. In 1750 Dargan's suit against John Combs in the Fairfax County court was settled; this was the last record of the family in Virginia. (12)

Exactly how long the newlyweds stayed in South Carolina before returning to Virginia is not known. Burr did have a tract of 150 acres on the Congaree River surveyed for him in 1769 by Richard Winn, but the requisites for a grant of this land from the provincial government were never completed. (13) Nothing else has been found of Harrison in South Carolina or in Virginia until 1770. By then he was back in Fauquier County, where in August he made a 10-shilling purchase from Peter Hitt, whose account book has survived.

In his father's will proved in January 1774 Burr was devised a 408-acre plantation adjoining land of his brother William in the northern part of Fauquier and an equal share with William in 472 neighboring acres. He also was given four slaves and one-third of the stock his father had on the plantation "at the mountains." He was to sell one of the slaves to pay his debts. (In 1772 Burr had had to mortgage slaves, cattle, and household furniture to cover a debt.)

Unlike his brothers William and Benjamin, Burr was not appointed an executor of the estate. His oldest son Benjamin received a Negro boy named Ned, but his daughters, Mary and Catherine, were not remembered by their grandfather, although most of the other granddaughters were.

Only a few months after the death of his father the minutes of the Fauquier court recorded "a petition of sundry persons

154

called Baptists praying that the court would grant them leave to erect a meeting house on the lands of Burr Harrison." First on the list of signers was Burr Harrison, and several of the names on the original appear to be in his handwriting, no doubt acting for members of the congregation who could not write. Other signers included James Winn and James Winn Jr., very likely a brother and a nephew of Burr's South Carolina friends, and a John Wright who was the son of a longtime colleague of Burr's father on the commissions of peace for Prince William and later Fauquier. The petition requested:

> ---- we being dissenters bearing the denomination of Baptists and desiring to worship God according to the best light we have on holy scriptures and the dictates of our own conscience humbly prayeth that your worships would be pleased to grant us the liberty to meet together for the prosecution of what we believe to be our duty at the meeting house built for that purpose on a tenement of land occupied by Burr Harrison ----.
> (14)

The building had been constructed in 1771; apparently Burr had been living on the tract of 140 acres under a lease from Lord Fairfax for some time. It was part of the Manor of Leeds, 120,000 acres which Fairfax as Proprietor had granted in 1736 to his agent, who immediately reconveyed it back to him as a private person in a move to insure his title in case the Proprietorship was taken away by royal decree.

Colonel Thomas Harrison and Captain John Wright Sr. must have been greatly disappointed in their sons becoming Baptists. As an example of what they probably thought, the 1769 petition of members of the Parish of Hamilton that it be divided in two was largely based on the claim that many of the inhabitants of Fauquier County resided so far from a parish church that they could seldom attend services, "which causes dissenters to have the opportunity and encouragement to spread their pernicious doctrines." The request was promptly granted by the General Assembly, which split off Leeds Parish covering the northern part of the county. The next year John Pickett, a Baptist minister, was committed to the Fauquier jail for three months for "preaching contrary to an act of parliament." (15)

Pickett's crime was refusal to register as a dissenter as required under the 1689 Act of Toleration. That act had brought a degree of religious liberty to Virginia. It put a stop to persecution of the Quakers in the colony, and they became the largest dissenting denomination in northern Virginia in the first half of the eighteenth century.

In the Rev. Charles Green's compilation of the 1749 list of titheables of Fairfax County he made a note beside the name of each person who registered his membership in a non-Anglican denomination. His data showed that out of a total of 2035 white males over the age of sixteen there were ninety-one Quakers, seventy-six Catholics, sixty-four Presbyterians, and twelve Anabaptists or other dissenters. All the Quakers and Anabaptists lived in the Upper Parish, where the people were mostly small farmers. Not by a long shot were all of the nominal Anglicans church-goers. The Rev. Mr. Green called only 130 of his parishioners "constant communicants." At the Goose Creek Church, the farthest away from Alexandria and the older settlements, he never had a single communicant. (See Appendix A-Statistics.)

Very soon the picture painted by those statistics would change radically. The time was ripe, as shown by the lack of support for the Rev. Green in the outer reaches of Fairfax. Revival exploded when the country-wide Great Awakening arrived in northern Virginia in the 1760s. By 1772 within five years of its beginnings, the Carter's Run Baptist Church, of which John Pickett was the minister and Burr Harrison a member, counted "about 250 families, whereof 240 are baptized and in communion." (16) Obviously, they were ready in 1774 to set up their second church, Upper Carter's Run, in the building on Harrison's land.

Carter's Run was a Separate Baptist congregation. They were an evangelical group who stressed the importance of conversion and public confession of faith. Their unsalaried ministers were ordained but not necessarily educated men. Like the Quakers they rejected any creed or articles of faith and gave all authority to the local church. They aimed at the "true religion," where worship did not depend on ritual or hierarchical authority. And, of course, they practiced adult baptism by immersion.

These Separate Baptists, like their less shouting, more Calvinistic brethren, the Regular Baptists, were strongest in the Piedmont counties such as Loudoun, Fauquier, & Culpeper.

No doubt, however, they were looked on by their more settled and generally better-off neighbors as noisy, uneducated, intolerant, holier-than-thou upstarts who were subverting the youth and were a danger to society.

Burr Harrison's conversion (dated to 1768 by his obituary) was the byproduct of his marriage. Elizabeth's father had been

156

an Anglican, but her brothers Jeremiah and Timothy both became Baptist preachers.

Evidently, Burr and his wife had intended to move to South Carolina after his father died, for by October 1775 he had sold his interest in the land left jointly to him and William to the latter. In addition, he had obtained an act of the General Assembly freeing him from the entail imposed by the will on the 408 acres bequeathed to him and "the heirs of his body" and had sold the property to James Grigsby. (17) But the Revolution had disrupted the plan. By 1777 the family had moved to another nearby farm, and in 1781 he signed a three-year lease for that one with the option to extend it when the term was over. The lease was for "the plantation in his occupation for four years past containing 150 acres." Harrison was to build "one good hewed log barn with good oak plank," twenty-four feet square and to plant "150 good apples of the winter kind." (18)

Burr Harrison was "recommended" by the Fauquier court to Governor Patrick Henry as first lieutenant of the militia in the company of which William Grigsby was captain and William Nash second lieutenant in March 1778 and took the prescribed oath in April 1779. (19) Surely Harrison, a 40-year-old who had been an officer in the French and Indian War, should have been given a higher rank than first lieutenant, especially considering that Grigsby, his immediate superior, was a younger man married to his cousin, Elizabeth Bullitt, sister to Thomas Bullitt. His own younger brother Benjamin was a captain. Was it his religious affiliation that held Burr back?

How much active duty Burr saw is uncertain. He did not obtain a military grant in Kentucky from Virginia; they were not given to militia officers. Although his obituary states that he served as a captain under Lafayette at Yorktown, he was never referred to as "Captain" in the records in Virginia or South Carolina. Nevertheless, there were Fauquier companies at Yorktown, even though the two regular regiments under Fauquier commanders had been decimated at Charleston in May 1780 and most of their personnel captured there. Furthermore, there was a "Captain Harrison" (no first name given) at Yorktown reported in a pension application by a David Ellington. (20)

There is an even more tenuous and indirect indication that Burr may have been the Captain Harrison. The family of his brother William's descendants who have his Maryland commission also own a table that Lafayette is said to have dined at. If true, it could be that Lafayette had visited his subordinate. Although only a captain, Burr came from an important family. Then one would have to assume that on leaving Virginia, he either gave the table to his nephew, a namesake and probably his godchild, or at least left it with him for safekeeping. (The number of tables that "Lafayette ate off" must closely approximate the count of beds that "Washington slept" in.)

Between August 1772 and July 1783 there are more references to this Burr Harrison in the minutes of the Fauquier court. In 1774 he and William asked for and obtained counter-securities for their bond with Hannah Boggess for her administration of the estate of her deceased husband. The following year he brought a runaway servant into court and got the man's indenture extended. In 1778 and again in 1779 he was licensed to keep an ordinary in his house. (21)

By 1783 the Harrisons were again planning their move to South Carolina. They started a suit to recover a debt owed them and another for damages due to trespass by a neighbor. In March their son Benjamin, Burr himself, John Moffett, and Minor Winn, brother of the Carolinians, sold a Negro lad named Ned to Josiah Fishback for eighty pounds in gold and silver. Ned was the name of the slave left Benjamin by his grandfather. Moffett was Harrison's landlord, and it may be he was owed for rent, but why Winn was included on the bill of sale cannot even be guessed. Benjamin signed the receipt. He was probably about fifteen years old. (22)

It took the family a year to wind up their affairs in Virginia, but in 1784 they arrived in South Carolina. Their new home was on three hundred acres on Little Creek of Little River in Camden District bought from Richard Walker in May 1782. (23) The new farm was about five miles west of Winnsboro. That town, named for Richard Winn, became the seat of Fairfield County when it was set up in 1785. Settlement in the area had begun about 1750, mainly by people coming from Pennsylvania, Maryland, and Virginia. The influx had increased greatly after the end of the French and Indian War and again after the Revolution. Generally, one thinks of the Cumberland Road into Kentucky being the great migration route for Virginians, but at this earlier time the way down the edge of the Blue Ridge into the Carolinas was also important.

Soon after arriving, Burr was made a justice of the peace. In that capacity he took the oaths of several Revolutionary veterans in their claims on the state for war service. At the first court for the new county, he was appointed coroner, an officer of the court who had more responsibilities than just investigating deaths. He retained that post at least through 1792. The last mention of Burr in the minute books came in 1796 when he "delivered the body [the person] of Joseph James

158

in discharge of his bail bond." (24)

In 1786 he was one of three commissioners charged with marking out a road from Mobley's Meeting House to Winnsborough. Mobley's Meeting House was a Baptist church built about 1760. About four miles from the home of the Harrisons, it appears to have been the congregation to which the family belonged. Unfortunately the minutes of this church have been lost.

Deeds of lease and release, in the forms commonly used in Virginia, have been found in Barnwell County that show that Harrison had at least one investment in land there. The deeds record the sale by Burr Harrison of the County of Fairfield to Joseph Duncan of 150 acres in Winton County, formerly the County of Colleton. The land had been granted to Thomas Morrison in 1771. At that time it was surrounded on all sides by "vacant land." When Harrison had bought, the property was not delineated. The sale for twenty pounds sterling was made in November 1787.

A clue to why Burr would have purchased land there some hundred miles away is given by the 1790 census of South Carolina. It shows Mary Foulke as a resident of Colleton County. She was Mrs. Chandler Fowke, nee Mary Harrison, Burr's sister.

Burr and Elizabeth Harrison had the following children live to maturity:

Benjamin - (ca. 1768–1837), m. (1) Eliz. Hart (?), (2) Mary Grice (?).
Mary - m. Benjamin May.
Catherine - m. Samuel Johnstone.
Jonathan - (1775–1851), m. Sallie Tyler.
Elizabeth - did not marry; died young.
Rebecca - m. Nathaniel Cockrell.
Susanna - m. William Head.
Sophia - d. 1824, m. 1797 Christopher Thompson.
Dorcas - d. 1866, m. (1) James Russell, (2) Hartwell Macon.
Narcissa - m. James Ragsdale.
Ann - m. James McClelland.
Mordecai - m. Susan Alston. (25)

In March 1798 Burr wound up his affairs in Fairfield County. He made deeds giving a slave each to eight of his children: Sophia Thompson, Dorcas, Susanna Head, Rebecca Cockrell, Mordecai, Elizabeth, Ann, and Narcissa. The slaves ranged in age from sixty years to six months. Five were over nineteen, and four were six or younger. (Ann got a man of sixty and a

159

baby girl.) Simultaneously he sold the three hundred acres bought in 1782 to a John Simonton. Burr's son Benjamin of Richland County gave bond to the buyer guaranteeing the title. (26)

Thereafter Burr, Elizabeth, and the unmarried children must have lived with the married ones. Burr died in 1822 and his wife in 1825. His obituary explains the probable reason for the break-up of the household.

> *Died on the 18th Aug., 1822 in Chester District, S.C. in the 84th year of his age, Burr Harrison, Esq. He was a native of Va., but had resided in this state for the last thirty-eight years of his life. ---- He served as Captain under Major General DeLafayette in the Rev. army. He was a tender parent and humane master. He had twelve children, eighty-four grandchildren, and sixty great-grandchildren. He embraced religion when about 30 years of age. ---- His mind was much impaired for the last thirteen years of his life, but to the joy of his children ---- they had reason to believe his right mind was restored to him again a short time before his death and that he fell asleep in the arms of Jesus. (27)*

Both Burr and Elizabeth were buried in a plot in Columbia, but a buyer of the property about the time of the Civil War tore down the fence and gravestones and built a house on the site. (28)

The legion of descendants of the couple are scattered over the United States by now, although concentrated in the tier of southern states from South Carolina to Texas. This review may give some of them a better picture of their ancestor and his accomplishments.

Notes:

1. While 1738 agrees with his obituary, the original source of the Sept. 20 birth-date has not been traced.
2. Alexander Beall recruited other Virginians besides Harrison, as evidenced by Record No. 951, Old Military and Importation Warrants of the Va. State Land Office. It reads:

> *Yohogania County, December Court, 1779.*
> *On the motion of Michael Van Bushkirk pray-*

ing a certificate of his military service ---- the
said Vanbushkirk served as an Ensign under a
commission from his Excellency Horatio Sharpe,
dated 2nd of May 1756 in a corps raised by
Alexander Bealle for the service of Maryland.
---- ordered to be certified.
   Assigned to Burr Harrison.
   Michael Vanbuscark.   2000 acres issued.
       per Test. Dorsey Pentacost.

Harrison had an interest in the area, now part of Pennsylvania. An order of the Yohogania court in 1777 dismissed his suit against William Williams.

3. *Maryland Archives*, Vol. 31, p.281. In a covering letter for the report of the agents charged with maintaining the Maryland regiment, the auditors comment on irregularities. The agents have not assured that men receiving enlistment bounties have showed up for duty.   Evidently the Maryland regiment in 1757 had companies commanded by Captains Dagworthy, Alexander Beall, and Joshua Beall.   Each unit had a first lieutenant, a second lieutenant, and an ensign.

4. Ibid. 25-262. The meeting was requested by three Cherokee warriors who complained that gifts promised for their loyalty in fighting the Indians of the French had been denied them by the officer who was the interpreter at a prior meeting in Fort Cumberland. Bullitt's report indicates that he distrusted that officer and thought he might have been trying to alienate the Cherokees.

5. June Clark Murtie, *Colonial Soldiers of the South*, p.533. Harrison was listed as a Marylander.   When forces under General John Forbes first attacked Fort Duquesne in September, 1758, they were repulsed with heavy losses. Its capture on November 25, 1758 gave control of the Ohio River Valley to the British.

6. Original parchment in possession of the author's wife, a direct descendant of Burr Harrison, nephew of Burr of South Carolina, who may have received it as a memento from his uncle.

7. State Archives, Annapolis, Md. Accounts of Anne Arundel County, July 10, 1762.

8. South Carolina State Archives, Columbia, S.C.   Computer Index 0151 002 065A 0096A 00. Judgment 1766 John Ward vs. "Barr" Harrison. The seventy-eight pounds of the tailor's bill would have been sufficient to provide for a colonial family of five for nine months. (Edwin J. Perkins, *The Economy of Colonial America* as quoted in V 92-430.)

9. John and Richard Winn were sons of Minor Winn Sr. of Fauquier Courthouse (Warrenton, Va.). Richard Winn commanded a regiment under General Sumter during the Revolution and after it became major general commanding the South Carolina militia and a U.S. Congressman. He died soon after removing to Tennessee from Winnsboro in 1812.

10. There is considerable confusion about the William Strother who married Catherine Dargan in 1759. William died in 1779 and Catherine in 1821. In his will children Kemp, John D., William, and Catherine are named. A James Strother, his sons, and his stepson, Daniel Flowerree, lived in northern Fauquier at the time of the Revolution. Flowerree had a son named Kemp. If, as appears likely, James was the uncle of William, Harrison may have known William before the latter went to South Carolina.

11. The year of the marriage is given in a 1923 letter from Mrs. Wildie H. Courie to Mrs. Eliza Wylie in the Winthrop College collection of the latter's papers. No source is given, but other data in the letter are consistent with known facts.

12. PW W C-20, 1736 and C-255, 1740 give the estate accounts of Edward Markham and Valentine Barton. S D J-392 has the Accoteek purchase. PW D A-185 records the sale of Cedar Run property, but NN F-124, 1743 is a grant for 254 a. on the Walnut br. of Cedar Run. M-34 has the arrangement with the Lords. (Owen Lord owned land on the Accoteek in 1719.) The will of Timothy Dargan Sr., (Charleston, S.C., Will Book 1760-67, p.218) written in 1761 and proved in 1762 makes bequests to wife Catherine; children Timothy, William, Jeremiah, Catherine Strother, Elizabeth, John, and Dorcas Milner; and grandchildren Charles and Mary Russell. (Daughter Ann had married Charles Russell in 1754.)

13. S.C. Archives Comp. Index 0009 018 0002 06555 00. "Pursuant to a presept directed by Egerton Leigh Esq., Surveyor General, dated Feb. 17, 1769 I have surveyed and laid out unto Burr Harrison a tract ---- Cert. June 16, 1769. Rich'd Winn District Surveyor."

14. F M 1773-84, p.196, 1774. The original petition found in the clerk's office in 1920 was published in T 4-260.

15. Idem., 1768-1773, p.163, Jan. 1770.

16. John K. Gott, *Carter's Run: Mother Church, The Virginia Baptist Register*, Number 2, 1963.

17. F D 6-170, 1774. Burr Harrison to brother William. F D 9-16, 1785. Grigsby to Kenner recites purchase from Harri-

son of 408 a. in 1775.

18. F D 7-327, 1781. Lease from John Moffett.

19. F M 1773-84, p.312, 1778; p.364, 1779.

20. Dorman, *Virginia Revolutionary Pension Applications*, Vol. 33, p.41.

21. F M 1768-73, pp. 423, 492; 1773-80, pp. 135, 186, 204, 234, 238, 245, 357, 455; 1780-84, 89, 128, 166 (July 1783). Operation of the county court was disrupted by the Revolution, among other reasons because the county clerk and many of the justices were officers on active duty. In April 1779 the minutes contain a long list of suits discontinued by the death of a party.

22. F D 7-483, 1783.

23. Fairfield D B-220, 1782.

24. Brent Holcomb, *Minutes of the Court of Fairfield County, 1785-99.* See pp. 1, 27, 28, 30, 35, 64, 75, 118, 130.

25. Winthrop College Archives, Rock Hill, S.C., Collection of Mrs. Eliza (Ragsdale) Wylie, a great-granddaughter of Narcissa (Harrison) Ragsdale. Principal source for tabulation. Except for order of birth of children, data has been confirmed by original records. Richland (SC) District Vol. 2, W K-108, 1837. Will of Benjamin Harrison names wife Mary and mentions children without naming them.

26. Fairfield D L 157, 158, 164, 220, 236, 237, 246, and 250. Gifts of slaves. L 182. Sale of farm to John Simonton. L 183. Bond by Benjamin Harrison guaranteeing title.

27. *Daily National Intelligencer*, Washington, 8/24/1822. Burr Harrison "on the 18th ult."

28. 1915 letter to Mrs. Wylie from her Aunt Kate (Ragsdale) Morrison. "Old Jack Caldwell of Columbia bought the lot where grandfather and [grand]mother Harrison were buried when Columbia was building up and took the tombstones off of our grandparents' graves and built a house over the graves. I have been in the house many a time when I was a child."

Chapter XIV

Benjamin Harrison (1744-1797)
(Benjamin 4, Thomas 3, Thomas 2, Burr 1)

A notation in the Dettingen Parish Vestry Book gives August 17, 1744 as the date of birth of Benjamin Harrison, the youngest son and next to the youngest child of Colonel Thomas and Anne (Grayson) Quarles Harrison. The baby was named after Anne's brother, Benjamin Grayson. (1)

This Benjamin Harrison, no relation to his contemporary who signed the Declaration of Independence, next appeared in the records when he married Mary Short of St. Paul's Parish of Stafford County on November 17, 1770. (2) Bride and groom were possibly distantly related, since Ben's Harrison grandmother is said to have been a Short. Ben's cousin, Frances Harrison, married Thomas Short, Mary's brother, a few years later.

Benjamin and Mary began their married life living on a tract belonging to his father, Colonel Thomas. When the Colonel died three years after the wedding that land was given to his grandson Thomas Gibson, and Benjamin was bequeathed all the rest of the home plantation including the house in which he had been born and raised. Clearly, Ben was his father's favorite, for he was given a much greater share of the estate than anyone else. As well as land, his inheritance included seventeen slaves, all the household furniture except a few pieces that two of his sisters were to have, all the farm animals except those at the "plantation at the mountains," and even all seven head of oxen. Benjamin was also the residual legatee to get anything that his father had not specifically mentioned in the will. At age thirty he had become a rich man.

Before his father's death, Harrison's role in the community was limited. In fact he did not appear in the court records until October 1775, when he and his brother-in-law, Jonathan Gibson, were appointed appraisers of a deceased neighbor's estate. Six months later he was named to "view a road," that is, to recommend the route for a new thoroughfare. His report was submitted the following October. (3)

In February 1778 he was appointed to the commission of peace for the county, but he never sat on the court. In July 1787 he was one of several gentlemen who refused to take the oaths prescribed by law for members of the commission. Presumably their objections were due to politics. Perhaps the dispute was related in some way with the Constitutional Convention going on at the time, but we have not determined whether Harrison was a Federalist or an Anti-Federalist. (4)

Ben could hardly have been a dyed-in-the-wool conservative, for in at least one respect he was ahead of the times, as a minute from July 1777 proves. Harrison was authorized "to inoculate his family with smallpox at his house in this county." (5) That he required permission from the court shows how new, risky, and controversial the procedure was. It used material taken from someone who was recovering from a mild case of the dread disease to infect persons who had not yet been exposed, hoping that they would then be protected. Both Harrison and the court had wavered for several months over the decision before it was finally taken, twenty years before Dr. Jenner discovered vaccination with the cowpox virus. As far as one can tell, Harrison was the first in the county to try the technique.

Such court minutes imply that Harrison was at home in Fauquier and not away in the Revolutionary army. Nevertheless, he was surely a captain in the county militia, even though he was not on the long list of Fauquier militia officers commissioned in 1777 and 1778. The proof comes from the pension applications of two veterans, both of whom swore they had served under Captain Benjamin Harrison, Major Samuel Blackwell, and Colonel Armistead Churchill. The latter two officers are known to have commanded one of the two Fauquier militia regiments. The county militia was on call only for duty within the state. After the war the records often refer to Harrison as "Captain." (6)

Captain Ben Harrison was affected by the outcome of a trial in 1782:

> ---- negro Peter a man slave of the price of eighty pounds the property of Benjamin Harrison Esquire with force and arms feloniously and burglariously broke open and entered the meat house of a certain Thomas Maddux ---- and then and

*there stole took and carried away five pieces of
bacon of the value of five shillings each the
property of him the said Thomas Maddux ---- and
on his arraignment pleaded "Guilty" and it being
demanded of him if he had anything to say why the
courts should not proceed to judgment and award
sentence of death against him he prayed the benefit of Clergy. Therefore it is considered by the
court that he be burnt in the left hand in the
presence of the court and that he receive 39 lashes
on his bare back well laid on at the public whipping post and that he be discharged from his im-
prisonment. (7)*

Benefit of Clergy had developed from the period in which
certain crimes had been tried in English ecclesiastical courts.
When the civil authorities had reduced the jurisdiction of the
Church, they granted the clergy review of capital offenses.
Well before Independence the "benefit" had become a legal
device for avoiding the death penalty prescribed for criminals,
especially if they were slaves, convicted of committing such
offenses "against the peace of the Commonwealth and the
Dignity thereof." The guilty but valuable Peter had been inherited by Ben from his father. The punishment meted out to
Peter was only a little more harsh than that given "Charles, a
negro slave" by the Prince William court some years earlier.
Notwithstanding that Charles had been found "not guilty" of
feloniously breaking and entering and stealing, the court ordered that he receive the "39 lashes on his bare back" before
he was "discharged and sent back to his master's service."

The whipping post and the branding iron were standard
means of punishment in eighteenth-century Virginia. Because
serious crimes, such as Peter's theft of the hams, when
committed by whites were outside the local jurisdiction and
tried in Williamsburg, the county records give no basis for
comparing the severity of the sentences imposed on white
versus black criminals.

In the judicial system after Yorktown, lawyers really came
into their own, as a multitude of cases postponed during the
troubled years were brought forward and new ones added.
Harrison was a party to a number of such suits, in some,
against close relatives. One had its beginnings early in 1784.
Jane Harrison, the mother and guardian of Benjamin's nephew
Burr, had recently remarried. The boy, who was fifteen or
sixteen, at first did not want the management of the estate left
him by his father to be turned over to his stepfather. With

166

court permission he took his Uncle Ben as guardian, but a little over a year later he went back to court asking leave to choose a replacement. When the request was granted, Benjamin appealed, but either he later withdrew his objections or they were overruled. This time the nephew did pick his stepfather to be his guardian. (8)

Only two months before this quarrel with Burr came to a head, Benjamin and his wife "for natural love and affection" ceded their rights in a parcel of land "formerly part of the Glebe of Hamilton" to another nephew, Thomas Gibson. (9) The tract had been left Gibson by Ben's father, Colonel Thomas. A possible reason for this apparently unnecessary "deed of gift" came to light in a case brought against "Harrison's Trustees" by "Maddux's Adms." in 1807. The administrators had found a receipt dated March 25, 1794, for one hogshead of tobacco received by Burr Harrison from Thomas Maddux. Ben Harrison signed as witness. Depositions given in the suit revealed the story of a dispute between Burr and his Uncle Ben about some land. Ben had offered to relinquish his claim to the land for a hogshead of tobacco. Burr, not having the tobacco, had borrowed it from Maddux and later repaid all but one guinea to Maddux. (10)

Finding the papers of this suit solved a mystery for us. We have the original of a 1795 deed by which Benjamin and Mary Harrison "for natural love and affection" gave Burr a tract of 470 acres with no further description than "where he now lives." (11) The deed was never recorded in Fauquier County, nor in any of the neighboring counties, and where and what it referred to had been forgotten. Now it became clear that the dispute between nephew and uncle was over two adjoining parcels inherited by Burr from his father, William Harrison. They had been owned by Burr's grandfather, Colonel Thomas, whose will had stipulated that William was to receive "one half the land wheron I now have a quarter purchased of Elias Edmonds to be equally divided between him and his brother Burr Harrison." The intent of the bequest was evident, even if the wording was ambiguous. Benjamin had been one of the executors of the will and had not objected when his brother Burr sold his half of the tract in question "supposed to contain 225 acres" to his other brother William.

By 1785 William was dead; Burr, the brother, had moved to South Carolina; and Thomas, the other brother, had gone to Kentucky. It looks as if Benjamin, as the residual legatee due anything not specifically devised to another by his father's will, decided to take advantage of its wording and lay claim to "his half" of the parcel. By the earlier parallel deed to nephew

Thomas Gibson, that teen-ager and his father may have obtained the release from Benjamin to avoid the trouble cousin Burr was experiencing, even though the boundaries of the former Glebe of Hamilton were described carefully in the will.

Whatever the reason for the deed, Jonathan Gibson, the father of Thomas, made Benjamin Harrison the principal executor of his will dated 1788 and proved in 1791. (12) That may have caused another family squabble. In August 1793 the court took the unusual action of ordering Harrison to settle the estate. This prompted several suits by the estate including one against Thomas Gibson. In February 1796, Benjamin submitted an initial accounting and reported an agreement with the co-executor that there would be no commission charged for his work. Even so, next month the court on the motion of Thomas and his brothers John and Jonathan ordered Harrison to surrender the administration to John Gibson. (13)

Bickering within the family in this period was not limited to the disagreements Ben had with nephews. In 1795 he was sued by his sister Anne and her husband James Gillison over a trust set up seventeen years earlier for the education of their children, because Gillison had been having financial problems. The couple had made Harrison and Jonathan Gibson the trustees. (14)

All these controversies may have affected the health of Benjamin, for he died in December 1797. (The suit by the Gillisons had not been settled yet.) His will left ten pounds to his daughter, Margaret Wagener, and an equal amount to David Arrington, probably an employee. A slave named Samuel received his freedom. All the rest of the estate went to his grandson, Benjamin Harrison Wagener. Colonel Peter Wagener and Benjamin Botts, an attorney, were named executors. A codicil to the will asked that the estate be detained by them until the boy reached the age of twenty-one. (15)

Margaret, the only child of Ben and Mary, had married Beverley Robinson Wagener, son of Colonel Peter, in 1792. Their young son must have died as a child, for in the 1800s several sales of tracts that had belonged to Harrison were made by the Wageners and the widow Mary Harrison with no mention of him. (16)

In one such, accomplished in 1817, John Gibson Sr. (the nephew who had taken over from Benjamin Harrison as executor of Jonathan Gibson) acting as trustee for "Beverley R. Wagener, deceased; Russel B. Harrison and Mary Eliza, [daughter of the Wageners]; Mary Harrison, and Margaret S. Wagener" sold John Gibson Jr. 280 acres, "late the property of Benj. Harrison, commonly called by the name of Mansion House or Brenttown Tract," partly in Prince William and partly in Fauquier. (17) The house was the one in which Benjamin had been born, and the land was part of the 1707 grant to his grandfather.

Harrison's emancipation of his slave Samuel evidenced again a progressive bent. Our impression is that such action was rare in the eighteenth century. The earliest example that we have seen came in the will of William Carr of Dumfries written in 1790. He freed one man and ordered that under no circumstances were any of his other slaves to be separated by a sale. If any attempt was made to sell one, all were to be liberated immediately.

A contemporary picture of Ben Harrison was given by the German traveler, Johann David Schoepf, previously quoted. On the day Schoepf and his companions left the house of the man who hoped to sell out and take his family to Kentucky, they took a wrong turn and got off the "Carolina Road" and headed southeast instead of southwest. After wandering through an unpopulated wooded area on a wintry December day in 1783, they eventually met a man on the road near the ford of Cedar Run who:

> indicated to us the plantation of a Captain B. H., whose house, as he said, stands open to every traveler, and the man himself is obliged to strangers if they will call upon him. We finally reached this belauded house, which stood on a very pleasant hill, with much open land about it. The customary negro cabins and other farmbuildings formed together a little village in which the finer and larger house of the Captain stood out well by contrast. We described our adventures to the Captain and the necessity we were under of asking for refreshments and a night's lodging, which he was willing for, but at the same time remarking that his house was no tavern. A reminder which we scarcely expected in a hospitable house [as later he boasted his was known throughout the country], and one not sustained by the hay, maize-bread, water, and fish [of which they take 2000 at a catch] we and our horses were entertained with.
>
> Of the 4000 acres which the Captain owns, only a very small part has been made tillable for he himself, through his negroes, finds it impossible to work the whole or put it to use. He has a few leaseholders, and wished there were more of them,

*because with them one may grow rich without
work. He would prefer Germans for tenants, but so
long as land is to be bought in the interior of
America these will be wise enough not to spend
their sweat on any land that is not their own, even
if they must be content with very little. (18)*

Schoepf also noted that the leaseholders "must gradually
bring into an arable condition the land they take over, giving for
one hundred acres about 1000 pd. tobacco. One acre of good
new land yields a hogshead of tobacco or 1000 pounds, the
medium worth of which is 10 guineas. The leases run for short
terms only and are then renewed." (Short-term leases were
certainly not the rule before the Revolution. Up to 1800 we
have seen none for a short term recorded in deed books, although the parties may have agreed sometimes to save the
clerk's fees and other costs of documentation.)

The German visitor was also shown a narrow vein of copper
ore that had been discovered by the grown-up banks of a small
stream. The Captain was going to have his Negroes dig it out
when they were not otherwise busy.

A little more than half of his total acreage had been inherited by Benjamin from Colonel Thomas. Most of the rest had
been acquired in a purchase of 1855 acres on the south side of
the Chopawamsic from John Ralls in 1778. As the German
visitor predicted, Harrison was not very successful in getting
renters for his properties. Only five leases for about one
hundred acres each were recorded by him in the deed books of
Prince William and Fauquier. (19)

One assumes Captain Ben Harrison was joking when he
confided to his guest his desire to get rich without work.

With reference to the disputes with his nephews, it is clear
that Ben got along well with his relatives when he was younger.
In 1771 he and his wife witnessed the bond for the marriage of
his cousin, Elizabeth Bullitt. His half-sister, Betty Quarles,
made a bequest to him in her 1774 will. His cousin, Thomas
Bullitt, willed him two prize colts in 1778. That year he and
Jonathan Gibson were chosen by his sister Anne Gillison and
her husband to set up a trust for the "support and education" of
their children. In 1783 he signed the bond along with John
Gibson for the marriage of John's brother, Jonathan to Ann
Eustace. (John was the nephew who took over the administration of his father's estate from Ben twelve years later.)

We should add that our inferences drawn from the troubles
between Benjamin and his nephews may be inaccurate. In 1825
a grandson of nephew Burr was born. He was named Benjamin

Harrison; time must have healed whatever wounds there may have been.

Notes:

1. *Records of Dettingen Parish.* Immediately preceding the first page of the section on indentures is the following record: Benja. the son of Thomas and Ann Harrison was borne a Saturday at six a clock in the morning the 17th day of August, 1744. Ann daughter of Thomas and Ann Harrison was borne a Sunday the 29th day of October 1749."
2. King, *The Register of St. Paul's Parish,* p.63. Benjamin always signed his name as Ben Harrison.
3. F M (Apr. 1773–Jan. 1780), p.243, 253, 270.
4. Idem. p.292, 302. (June 1786–Apr. 1788), p.240.
5. Idem. (1773–1780), p.280.
6. US Archives S 32439. John Peake of Fauquier served first in Lee's Light Dragoons and later in Capt. Benjamin Harrison's militia company. Dorman, *Virginia Revolutionary Pension Applications,* 31–74, quotes an applicant as having served in 1777 under Harrison, Blackwell, and Churchill. Gwathmey lists only a Captain Benjamin Harrison of the 13th Virginia Regiment of the Continental Line, enlisted 1776, retired Feb. 1781 with the rank of major. That officer was from Augusta County, we think; he was not Benjamin Harrison of Fauquier.
7. F M (Feb. 1781–May 1784), p.56. The sitting justices of the county court reconstituted themselves for the trial as a special court of oyer and terminer authorized to try slaves for capital offenses, such as that of Peter.
8. Idem., p.247 and (Jun. 1784–May 1786) p.193, 245, 253.
9. F D 9–38, Sept. 1785.
10. The original papers of this chancery suit are in the Fauquier courthouse. Depositions are made by Lucy Pickett Harrison, wife of Burr, and Philip Mallory, son of Burr's stepfather.
11. F M (Oct. 1795–Mar. 1797), p.43. The deed was presented in court and certified, but it was never recorded. We have the original.
12. F W 2–204, pr. September 1791. Gibson's will named children Thomas, John, Anne Grayson Blackwell and "three youngest," Jonathan Catlett, Susanna Grayson, and Mary.
13. F M (1795–1796), pp.3, 65, 120, 166, 185, 233, 520.
14. Idem. pp.52, 53.
15. F W 3–90, 1798. Will dated 1/2/1798 was presented to the January court. By F D 12–329 and 12–385, both dated

February 1796, Benjamin and Mary had given much of the land inherited from his father to their grandson and 246 a. to Beverley and Margaret Wagener.

16. PW D 1-20, 1800. To the Reverend Thomas Harrison. PW D 1-306, 1800. 101 acres to Thomas Homes.

17. F D 22-62. Mary Eliza was the granddaughter of Benjamin; Since she was not mentioned in his will, she may have been born after Benjamin's death.

18. Schoepf, *Travels in the Confederation, 1783-1784*, op.cit.

19. Other deeds to which Harrison was a party include: PW D T-414, 1778. Purchase of 1855 a. on S. branch of Chopawamsic from John Ralls. F D 6-479, 1774. Purchase of 235 a. from Peter and Sinah Wagener of Fx. F D 7-485, 1783. Sale of above 235 a. to Cuthbert Bullitt. PW D U-307, 1782. To John Edington. PW D U-426, 1783. Lease of 200 a. to Thomas Dowdall. F D 8-169, 1784. Lease of 180 a. to Benjamin George. F D 9-18, 1785. Purchase of 192 a. from Joseph and Mary Combs of St. PW D W-278, 1785. Purchase of 95 a. from John Pope. PW D X-73, 1787. Lease of the 95 a. to Joseph Brady. F M 1787, p.239. Purchase from John Coppidge. F M 1787, p.347. Lease to Thomas Bland. F M 1789, p.161. Lease to Samuel Burroughs. F M 1790, p.275. Lease to George Grant.

Chapter XV

The Calvert-Harris-Harrisons
Descendants of Burr Harrison Jr.

A single deed registered in Prince William in 1739 affords the only manifestation that the second Burr Harrison, son of the immigrant, had descendants.   By it Thomas Calvert alias Harrison and his wife, Sarah, transferred to John Carr "all my right and title of that track [sic] or parcel" containing two hundred acres "on the north side of Quanticott Creek and Run, it being the land that Burr Harrison, deceased, left between George Calvert alias Harrison, Burr Calvert alias Harrison and Thomas Calvert alias Harrison."   The sellers "covenant" that Thomas "now is the true, lawful and rightful owner of the said land and is rightfully seized in his own right of a good, shure, perfect, absolute and indefeasible [cannot be annulled] estate of inheritance in fee simple."   The buyer was to pay 5500 pounds tobacco in 1739 and 5000 the following year.   The clerk who copied the document showed the signatures as Thomas T (his mark) Calvert alias Harris (not Harrison) and Sarah X (her mark) Calvert alias Harris. (1)

This deed has caused genealogical researchers no end of problems, and indeed no certifiable resolution of most of them has been achieved. However, since Burr Harrison Jr. had received a patent for two hundred acres on Quantico Creek in 1700, land that had escheated on the death of his wife's first husband, it was unquestionably he who made the bequest to the three brothers.

Less certain is the relationship of the three Calvert alias Harrisons to Burr Jr.   "Alias" was used occasionally by orphans who had been raised by a relative of their mother, in essence an adoptive father. Therefore, some descendants have suggested that the brothers were children of a daughter or sister of Burr Harrison Jr., one who had married a Calvert.   They proposed that Burr had raised the boys from an early age after the death of their father. Admittedly this possibility has not been disproved, but no one yet has found a Harrison woman or a Calvert man in the right time and place to have been a parent of George, Burr, and Thomas.

More commonly, the term "alias" was applied to illegitimate children who had been recognized by the father. The mother's surname was used for legal purposes for the child, even if he preferred to be called by the name of the father; hence the alias. Public opinion at the beginning of the eighteenth century took a somewhat tolerant attitude to children born out of wedlock, provided their fathers supported their up-bringing. After all, kings, nobles and even churchmen had such progeny. While the court minutes of the time were replete with cases of the mothers of "base-born" infants being punished for their "crimes," invariably they were servant girls, and the fathers were either unknown or of "the lower classes."

Thus we believe it likely that sometime after 1700 Burr Harrison Jr. had a liaison with a Calvert woman. Burr's unions with Lettis Smith and Mary Mansbridge had not yielded an heir in an era when that was at least as important as it is today. We don't know what happened to Mary Harrison after 1705. Even if she had died, marriage might have been out of the question for the couple. The Calverts were Catholic (at least in Maryland) and the Harrisons firm Puritans.

The earliest Virginian record we have found of the Calvert family pertained to George Calvert, witness to the deed of sale for the cattle that Burr Harrison Sr. bought from Richard Nixon in 1691. As one would expect, he was a neighbor of the Harrisons, residing just north of the Quantico. John Calvert, probably George's brother, was paid the bounty for killing a wolf in Stafford in 1703. No other Calvert men lived in the Quantico area in that time period. (2)

Therefore, a daughter or sister of of one of these Calverts was probably the mother of the Calvert-Harrison brothers.

A Jane Colvert living in Stafford in 1701 was a Frenchwoman unrelated to the Virginia family. A more feasible alternative would be the Sarah Colbert or Colvert who was on the quitrent rolls in Prince William holding 109 acres in 1723, 1740, and 1752. The earliest listing had the notation "not demanded." No clue was given as to where her acreage was located, how it was obtained, or what happened to it. (3)

Another difficulty that genealogists have had with the Calverts-alias-Harrisons stems from the failure of Burr Harrison Jr. to provide for the education of his three sons, an indication that he died before they reached school-age. They were unable to sign their names. As a result, neither the lawyers who drew up documents referring to them nor the clerks who copied those papers were sure about their surname. In addition to Calvert alias Harrison, they or their children were called Calvert, Colvert or Colbert, Harris, Harrison, and Calvert Harris. Many of their descendants seem to have chosen Harris as the name, but others may have picked Harrison or Calvert.

A minor unsettled matter is how Thomas came to be in possession of the full 200 acres, when it had been left jointly to George, Burr, and him. Evidently George had died before the deed was written, but Burr seems to have survived Thomas by many years. Maybe the two had divided their inheritance before Thomas made his sale.

None of these questions can be answered satisfactorily. So leaving aside the speculation, we should look at the record, starting with Thomas, the youngest of the brothers. In 1740 a survey was made of 110 acres on branches of Powells Run for Thomas Harrison but the name of Thomas Colvert was written in over the "Harrison." Five years later Thomas and Sarah again sold land, 400 acres this time, still on the north side of the Quantico. It was further described as the plantation where John Carr (of the earlier deed?) and Sharlett Barker "now live" and as being near the uppermost marsh of the Creek. (4) A suit brought by Thomas against John Carr for trespass was dismissed in 1753. The dispute may have been over the boundaries of one or both of the tracts sold by the Calvert-Harrisons or over adjoining land retained by them.

In 1749 Thomas leased 130 acres on Bull Run from Frances Watts for the term of the "longest-liver" of himself, Sarah, and their son William. Thomas Smith, who had witnessed the deed to Mr. Graham, also witnessed this contract. Furthermore, Smith leased the other half of Watts's land. Could he have been Sarah's brother? Whether the Calvert-Harrison family moved inland from the Potomac to the leased tract or worked it in some other way is unknown. (5)

Thomas died in 1754. His widow, Sarah, submitted the will of "Thomas Colvert" to the Prince William court and gave a bond co-signed by John Colvert for her administration of the estate. (6) Sarah was last heard from in 1757, when as "Sarah Harrison Calvert" she was paid 300 pounds tobacco by the Dettingen vestry for burying Griffith Watkins.

In summary, this much is certain: Thomas Calvert alias Harrison first appeared in the records in 1739; his wife's name was Sarah; he lived near the Quantico; he was illiterate; he had at least one child, William, born before 1749; and he died in 1754.

Very likely the son named in the lease for the Bull Run tract was the man who in 1779 sold 110 acres on Powell's Run (two or three miles north of the Quantico). This plot had belonged to his wife's grandfather, William Davis, and had come down to her through her father, Joshua Davis. The sellers are called Harris in the body of the deed, but it was signed William Harrison and Elizabeth E (her mark) Harrison. (7) William later deserted Elizabeth and ran off to Danville, Kentucky. There he promoted himself to Major William Harrison and married twice more. He died in 1822.

Thomas's brother, Burr Calvert alias Harrison, named in the deed to John Carr, resided on Powell's Run; first a grant to Charles Cornwall, then one to John Gregg, and another to Thomas Reno showed "Bur Calvert" there. In 1750 a minute of the Dettingen vestry resolved that the new vestry house should be built "at the most convenient place by Burr Colbert's plantation." That would set the building near the Quantico church, a little to the south of Powells Run. Burr Calvert still owned land in the vicinity in 1757. (8)

A further sign of Burr of the multiple names was provided by a 1755 Fairfax deed. It covered the lease of 243 acres in Cameron Parish on branches of Cub Run made by Robert Carter to Burr Calvert Harrison for the lives of "Burr Calvert Harrison Jr.; Jane Harrison, his mother; and Micajah, her fifth son." The "Jr." was inserted in the record copy, either when the clerk reread his work or later. Although the lessee might conceivably be Burr Calvert alias Harrison Sr. and thus the husband of Jane, more likely it was granted directly to their young unmarried son. We have never seen a lease for "three lives" in which the lessee himself was not the first of the three "lives" named. Furthermore, the lease identifies Calvert alias Harrison as being of Fairfax, not Prince William where Powell's Creek is located. The minute of the Fairfax court by which Carter acknowledged the lease called the lessee Burr Harrison. (9) Four years earlier a Burr Harris had been paid for attending Fairfax court for thirteen days as a witness, without a travel allowance.

Carter's lessee was required to build "a good dwelling house, 20 ft. x 16 ft. and a house 32 ft. x 20 ft. as good as the common tobacco house" and to plant fifty apple trees and fifty peach trees and "enclose the same with a sufficient and lawful fence."

Cameron Parish became Loudoun County in 1757. Sampson Turley sold a slave to Burr Calvert alias Harrison there in 1764 and another in 1765. The Loudoun clerk's fee book lists a Burr Harris in 1764. (10)

176

Lastly, a Bur Harris of Ninety-Six District of South Carolina wrote a relatively brief will in 1783. After the standard preamble that he was sick in body but of perfect mind and memory, in the first of five short items he "lent all my estate both real and personal to my loving wife Jean Harris as long as she lives." By the second item he gave "after the death of my wife all the land I now live on to be equally divided between my four sons Obed, Thos., George, and Cage Harris." The other items gave instructions for the division of his slaves among his sons. The will was signed Bur B Harris. The mark B was the one used thirty-five years earlier by Burr B Calvert when witnessing a deed for land sold by a neighbor on Powell's Run in Virginia. The will was submitted to the court in March 1787.

Jean Harris of Newberry County (part of Ninety-Six District) wrote her will in June 1786. She gave her "son Bur Harris one cow and calf." All the rest of her estate was to be divided equally "between my three daughters namley Lettes Cockrell, Jean Dawkins, and Cloey Liles." Sanford Cockrell, Wm. Dawkins, and James Liles were designated her "Extrs." (Dawkins had married Mary Harris first and then her younger sister, Jean.) The will was witnessed by George Harris, Micajah Harris, and Robt. Rutherford. The last had also witnessed Burr Harris's will and was one of the appraisers of his estate. Unfortunately the date that the will of Jean Harris was proved is illegible. (11)

We conclude that Burr Harris of the 1783 will in South Carolina was the brother named in the 1739 deed of Thomas Harrison alias Calvert and was the man known variously as Bur Calvert and Burr Harris who had lived near Powell's Creek until after 1761.

We believe he was the father of the Burr Calvert alias Harrison who obtained the lease for lives in Fairfax in 1755. His oldest son, the lessee, must have been in South Carolina in 1786 for his mother to leave him a cow. He would be the Burr Harrison of Ninety-Six District recorded in the 1790 census. In his household were two males over sixteen, one under sixteen, and two females, and he owned nine slaves. He had married Mary Haynie, the daughter of Maximilian Haynie, said to have arrived in South Carolina in 1773. (12)

Burr and Micajah were specifically mentioned in the 1755 lease; the second, third, and fourth sons of Jean would be Obed, Thomas, and George. Cage may have been born after 1756 or he may have been a sickly child, less likely to survive and thereby add to the length of the lease.

Gwathmey reported that a Burr Harris was a corporal in the

Third Virginia Regiment during the Revolution but gave no source and no further details. To which generation this patriot belonged has not been determined. Micajah Harris, who was without much doubt the "fifth son" of the 1755 deed, was also said to be a Revolutionary War soldier.

The family probably had left Virginia soon after Yorktown. A Public Service Claim for "horse hire furnished the Continentals" during the war was filed by Gavin Adams, assigneee of Burr Harris of Prince William. It looks as if Harris transferred his receipt to Adams before moving. However, an Obed Harris was allowed a claim for beef, and he was still in Prince William in November 1784 when he was appraiser of an estate. Maybe he went south somewhat later than his father and other members of the family, or perhaps the claim belonged to another person, such as a son or nephew.

There are still Harrises in Newberry County, South Carolina, over two hundred years after their ancestors Burr and Jean moved there.

Obed Harris had leased 150 acres from Thomas Blackburn in 1768 for the lives of himself and his sons Burr and Obed. He signed without having to make his mark. In the contract he was allowed to take from a neighboring tract any timber needed to erect or repair buildings on the premises. He too was required to plant an orchard "of at least 100 winter apples at thirty feet distance and 200 peach trees at sixteen feet distance." Cider, applejack, and peach brandy must have been in great demand. (13)

The only other times an Obed Harris was named in the sparse Prince William records between 1750 and 1785 came in 1760 in an order concerning a suit "advs. Rex" (the authorities of the colony). However, in 1758 he was a customer of both the Dumfries (Quantico) and the Colchester (Occoquan) stores of John Glassford and Company. On June 29, 1768, he, Burr, and Thomas Harris made cash purchases at the Colchester store. Their separate charge accounts were indexed as on page twenty-seven of the ledger. (The page is missing from the book.) (14)

In 1757 Bertrand and Jesse Ewell leased 100 acres on "the main road between Powells Run and the plantation where Francis Jones lives" to Thomas Harris for the lives of him, his wife Maryanne, and his son John. The annual rent was fixed for a lifetime of fifty years or more at four pounds plus quitrents and taxes. Clearly, the lessors did not consider inflation to be a problem. (15)

A major unresolved question is whether Thomas and Burditt Harrison, who in partnership with Andrew Smarr received a

178

grant of 501 acres on the south branch of Pohick Creek in 1729, were later known as Thomas and Burr Calvert alias Harrison.

When Thomas Harrison sold his share of the Smarr-Harrison-Harrison grant in 1734, he was identified as a resident of Truro Parish, he made his mark in signing, and no release of dower rights was appended to the deed. The indication is that he was unmarried.

Burditt sold his third of the Pohick grant with his wife Jane's formal agreement in 1731. His signature was copied Burditt B (his mark) Harrison. Also in 1731 Burditt Harrison patented 185 acres on the south branch of Powells Run. However, the next year a man identified as Burr Harrison, so named several times in the body of the deed, and his wife, Jean, sold 100 acres on the same branch of Powells to Peter Cornwall. In the register copy Jean was shown as signing with her mark, but the grantor's signature on the deed and the receipt for payment was copied as Burr Harrison without any mark. Nevertheless, the seller had to be the man previously called Burditt Harrison for the land was identified as part of the 185-acre grant of 1730/1, when Cornwall resold it in 1773. (16)

The 1736 quitrent roll listed "Burr Harrison Jr." with 185 acres, referring undoubtedly to "Burditt" Harrison's patent. Apparently the sale of 100 acres of it had not been picked up by the collector's office. The roll listed no one else who might have been Burr Calvert alias Harrison by any of his names and no one at all who could have been the Thomas Harrison of the 1729 Pohick grant or Thomas Calvert alias Harrison.

In the next surviving roll, that of 1751, the name Burr Harrison Jr. is gone, but Burr Colbert Harrison is shown with 93 acres. Again there is no one who could be either of the Thomas Harrisons.

The 1741 poll for burgesses had a Burr Harris who voted for Valentine Peyton and Thomas Harrison (Jr.), but as with the quitrents no "suitable" Thomas.

Although the name Burditt Harrison disappeared forever from the Prince William records in 1731, it reappeared in King George's 1787 titheables list and in an 1833 pension application of a Revolutionary War veteran residing in Orange County. Burdet Harrison, born in 1758, affirmed that he had enlisted in 1779, apparently on an impulse while away from the King George home of his father, for whom he was named. He had served in the regiment stationed at the Albemarle Barracks guarding prisoners (mostly Hessians captured at Saratoga). In the spring of 1781 after the POW's had been marched from Charlottesville to Winchester (on fears of their release by the approaching Tarleton), Burdet was honorably discharged.

179

However, he was drafted into the county militia and was "on march to Yorktown when the surrender news came." His brother John Harrison confirmed his testimony. (17)

The bewildering confusion of similar first names and variable surnames continues after the Revolution. The 1793 will of William Fairfax named six daughters including Eadah Calvert. Three years later Burr and Adah Calvert relinquished to William Fairfax Jr. any claim they had on the estate of her deceased father. Burr signed Burwill Calvert. One of the British Mercantile Claims was against Burwell Harrison. (18)

The intact part of the 1790 Virginia census has a Burr Harrison in Shenandoah County, the head of a household of five with no slaves. We think we have accounted for all the Burr Harrisons who were (or could be at that date) descendants of Captain Thomas Harrison.

Another loose end that needs to be fastened down concerns a William Burr Harrison known to us from a single reference. In 1784 George Kitchen, a relatively young man, made his will and named his "friend William Burr Harrison" executor. Definitely not of the line descended from Thomas Harrison (1665-1746), Kitchen's friend was most likely one of the Calvert-Harris-Harrisons, possibly the son of Thomas Calvert alias Harrison named in the lease for lives on Bull Run. (19) The land leased by Burr Calvert Harrison Jr. was also located in this area where Fairfax, Prince William, and Loudoun meet. In the Civil War era an Obed Harris and a Burditt Harrison resided thereabouts.

Our effort to determine the ancestry of these later Harrises and Harrisons leads us back to the basic question of whether the Harrisons of the 1729/30 Pohick grant were or were not Thomas and Burr Calvert alias Harrison. If we had only to account for Burditt and Burr, we could decide affirmatively. But to make Thomas who sold his land on the Pohick in 1735 mesh with the Thomas who sold the Quantico tract in 1739, he would have to have married and moved from Truro Parish to Hamilton in the interim--not impossible, but unlikely.

We have not found the key to unlocking the conumdrum. So like others who have searched, we are left with the confusion of Harrisons, Harrises, Calverts-alias-Harrison, and Calverts. Some are clearly descendants of the first Burr Harrison. If any are not, then they could conceivably trace back to an unidentified brother or other relation of the immigrant.

We can conclude, however, that all the known and all the putative eighteenth-century members of these families were considerably less well-off economically than their cousins of the lineage of Captain Thomas. Clearly the illiteracy of the progenitors in the middle years of the eighteenth century was primarily responsible for their condition, shared with the Bartons and Wallises, but not with the Whitledges descended from the literate son-in-law of the immigrant Burr. One wonders how many generations it took to equalize the average economic and social status of each of the various colonial branches of the family tree.

Notes:

1. PW D D-47, 1738/9. Thomas Calvert alias Harrison and wife Sarah to John Carr, 200 a. on N. side of Quanticott Creek. The land remained in the Carr family for at least fifty years. In 1790 William Carr bequeathed to his young son William "part of my land adjoining the town of Dumfries from the Church Branch below the Quarry Hill to the Beaverdam Branch including all the land my father purchased of Thomas Calvert Harris except the meadow below the house where I now live." PW O p.173, 1753. Thomas Calvert alias Harrison vs. John Carr for trespass. Suit dismissed.
2. See Chapter XIX.
3. Undated PW quitrent roll, original in Huntington Library, ca. 1736. Sarah Colvert, 109 a.; Capt. Burr Harrison, 712 a.; Burr Harrison Jun'r., 190 a. PW Rent Rolls, 1751, 1752, Sarah Colvert, 109a.; Burr Colvert, 93a.
4. Joyner NN Surveys, 3-101. Warrant for survey of 110 a. on Powells Run. PW D I-15, 1745. Thos. Calvert alias Harrison and Sarah his wife to John Graham 400 a. on N side Quantico Cr. where John Carr and Sharlett Barker now live. Witnesses include Thomas Smith.
5. PW D L-195, 1749. Frances Watts to Thomas Calvert alias Harrison, lease for lives of Thomas C. al. H, wife Sarah, and son William. 130 a., part of 266 a. on S side of Bull Run. Witnesses: Thos. Smith and John Combs. PW L-197, same date. Other half, 133 a., leased to Thomas Smith. Witnesses: John Combs and Obed Calvert.
6. PW Bond Book, p.7, 1754. Thomas Colvert dcd., Sarah admx. and John Colvert, security. PW O p.117, 1754. Thos. Calvert alias Harrison will proved by Sarah Calvert.
7. PW D U-22, 1779. William Harris and Elizabeth, his wife, sell Richard Graham 110 a. on Powells Run. Probably this was the tract surveyed for Thomas Calvert Harrison in 1740. Culpeper Land Causes 2-79. Wm. Harris (Harrison) m. (1) Elizabeth Davis, deserted her and went to Danville KY, m. (2) Margaret Miller, and (3) Isabella McDougle.

8. NN E-405, 1741. Charles Cornwall, 326 a. on Powells Run adj. Burr Calvert or Harrison. NN E-481, 1742. John Gregg, 380 a. on Powells Run adj. Burr Calvert. NN F-38, 1742. Thomas Reno, 531 a. on Lick Br. of Occoquan, adj. Bur Calvert. PW W C-376, 1742. Frances Wright will. Jane Colvert, her mark, witness with Moses Linton. PW D L-55, 1748. Joseph Chapman, planter, to John Graham, 300 a. in Lord's patent. Witnesses include Burr B (mark) Calvert. NN I-32, 1757. William Linn, 48 a. adj. Burr Calvert.

9. Fx D D-334, 1755. Robert Carter of Westmoreland to Burr Colvert alias Harrison lease for lives. 243 a. in Cameron Parish on branches of Cub Run, part of 6030 acre Bull Run tract.

10. L D D-430, 1764. Sampson Turley sells slave to Burr Colvert alias Harrison. V 17-274. 1771 Loudoun titheables lists Burr Harris with three slaves.

11. King Papers. Letter to Mr. King from descendant of Burr Harris enclosed typed copies of wills citing Abbeville SC Courthouse Box 107, Pack 2890, will of Bur Harris and Pack 2888, Jean Harris. The latter copy read "Hamley" Lettes Cockrell which we believe was really "namely." According to the letter Wm. Dawkins m. (1) Mary Harris and (2) her younger sister Jean. Wm. died in Jefferson Co., GA in 1801. In 1777 Wm. Dawkins and wife Jane had sold Maximilian Haynie land.

12. Judge Belton Oneall, *Annals of Newberry, SC*, p.224. Maximillian Haynie from PW ca. 1772-3, died 1812, aged 93, had married (1) -----Faulkner & had two daughters; one of whom married a Mr. Courtney in Va. and the other Burr Harrison in Va. PW W G 62, 1779. Division of Thomas Faulkner's estate: "to each of 14 grandchildren -- 5/14/3; to heirs of Mary Harris alias Calvert and Sally Cortney -- 108/1/5 and four negroes; other half between the 12 children of Mary Elliot." Evidently Mary (Haynie) Harris, one of the fourteen grandchildren of Thomas Faulkner, was a deceased wife of a Burr Harrison, also known as Burr Harris alias Calvert. He would have been the son of Burr and Jean Harris who died in Newberry County about 1787.

13. PW Q-594, 1768. Thomas Blackburn lease to Obed Harris 150 a. part of larger tract granted to Anthony Seale Jr. Harris may take from the lot demised to Henry Hampton any timber needed to erect or repair houses on the premises. PW Q-598, same date. Lease to Henry Hampton of remaining 1112 a. for lives of Henry, Elenor, and Henry Jr. Names other tenants on original tract: Henry Hope, James

Kitchenride?, Obed Harris, Christopher Hopwood, and William Jones.

14. Library of Congress, Manuscript Collections, John Glassford and Company.
15. PW D R-354, 1758. Bertrand and Jesse Ewell to Thomas Harris, 100 a. on W side main road.
16. NN C-33, 1729/30. 501 a. to Andrew Smarr, Burditt Harrison, and Thomas Harrison, on S branch of Pohick and Sandy Run. NN C-116, 1730/1. Burditt Harrison 185 a. S. branch of Powells Run. PW D A-79, 1731. Burdet Harrison of Hamilton Parish to Robert Stephens 161 a. for 16,000 pounds tobacco. Part of land that he, Andrew Smarr, and Thos. Harrison took up by warrant bearing date 1729. Signed Burditt (his mark) Harrison. Wife Jane relinquished her right of dower. PW D A-350, 1732. Burr Harrison and Jane his wife to Peter Cornwall, 100 a. beginning on branch of S. run of Powells Creek. PW D B-471, 1735. Thomas T Harrison, planter, of Truro Parish to Joseph Reid, 153 a., one third of 1729 grant to Andrew Smarr, Burditt Harrison and self.
17. Revolutionary War Pension Claim, US Archives, Burdet Harrison.
18. PW W H-82, 1793. Wm. Fairfax will, pr. 12/2/1793, names wife Elizabeth and six daughters including Eada Calvert and three sons including William (Jr.). PW DB Z-70, 10/14/1796. Burr Calvert and wife Adah to William Fairfax, all of PW. Signatures: Burwill Calvert and Adah Calvert. V 20-52 British Mercantile Claims. James Ritchie & Co., Fredericksburg store had claim against Cuthbert and Burwell Harrison.
19. PW W G-312, 1784, pr. 1785.

Chapter XVI

The Whitledge Family

Sybil (Harrison) Whitledge, the wife of Thomas Whitledge, was the only verified daughter of the first Burr Harrison. Her sons and grandsons lived until after the Revolution in the same neighborhood as many of the descendants of her brother, Thomas Harrison. The region was located in what is now Prince William near its boundary with Fauquier, on Cedar Run and its tributary called Lucky Run.

Thomas Whitledge (ca. 1665–1726)
(Thomas 1)

Thomas Whitledge m. Sybil Harrison, dau. of Burr Harrison Sr. Children: Thomas, William, John, Elizabeth m. Lewis Reno, and Sybil m. (1) Abram Farrow, (2) Benjamin Bridges.

The first appearance in Stafford County of Sybil's husband (or husband-to-be), Thomas Whitledge, came in 1691 when he was paid for his time as a witness for the plaintiff Richard Gibson in the suit over the Holmes/Nixon/Harrison cows.

We don't know when Whitledge had arrived in the Chopawamsic area, but there is reason to believe that he was a son of the Robert Whitledge who was one of the headrights claimed by Samuel Mathews for his 1657 patent of 5211 acres on the north side of the Chopawamsic. (1) Burr Harrison's plantation was situated on part of that grant. It's possible that Whitledge or his father owned or rented part of the Mathews tract, but, if so, all record of a deed or rental contract disappeared. More likely, the young man was an overseer or tenant of a landowner such as one of the Brents or of Harrison himself. (Even in that era it wouldn't be the first time that someone married the boss's daughter.)

184

Thomas Whitledge and Thomas Barton were the two corporals in Captain Thomas Harrison's company of "foot" in the 1702 Stafford militia. Whitledge was again tied to his brother-in-law, Captain Harrison when the two obtained their grant of 938 acres on Cedar Run. On his own the next year he patented 272 acres nearby. (2)

For the 1723 census of tobacco plantings Whitledge reported 34,537 plants grown with the help of Thomas Jr., William, and John, all over sixteen. Judging from the fact that none of the sons had separate households, one can surmise that the elder Whitledge married Sybil Harrison after he had testified in the Gibson vs. Harrison case.

Whitledge died intestate in 1726; his inventory, but no will, was recorded in the lost Stafford Liber K. (3) Sybil died sometime before 1733, whether before or after her husband we can't say.

Thomas Whitledge Jr. (ca. 1695 - ?)
(Thomas 2, Thomas 1)

About all that is known about Thomas Whitledge Jr. is that in 1731 he purchased 130 acres on Lucky Run near his father's portion of the Harrison/Whitledge grant, and a couple of years later sold the 200 acres on the south side of the Chopawamsic that his Harrison grandfather had willed to his mother. (4)

No indication that he ever married has survived. If he did, no sign of any children has remained. No inventory or will of his could be found in the Prince William archives, where will books D, E, and F from 1744 to 1778 have been lost.

William Whitledge (ca. 1702-1782)
(William 2, Thomas 1)

William Whitledge m. ---- Allen. Children: William, Sibby m. William Grant, Frances m. ---- Overall, Mary m. William Coppedge.

In 1731 William Whitledge bought 50 acres on Cedar Run having a corner to Capt. Thomas Harrison and Thomas Whitledge. It adjoined his own land, obtained no doubt as a gift from either his father or his older brother. (5)

In 1750 William and his brother John entered a formal agreement to build a mill race on Lucky Run. The brother's properties lay on opposite sides of the brook. Somewhat surprisingly, William made his mark, an inverted W, while John signed his name as did a Thomas Whitledge, who witnessed the contract. We can't tell whether the last was John's son or the brother of the two principals. Perhaps the partners dug the race, but evidently they never got around to constructing the mill.

Some years after John's death, William petitioned for an acre of land (now his nephew's) on which to put the mill. Following procedure, a jury of neighbors appointed by the court visited the site and adjudicated the location. This time "Whitledge's mill" was built. (6)

The will of William Whitledge, dated May 1782 and proved that August, made bequests to his son William; daughter Sibby Grant; daughter Frances Overall and her children: William, Parthenay, Fanny, Caty, Harrison, Thompson, Nathaniel Saley, John Thomas, and Robert; his other grandchildren: Overall Whitledge, John Grant, and Baldwin and Frances Coppedge (to be held for the last two by their father, William Coppedge); and finally to his sister-in-law, Caty Allen. (7)

John Whitledge (ca. 1706-1761)
(John 2, Thomas 1)

John Whitledge m. 1733 Elizabeth Overall. Children: John, Thomas, Robert, Sibel.

Except that he lived near his brothers, probably on a part of the Harrison/Whitledge grant inherited from his father, little is known of John, the youngest of the three Whitledge grandsons of Burr Harrison Sr. In 1768 his estate was divided among his widow Elizabeth and his children, who were not named. Elizabeth died in 1771. (8)

The son named for John 2 apparently inherited his land and lived on it throughout his life. This John 3 (ca. 1735-1788) was an administrator of his Uncle William's estate. We assume it was he who sold 305 a. on Cedar Run to the Rev. Thomas Harrison. (9)

Unlike John 3, his brother Thomas 3 removed to Kentucky, possibly about the same time as his neighbor and second cousin, Thomas Harrison (Thomas 4, Thomas 3). The 1800 census of Kentucky found three Whitledges living in the new state: Thomas in Bourbon, Robert in Henderson, and John in Nelson.

William Whitledge (ca. 1730 - ?)
(William 3, Wm. 2, Thos. 1)

William Whitledge m. Sybil Farrow. After being named executor of his father and inheriting part of his real estate, William 3 and his wife Sybil sold some acres of their land on

Cedar and Lucky Runs. The tract was next to property of his brother-in-law, William Grant. After that transaction we lost track of him. (10)

Sybil (Whitledge) Farrow Bridges
(Sybil 2, Thomas 1)

Sybil (Whitledge) Farrow m. (1) Abram Farrow, son of Abraham and Margaret F., m. (2) Benjamin Bridges. Her Farrow children: Isaac, Lidia, Abram, John, Elizabeth, Sibell, and Margaret.

Abram Farrow died in 1743. His will was witnessed by Thos. Whitledge, and his widow's bond as executrix was co-signed by Thomas Harrison Jr. (Thomas 3, Thomas 2). John Farrow, the son of Abram and Sybil, became a trusted employee of Leven Powell, both in Virginia and in Kentucky.

By the beginning of the nineteenth century, the last person named Whitledge had disappeared from Prince William County. Apparently the third and fourth generations had all died or moved to Kentucky. John Farrow may have had much to do with settling his Whitledge cousins in that state.

Notes:

1. Pat. Book 4-106, 1657. Samuel Mathews 5211 a.
2. NN 4-8, 1710. Harrison and Whitledge. NN 4-52, 1711. Thomas W. 272 a. adj. John Hogan, William Bland, and John Bennett.
3. St Index to Liber K, p 24, ca. 1726. Inventory of Thomas Whitledge.
4. PW D A-1, 1731. Thomas W. Jr. from John Homes 130 a. on S side Occoquan on Lucky Run. PW D A-61, 1731. Thomas W. Jr. witness to deed. (We know of no other instances in the 18th century when someone retained the "Jr." after the death of his elder. Still we think the references are to Thomas 2, Thomas 1.) PW D B-263, 1734. Thomas Whitledge to Burr Harrison 200 a. on S of Chopawamsic, that his grandfather, Burr Harrison, had willed to his mother, Sybil Whitledge.
5. PW D A-7, 1731. William Whitledge from Philemon Waters; (brother-in-law) Lewis Reno a witness.
6. PW D M-147, 1750. Agreement between William and John W. PW D R-88, 1769. William W. petitions land on Lucky Run belonging to John W. be laid off for building water mill.
7. PW W G-170, 1782. Will of William W. William Grant

was on the first Fauquier commission of peace in 1759.

8. PW D R-58, 1768. Certifies that estate of John Whitledge was divided among widow Elizabeth W. and children, but gives no details. PW Bond Book, 1771. John W. adm. of Elizabeth W., dec'd. John Glassford Company Ledger, Dumfries Store, 1772. Accounts of John W., Robert W., and estate of Elizabeth W. A printed copy of the St. Paul's Parish Register includes the following marriage dates: 9/15/1733. John Whitledge of Hamilton and Elizabeth Overall of this parish. 10/27/1733. Nathaniel Whitledge of Hamilton and Frances Overall. 3/29/1746. Lydia Whitledge of Hamilton and Thomas Green.

9. PW W G-212, 1775. Guardian's account by John W. for orphans of Anthony Kitchen. PW D U-509, 1784. Receipts to John W. and William W., executors, for delivery of one-fifth shares of William W. (Sr.) estate, to each of grandchildren John Grant and Baldwin and Frances Coppedge. PW D 3-268, 1806. Thos. and Sarah Harrison give their son Thomas 305 a. on Cedar Run, purchased of John W. in line of Grant and corner to Wm. Fitzhugh.

10. PW D W-347, 1786. William W. and wife Sybil sell land on Cedar Run and Lucky Run adj. William Grant to Wm. Fitzhugh.

Chapter XVII

Barton and Wallis Families

Although Sybil (Harrison) Whitledge was the only confirmed daughter of the first Burr Harrison, there must have been others. Two prime possibilities were, as noted previously, the wives of Thomas Barton and John Wallis. While even the given names of the two women have been forgotten, each had a son and at least one grandson with that uncommon first name "Burr."

Tracing the eighteenth-century descendants of these early off-shoots from the Harrison family tree has been hindered by the large gaps in the surviving records of Stafford and Prince William counties. Furthermore, these families were less prominent in county affairs, less well off, and generally less educated than their Harrison cousins. While our analysis is incomplete, especially with respect to the Bartons, the available firm data is presented in the current chapter along with our inferences about relationships within each of the two families.

Two men named Barton, probably brothers, owned land in Stafford before 1680. Possibly they were "poor relations" of Captain William Barton, member of the Maryland Council from Charles County, but socially as well as economically, they were not on a par with him.

Nathan Barton was one of two. Although his oldest son was born in Maryland in 1667/8, he had a plantation in Stafford before 1679. He died in Maryland about 1685. (1)

William Barton (1667/8 - ?)
(William 2, Nathan 1)

William Barton, the son of Nathan, also had interests in both Provinces. He and his wife, Elizabeth, had three sons, Thomas, William, and David born at Mattawomany, Charles

189

County, Maryland, between 1689 and 1695.

In 1689, after nearly two years of legal action, William obtained an order in Charles County requiring that Francis Hammersly, the executor of the will of Barton's father, Nathan, who died at Mattawomany "sometime in 1684 or 1685," pay William the rent of a plantation formerly belonging to his father and deliver to him on behalf of his sister Martha a Negro girl who had been bequeathed her.

Simultaneously with pursuing Hammersly in Maryland, William was going after him in Stafford proceedings. He complained that Hammersly was detaining from him his orphan brothers Nathan and Thomas, and he feared that Hammersly, a Roman Catholic, would bring them up as Papists. The court ordered that the two boys be placed in temporary custody of two Stafford citizens and made William guardian of his sister. (2)

William Barton evidently returned to Maryland. Nathan (Jr.) also disappeared from the Stafford scene; either he died or moved back to Charles County. Their brother Thomas may have been the Barton whose children were massacred by Indians in 1700, probably on the Neabsco plantation. Perhaps he too went back to Maryland after the tragedy.

Thomas Barton (ca. 1635-ca. 1698)
(Thomas 1)

The initial record regarding an earlier Thomas Barton, progenitor of most of the northern Virginia family, came in 1678, when he bought 400 acres, the upper part of a 2000-acre patent to William Borne. Barton had been one of the Brent/Broadhurst tenants who had challenged Burr Harrison's title to the Chopawamsic plantation bought from Gerrard Broadhurst. He must have moved to his newly purchased property after Harrison straightened out the situation by the deal with the heir of ex-Governor Mathews.

Barton was occasionally mentioned in the records from then on; for example, the first church services in the area that eventually became Prince William were held at his house. He was last differentiated from his son, Thomas Barton Jr., in 1697 and died between then and 1700. (3)

Thomas Barton (1660-ca.1730)
(Thomas 2, Thomas 1)

In spite of the initial controversy between Thomas Barton Sr. and Burr Harrison Sr., we know the two families became friendly, as witnessed by their joint parties with Richard

Gibson, William Borne, and the folks from Maryland. Thomas Barton Jr., the only proven son of Thomas 1, is the man who is supposed to have married a Harrison. The case derives mainly from his naming a son Burr, but circumstantial evidence also favors the hypothesis. Having grown up within a mile or two of the Harrisons, he was in the right place to have courted one of the Harrison girls. Furthermore, since he was about the same age as her brothers, Thomas and Burr Jr., he probably was a frequent visitor in the Harrison household.

Thomas Jr. was paid the bounty for a wolf in 1687. It was he who in 1691 testified in the Gibson vs. Harrison case. In 1697, still designated as Thomas Barton Jr., he obtained an escheat grant for one hundred acres that had been a part of the Thomas Dyas/Days patent sold by Dyas to Edward Fisher, whose only heir had died childless. On the northeast side of the Quantico, the lot was adjacent to William Mansbridge's sector that later passed to Burr Harrison Jr.

Barton paid quitrents on five hundred acres in 1723, one hundred for that Quantico parcel plus four hundred inherited from his father. The next year, helped by Valentine, Burr, and James Barton, the last a boy of thirteen, he grew 12,565 tobacco plants.

In 1728, a year or so before Barton died, he sold the four hundred acres to Abraham Farrow Sr. His wife Grace released her dower rights. We doubt that Grace was Barton's first wife. In 1731, now the Widow Barton, she deeded property to her children: Lydia, the wife of Benjamin Drummond, and William, who was to receive his share when he came of age. Assuming that James was her oldest child and that he did not share in her gift, because he had died before it was made, Grace married Barton around 1710, when he was close to fifty. (4)

We wonder why Thomas Barton named a son "Valentine" before calling one "Burr." His choice raises doubts about Barton's wife being a daughter of Burr Harrison, because the usual practice was to name the next-to-oldest son for his maternal grandfather. A possible rationale is that Valentine was the child of a wife who had died before Barton married a Harrison. Another possibility is that Valentine was an orphaned nephew raised as son by Thomas.

A hint that the latter guess may be accurate comes from three references in 1700 to a Charles Barton. He witnesses a will in January, testifies in Stafford Court in August, and witnesses Mary Harrison's release of dower rights in her husband's 600-acre part of the Horsington patent. Then he disappears forever from the Stafford records. His relevance to the question at hand is that the only proven son of Valentine

191

Barton was named Charles. (5)

Edward Barton (ca. 1655-1711/2)

A third Barton, Edward, lived in the part of Stafford that is now Prince William at the end of the seventeenth and beginning of the eighteenth centuries. Just where he fits on the family tree is unknown. He was younger than Nathan and Thomas Sr., but older than Thomas Jr., judging from the ages of his children. He apparently lived nearer Nathan's plantation on the Neabsco than those of the two Thomases on the Quantico. Like the two Thomases he was associated with the Harrisons in that he and Burr Harrison Jr. married the sisters, Ann and Letice Green. Undoubtedly related to the others, he may have been a son of Thomas Sr., but no known descendant of the latter was named Edward. Perhaps further searches in Maryland would establish his antecedents.

Edward and Ann (Green) Barton had four daughters, Constance, Margaret, Ann, and Letice, none of whom were married in 1700. The oldest, Constant, was probably born about 1680, for she was given a horse in 1690 by her uncle by marriage, Edward Smith. The daughter Ann married John Linton, Margaret probably married Moses Linton, but no trace of Constant and Letice was left after 1700. The Bartons had no son that lived to maturity.

Edward Barton died in 1712. His will dated January 1711/2, among the lost Stafford documents, was cited in a deed made long afterwards by his grandson Moses Linton. (6)

Thomas Barton (? - 1752)
(Thomas 3?)

Perhaps we have erred in our assumption that the Thomas Barton Jr. on the 1724 list of tobacco tenders was the son and grandson of men of that name. When this Thomas died in 1752, his administrator was a David Barton. Because of his death, a suit for trespass by William Furr against him, William Barton, and Alexander Farrow was dismissed. We wonder whether he might have been the Thomas, son of William, born in Maryland in 1679. That Barton had brothers named William and David.

At any rate this Thomas Barton Jr. bought 175 acres on Cedar Run in 1725. This was one of the first moves inland of what became a total exodus of the Bartons from their original seat near the Potomac. The fact that he chose to settle near the tract patented in 1707 by Thomas Harrison and Thomas

192

Whitledge may have some significance. They would have been his uncles, if his mother was a Harrison. Later Barton and Thomas Whitledge Jr. had a survey made of 265 acres on Kettle Run, but for some reason they never "took up" the parcel.

However, Barton did obtain a grant for 491 acres on Hunger (now called Hungry) Run on the west side of the Bull Run Mountains in 1740. It became a new center for the Barton family. (7)

The 1737 quitrent roll had Thomas down for 100 acres. He was not on the next extant roll in 1752, but a Widow Barton appeared with 100 acres. In 1753 her 100 acres were marked "now John Simms."

Valentine Barton (? – 1740)
(Val. 3, Thos. 2?)

Valentine Barton bought land of his own in 1724, the year that he was shown helping grow tobacco on the plantation of Thomas Barton (Thomas 2, Thomas 1). As the assignee of his wife, the widow of Maurice Bevins, he got a grant of 377 acres "twixt Broad Run and Bull Run." Valentine added to his holdings in 1731 with 419 acres bought from Sarah Moss. On the 1736 Rent Roll he was charged with 1000 acres, 200 more than his known purchases.

Valentine Barton died in 1740, and his widow, Anne, was bonded for administering his estate. The inventory included two wolf traps and a beaver trap, four cider casks, a fiddle valued at five shillings, two "servant men," but no slaves. The estate account that his widow submitted showed among other disbursements three pounds for funeral expenses and 20/13/4 each to Maurice Bevin's three children. (8)

Charles Barton (ca. 1720–ca.1765)
(Charles 4, Valentine 3)

Barton had evidently had a prior wife who died before he wed the widow of Maurice Bevin. The Charles Barton who received a land grant in 1742 for 639 acres on Broad Run was designated in the deed as the son of Valentine Barton deceased. If he was of age, he was born before 1722.

Charles 4 sold Thomas Hogan 181 acres out of his grant in 1748. The collector of quitrents showed Charles with 419 acres in 1752 and 1760 and in the earlier year added a note "Charles Barton to Thomas Hogan 181." If the 419 acres was, as it seems to have been, the tract his father bought from Sarah

193

Moss, what happened to the balance of his own grant? His name wasn't on the 1767 list. (9)

Valentine Barton (ca. 1725 - ?)
(Val. 4, Val. 3 ?)

Another Valentine Barton, unlikely to be the son of the Valentine who died in 1740, was a "foot soldier" in the Prince William militia paid 990 lbs. tobacco in 1756 for serving in the French and Indian War. He lived in the part of Prince William that became Fauquier. Evidently, he was much less well-off than Valentine 3, and unlike his predecessor, could not sign his name. In 1769 he was forced to sell household furniture, all his "crop of corn, tobacco and oats now in the house and in the field," and much of his livestock for less than twenty pounds Virginia money and 630 pounds of tobacco. Two bills of sale dated six months apart and signed Vall. B (his mark) Barton Sr. were registered the same day. The second included many of the goods named in the first and added the year's harvest. Since the buyer was an agent for the Wm. Cunningham Company, it had probably carried Barton until harvest time and then foreclosed on him.

We think the Valentine Barton on the Fauquier tax list in 1800 belonged to the next generation. (10)

Burr Barton (ca. 1705 - ?)
(Burr 3, Thomas 2, Thomas 1)

Burr Barton was over sixteen years old in 1724, when he was tending tobacco on his father's plantation. On the rent roll of 1737 he was billed for 150 acres, probably a lease of part of the Brenttown tract. Some time before 1741 he moved to the Barton enclave near "Hunger" Run, joining Thomas, Valentine, Charles, and Lydia (Barton) Drummond, all of whom lived in the vicinity. His 1741 land grant of 300 acres "on the Bull Run Mountains" adjoined the land of the heirs of Maurice Bevin, (the stepchildren of Valentine Barton). However, the next year Burr and his wife, Elizabeth, sold Edward Feagan that tract, described as where they were living.

Burr apparently gave up the attempt to make a living farming his own land and became an overseer (share-cropper) for Thomas Keith, who owned a large property on the west side of Pignut Mountain, a few miles south of Hunger Run. In the list of British Mercantile Claims the note about Burr's small debt declared he was a "resident of Fauquier, never possessed of more property than personal possessions, an overseer depending on proportion of crop; for many years overseer to Thomas Keith."

In the period before the Revolution Burr Barton was in attendance at Fauquier Courthouse on various court days. On one occasion he was "presented" by a grand jury for non-attendance at church.

We have not found the date of his death and the names of his children, if any. However, one or more of the Barton men who resided in Fauquier in the latter part of the eighteenth century could have been his sons. (11)

James Barton

One of these people was the James Barton on the Fauquier tax list of 1787 who lived in the district to the east of the Falmouth Road (now Route 17). James had one white male aged fifteen to twenty-one in his household. He did not own slaves. A Levi Barton was a neighbor. Joseph Barton in another district headed a household with two white males over sixteen. The other, Thomas Barton, was said to be levy free, indicating perhaps that he was the elderly father of Joseph.

In 1773 James must have been hard up for cash, for he paid a debt of four and a half pounds to Wm. Cunningham & Co. with a "sorrel mare." (12)

The poor fellow suffered another setback recorded for posterity by the Fauquier court: "James Barton has had the misfortune to lose one of his ears bitten off by George Asbury."

We doubt that James of Fauquier was the 13-year-old boy who worked on his father's tobacco farm in 1724. That lad was never heard of again. His namesake may have been a son or more likely a nephew.

Cuthbert Barton

A Cuthbert Barton was "discharged from paying county levy" by the Fauquier court in 1762. Generally exemption from taxation was granted to the poor and elderly and so it might have been in this case. On the other hand he or another Cuthbert Barton appeared in court as a witness in Fauquier in 1786 and was on the 1800 tax census with no slaves. (13)

How much the Harrison-type name of this man (or men) adds to the case for his being a descendant of Burr Sr., we leave to others to decide.

David Barton of Fauquier
David 4, Thomas 3

195

David Barton m. Ruth ----. Children: Elizabeth, Benjamin, John.

About 1759 Lord Fairfax began to offer leases for lives in his Manor of Leeds, the huge tract he had gone through the legalities of granting himself in 1736 when he was in the midst of the dispute with the government of the colony over the boundaries of his Proprietorship. The leases were aimed at a different market than the aristocratic owners of multiple plantations or the land speculators or even the smaller buyers who wished to "bank" their inheritance or their savings into land. The lessees were usually young men newly married with small children looking for their first farm much like today's buyers of their first house. After the Revolution their younger children and many of themselves departed Fauquier in proverbial droves for cheap land "of their own" in Kentucky.

The Manor of Leeds ran from along the south fork of the Shenandoah to about where Route 50 today crosses the river, then across the Blue Ridge and down along it and its foothills skirting the large tracts that had been sold to Burgess Ball and others a few years before, then headed east toward today's village of Marshall, next back along the boundary with the Rev. Scott to the Rappahannock and with it toward the beginning.

One of the first customers for a lease in the Manor was David Barton who took one of 200 acres in 1759 for the lives of himself; his wife, Ruth; and his daughter, Elizabeth Barton. Its northern boundary ran along the line of the Major James Ball tract, part of which was purchased by Colonel Thomas Harrison four years later.

In 1768 Barton leased another 225 acres in the Manor of Leeds from Lord Fairfax, not adjoining the first but nearby. This time the term was for the lives of himself and his sons Benjamin and John. A couple of years later he mortgaged this piece, described as the tract on which his mill stood, to secure a loan of 124 pounds to be repaid in four annual installments. Before the year was out, he sold the lease to Bryan Bruin of Frederick, including a payment plan for the buyer that allowed Barton to pay off his own mortgage. Next David sold "all my beds and furniture, potts and pans and pewter, and all and every other article of my household goods" to John Morehead for ten pounds. Finally, in 1771 he sold his 1759 lease to Thomas Nelson.

There are no later records of David in the county. That he left Fauquier is indicated by two Northern Neck grants made shortly before the Revolution to John, Earl of Dunmore, assignee of Samuel Pritchard, assignee of David Barton. The tracts were in Hampshire County (now West Virginia) on the South Branch of the Potomac and the "Great Waggon Road" west from Winchester. We have not tried to determine whether David actually moved there or changed his mind and went elsewhere. In the census of 1810 a Benjamin Barton in Culpeper and a Benjamin Jr. in Montgomery may have been his son and grandson.

Barton was obviously a capable man respected by his neighbors with such tasks as being the "road surveyor from his precinct to Goose Creek" and with two neighbors of "viewing," i.e., choosing the route for, a road from the Manor Road to the Upper Church. He was literate, at least to the extent of signing his name. (14)

David had a brother John who in 1771 took a lease of 100 acres in the Manor of Leeds close by the two leases David had had. The three lives were those of John himself; his wife, Rhody; and his son Benjamin. John Barton was still living on the site in 1800. (15)

The two brothers may have been sons of the Thomas Barton who died in 1752. At least they were related to him. The Fauquier minute books have a notation that Thomas Barton was ordered to make a deposition in a 1769 suit against David.

Kimber Barton

Kimber Barton, another of the Fauquier family, was married to Elizabeth Lewis in 1771. A few years later he witnessed a deed from James Lewis and his wife, Mary, who were selling land on Wolf Trap Branch in the northeast corner of the county near Hunger/Hungry Run. It looks like Lewis was either Kimber's father-in-law or brother-inlaw. (16)

According to Gwathmey, Kimber Barton was a soldier in Captain James Scott's company during the Revolution. Other Fauquier Bartons who served in the Revolution were Levy, James, Stephen, and Thomas. A Kimbel (sic) Barton was recorded as a titheable in Hampshire County in 1787.

In the 1810 census Levy and James were placed in Loudoun, Joseph and John in Fauquier, and Valentine in Prince William. Farther afield, but still men who most likely were born in the Hunger Run area were Thomas in Berkeley and Burr and Elisha in Bedford County.

No Bartons had wills, inventories, or estate accounts registered in Fauquier from its founding in 1759 through 1850. After Kimber's marriage the next one involving a Barton took place in 1808, when Thomas Barton wed Sarah Drummond, the daughter of William Drummond. Three daughters of Thomas were married a generation later: Maria to Edward Wyne in 1826, Jane to James Carter in 1829, and Roxsey Ann to Willis Athey in 1831. In 1819 a James Barton wed Peggy Farrow. Thomas lived in the Hunger Run vicinity; it should be possible to locate James through the census records, but we have not attempted to do so. We assume most of the family had left the county by 1810. (17)

John Wallis (ca. 1670–ca. 1725)
(John 1)

The possible daughter of Burr Harrison who married John Wallis had many fewer descendants than her "sister Barton" at least in the eighteenth century. In fact we know of only one grandson named Wallis and do not know if he had any sons who carried on the name.

Indeed, the fact that the younger son of John Wallis was called Burr is really the only indication that he may have been a grandson of the first Burr Harrison. Compared to Thomas Whitledge and Thomas Barton Jr., John Wallis was younger and lived somewhat farther away, but in both respects he was within reasonable limits to be a son-in-law. Unlike the other two men, he is not connected directly to Burr Harrison Sr. by any extant record. It's possible that Wallis named his son for either Burr Sr. or Burr Jr as a friend rather than a relative.

The first reference in Stafford County to the family came in 1666 on an application for a land grant; it listed a John Wallis among the transportees. He was probably the same man claimed as a headright for a different patent four years before in Westmoreland. In that county a Thomas Wallis was found "dead on a poynt of oyster shells in the Machoteck River" in 1676. The coroner's inquest ruled his death was accidental. John Wallis was named there in 1694 and in 1697.

A Thomas Wallis in 1695 received a grant of 369 acres in Stafford on the south side of Potomac Creek adjoining land that he already owned. John Wallis obtained 150 acres in Stafford in 1698, about the time he or his namesake disappeared from the records of neighboring Westmoreland. We presume these men were connected to each other and to the Westmoreland family, but we do not know what the relationships were, nor how to tie either of them to the John Wallis thought to have married a Harrison.

Almost all we know for certain about that John is that in 1724 he was granted 334 acres in Stafford between the Morumsco and Little Creeks on John Peake's "Rowling Road." (18)

198

Thomas Wallis (ca. 1695-1744.)
(Thomas 2, John 1)
Burr Wallis (ca. 1700-1736)
(Burr 2, John 1)

The next generation of Wallises showed up in the Stafford records in 1732, when Thomas Wallis and his wife, Mary, deeded his brother Burr a part of the land on which they were living. On Morumsco and Little Creek it had been "taken up" by their father John Wallis.

We gather from this gift that John Wallis had died intestate, and Thomas as the elder son had inherited his real estate. The Morumsco tract was probably the only parcel that the father owned at the time of his death. The younger brother, Burr, had been living with Thomas and Mary and was either recently married or about to become so. Their mother, thought to be the daughter of Burr Harrison, had died before 1732, because no mention was made in the deed of her dower rights.

The younger of the two Wallis brothers died in 1736. His widow, Jane, was bonded for the administration of his small estate; personal property was appraised at a meager twelve pounds. (19)

Thomas Wallis survived his brother by eight years. His inventory was recorded in 1743/4. Mary, his widow, was named administrator of the estate. (20)

Burr Wallace (ca. 1732 - ?)
(Burr 3, Burr 2, John 1)

In 1766 Benjamin Sebastian sold John Baylis 141 acres. The deed cited that the lot had been given to Burr "Wallace" by (his brother) Thomas, the son and heir of John Wallace to whom the land had been granted originally. Burr Wallace (Jr.) together with John Brown and his wife, Jane, who was relinquishing her rights as the widow of Burr (Sr.), had conveyed the property to Sebastian in 1753. The 1752 Prince William rent roll gibed with that history; it showed that Burr Wallace's orphan held 140 acres.

Burr Wallis/Wallace was apparently the only grandson of John Wallis of the 1724 patent and possibly the last of that line. He was living in Fauquier in 1759 and 1761 and in Shenandoah County in 1772. In all three citations he was the defendant in a suit. At that point, when he was about forty, the trail is lost. Whether he moved to Kentucky or the Carolinas or whether he died, and in either case whether he left descendants, we may never know. (21)

Notes:

1. Chas. Co., Md. Q1 reverse, Births and Marriages. Wm. Barton, the son of Nathan Barton, born 19 Feb. 1667/8. Pat. Book 6-691, 1679. Wm. Harris 1600 a. head of main run of Neabscoe adj. Nathan Barton & Robert King. St 1686-94, p.62, 1687. Deed Chr. Butler to David Darnell between Neabsco and land of Nathan Barton, dec'd.

2. Chas. Co. Q1, op. cit. Thomas Barton, son of Wm. and Elizabeth Barton of Mattawomany, born 17 July 1689. William Barton, son of Wm. and Elizabeth, born 11 November 1690. David Barton, son of Wm. and Elizabeth, born 25 June 1695. PW D A-176, 1731. Deed recites that Elizabeth Barton sold Charles Tyler 500 a. on Potomac R. and Powells Creek in 1711/12. Chas. Co. Q-17, 1689. William B., son of Nathan B. dec'd., brings copy of inventory of his father's estate and of the accounts of Francis Hammersly for his adm. of it. (Hammersly married Mary Brent, the daughter of the lawyer George Brent). Ibid Q-26, 1690/91. Wm. B. ag. Francis Hammersly. St 1689-1693, p.3, 1689. Ordered Nathan B. placed in custody of Augustine Knowlton, and Thomas B. in that of Maj. Andrew Gilson until next court when they can be bound to learn a trade. William B. to have custody of sister Martha.

3. St. J-292, 1726. John Underwood to Frances Purcell 150 a. on S. side Quantico, part of uppermost 1000 a. of Wm. Borne's patent. Borne had sold Thomas Barton 400 a. of the 1000; another 300 a. had belonged to "Mary, widow of Wm. Mansbridge."

4. NN 2-284, 1697. 100 a. of Thomas Dayes grant was purchased by Wm. Fisher who left one daughter, who died without child. Escheat grant to Thomas Barton Jr., assigneee of Thomas Barton. On NE side of Quantico. St D J-507, 1728. Thomas Barton Sr. (Jr. before father died), planter, to Abraham Farrow Sr., Gent., 400 a., the upper part of 2000 a. granted Capt. John Lord in 1664. This 400 a. conveyed by Lord to Thomas Borne; by Thomas's son William to Samuel Meese; in 1678 Meese to Thomas Barton, "father of said Thomas Barton." Adjoined land of Farrow on Quantico. Signed Thomas T Barton. Grace, wife of seller, relinquishes rights. PW D A-317, 1731. Grace Barton, widow of Thomas Barton, to children: Lydia Drummond (probably wife of Benjamin Drummond) and William Barton, when he becomes 21. Grace (X) Barton. Witnesses: Thomas Barton & John Metcalfe.

5. St Z-13, 43, and 108.
6. St Records 1686-94, p.162, 1690. Edward Smith gives Constant Barton a gray mare. St Z-2, 1699. Anne Carmalt, formerly of Maryland now of Stafford, binds son John to Edward Barton. St Z-103, 1700. Edward B. bond to George Mason for daughters' share of estate of their grandmother Anne Scarlett. Names wife Ann and unmarried daughters: Constant, Margaret, Ann, and Letice. PW D L-84. Cites will of Edward B. dated Jan. 1711/2.
7. PW D A-321, 1732. Mathew Moss, planter, to Thomas Barton, planter 100 a. on Fornication Branch of Broad Run at the foot of the (Bull Run) mountain. PW M 1752-53, p.26. Inventory of Thomas B. ordered.
8. NN B-86, 1724. Valentine Barton 377 a. on Broad Run and Bull Run, adjoining John Young, George Dawkins. Joyner, NN Surveys, 1727. Valentine Barton, assignee of Mrs. Maurice Bevin, widow now married to Valentine, 377a. "twixt" Broad Run and Bull Run. PW D A-320, 1731. Sarah Moss to Valentine Barton, 419 a. PW W C-103, 1737. Valentine B. cosigner of bond by Leonard Barker, adm. of John Walker estate. PW W C-106, 1736. Val. B. cosigns bond of Sarah Chapman, adm. of husband Nathaniel's estate. PW W C-203, 1739/40. Anne Barton's bond. PW W C-222, 1739. Valentine Barton's inventory. PW W C-243, 1740. Estate account of Valentine Barton. PW D I-235, 1746. Ann Barton, for love and affection to James Grigsby of Stafford, all her right of dower in lands sold by her son Maurice Bevin to Grigsby.
9. NN E-447, 1742. Charles Barton, son of Valentine dec'd., 639 a. on Broad Run. PW D L-69, 1748. Charles Barton to Thomas Hogan 181 a. part of 639 a. grant in 1742.
10. F D 3-521, 1769. Valentine Barton to John Waddell.
11. John Savage's 1737 map of Brenttown shows Burr Barton residing in the fork of the confluence of Broad and Cedar Runs. PW D E-473, 1740. Burr Barton and wife Elizabeth to Edward Feagan 300 a. F M Oct. 1763. Indicted by grand jury. V 20-63, Brit. Mercantile Claims, Colin Dunlap & Son Dumfries store.
12. F D 5-351, 1773. James X Barton pays debt.
13. F M Mar. 1762. Cuthbert Barton. F M Aug. 1786. Cuthbert B. a witness at court.
14. F D 1-47, 1759. Lord Fairfax to David Barton, F M May 1759. David B. to survey road. F M Jan. 1765. Thomas Watts, David B., Robert Ashby, and Enoch Berry to view road. F D 3-242, 1768. Lord Fairfax to David B. F M Sept. 1769. Deposition requested of Thomas Barton. F M

Nov. 1770. John McMillion ag. David B. F D 4-111, 1770. David B. to Brian Bruin. F D 4-203, 1770. Sale of household goods. F D 4-432, 1771. David B. to Thomas Nelson.

15. F D 3-391, 1771. Lord Fairfax to John B. VG 20-181. F 1800 tax list, district of Elias Edmonds Jr.

16. F Marriage Book 1-41, 1771. F D 4-278, 1776.

17. F Marriage Book 3-67, 1808. Thomas Barton. Ibid. 3-371, 1819. James B. Ibid. 4-192, 1826. Maria B. Ibid. 4-287, 1829. Jane B. Ibid. 4-355, 1831. Roxsey Ann B. F D 29-44, 1826. Thomas Barton to secure a debt to Aaron Drummond; taken by Barton to Burr Powell, justice of the peace in nearby Middleburg (Loudoun Co.), and by Powell acknowledged to the Fauquier court in Warrenton.

18. W O 1658-64, p.6a, 1662/3. Francis Hailes brought John Wallis into this country. St 1665-8, p.50, 1666. 40 persons transported by Henry Hudson include John Wallis. NN 2-135, 1694/5. Thomas Wallis 369 a. on main run Potomac Creek. Land surveyed for Richard Fossaker, who sold to John Pike who sold to Wallis. NN 2-297, 1698. John Wallis 150 a. NN A-49, 1724. John Wallis 334 a.

19. PW D B-13, 1732. Thomas and Mary Wallis to brother Burr part of land where we now live taken up by father John Wallis on Morumpsco and Little Creek. PW W C-94, Aug. 1736. Jane Wallis bond with Richard Crupper and George Byrn for adm. estate of Burr Wallis. PW W C-99, Mar. 1737/8. Jane W. adm. Burr W. presented inventory; total value 12/10/1. Appraisers: William Baylis, Richard Cogins, John Johnson.

20. PW W C-391 1743/4. Mary Wallis bond with Peter and Charles Cornwell for adm. estate of Thomas Wallis. PW W C-400, Mar. 1743/4. Thomas Wallis inventory submitted by Mary Wallis, taken by George Calvert, Burr Harrison and Thomas Dowell. No slaves. Value 11/2/10.

21. PW D P-9, 1766. Benjamin Sebastian and Priscilla to John Bayliss. F O p.24, 1759. Burr Wallis a defendant; F O p.162, 1761. Burr W. again a defendant. Sh O 1772-4, p.58. Burr W. defendant in a suit.

Chapter XVIII

The Lintons of Northern Virginia

About 1743 Jane Harrison, the eldest daughter of Captain Burr and Mrs. Ann (Barnes) Harrison, married John Linton, the son of the late Mr. John and Mrs. Anne (Barton) Linton. The bride was the granddaughter of Colonel and the late Mrs. Thomas Harrison and Captain and Mrs. Mathew Barnes. Very likely her three living grandparents witnessed the wedding, which would have taken place at the Quantico Church of Hamilton Parish with the Reverend Mr. Keith officiating.

The Harrison and Linton families had been good friends and neighbors for at least fifty years before the wedding. A cousin of the groom, Seth (Linton) Quarles, was named for the bride's paternal grandmother. Although not proved, we believe one of the groom's older brothers had married a Harrison, aunt of the bride.

John Linton, the groom's father, was first recorded in Stafford in 1701 when he was paid 1000 pounds of tobacco by the county for "post, two journeys." The next year his brother Moses was an ensign in Captain Thomas Harrison's militia company. (1)

The genealogy of the descendants of the brothers John and Moses is exceptionally confusing, because so many Lintons with the first names of John, Moses, and William lived in the region during the eighteenth century. Although our attempt to clarify some doubtful points touching the first three generations of the family has not been completely successful, we submit the analysis as an addition to the history of Harrison friends and relatives.

Anthony Linton (1624–ca.1699)

Although no one is sure where the brothers came from, they

probably belonged to a Linton family, three of whose members reached the area north of the Rappahannock river in the decade of the 1650s. One of this first generation was Anthony Linton, in Northumberland County by 1656. He was born about 1624, immigrated to Virginia in 1637, and died shortly before 1700. As a young man he was an indentured servant accused of being a runaway from York, but he had become a vestryman before he was fifty. He and his wife, Jane, had a son named Henry who died in 1678. Henry had married Sarah Swellivant and had a son named Anthony. In 1669 the first Anthony gave a heifer to his cousin William Linton and in 1678 mentioned having a brother John. (2)

John Linton (1632-ca.1705)

The brother John was in Westmoreland County by 1662 when he witnessed a document of William Freake who lived on Appomattocks (now Mattox) Creek. The next year Freake, justifying a request for a land grant, swore he had brought John Linton "into the Colony." John witnessed Freake's sale of land on Hollowes Creek to "Malachi Peale, merchant" in 1673. He may have become an employee of Peale, since he witnessed several deals made by Peale in subsequent years.

This John Linton, "aged 45 years," gave a deposition in 1677/8 that "being at the house of Mr. Originall Browne in Nominy with Richard Hancock, we were drynking of cyder at length." Most of the rest of his testimony is now illegible, making it impossible to decipher what disturbance was caused by the partying. The last time John Linton figured in the Westmoreland files came in 1703, when he owed money to the estate of William Clark. (3)

William Linton

William Linton was claimed as a headright in a patent granted in 1654.

It was he who partnered George Harrison in buying 450 acres from John Williams in 1671. Whether it was he who witnessed William Clark's will and appraised his estate or a William Linton of the next generation is unclear. (4)

We assume that one of these three men was the immigrant ancestor of the Linton family of Stafford. In our opinion, William was the most likely to be the father of the brothers John and Moses.

A Moses Linton Jr. died in Lower Norfolk County in 1677; his will names his son Moses and mentions that his wife was expecting a child. Another Moses Linton who died in the same county in 1693 had a son named William. Some have assumed he was the son of the man who died in 1677, but more likely the relationship was the other way around. On the basis of the similarity in Christian names, some connection between the northern Virginia Lintons and the ones in the Norfolk area seems likely.

John Linton (ca.1670–1728)
(John 1)

Few details of the life of the first John Linton of Stafford survived the destruction of many of the county records. For example, he apparently lived on the neck of land between the Occoquan and the Neabsco, but his deed of purchase was lost. However, he was clearly a man of considerable means, even though he was never a militia officer or justice of the peace. In the 1723 quitrent roll he was shown as holding 1050 acres. Later he added 382 acres on the Accotink and 500 acres on the Broad Run of Potomac through grants from the Proprietor and bought 120 acres on the main run of the Occoquan from James Bland. (5)

About 1700 Linton married Ann Barton, the daughter of Edward and Ann (Green) Barton. His wife was first cousin on her mother's side to William, Edward, and Katherine Smith, the stepchildren of Burr Harrison Jr. The Lintons had the following known children:

William (ca. 1702–1733).
Moses (ca. 1705–1752).
Ann m. (1) Scarlet Hancock, (2) William Hancock.
Frances (ca. 1710–ca. 1730) unmarried.
Constant, m. George Brett.
John (ca. 1715–1759).
Letice – (1728–?).

These children were provided for in Linton's will dated in February of 1727/8 and proved two months later. Bequests of land were made to son John, a quarter on the (Potomac) riverside; to daughter Ann, the "plantation where the Widow Kid now lives"; to Frances, the plantation "where John Wallis is now"; and to Constant, a "plantation with 150 acres of land purchased of James Bland lying on the main run of Occoquan."

Money for mourning rings was given to Seth Linton, "daughter of my brother Moses," and to Katherine (Smith) Hancock. The residue of his real and personal estate was to be divided among his wife and children, including one as yet unborn (Letice). His widow and his sons William and Moses were the executors. The lost Stafford Liber K recorded the division of the estate to Ann, William, Moses, Ann Jr., Frances, Constant, John, and Letice in that order. (6)

Moses Linton (ca. 1675-1729)
(Moses 1)

Moses, the brother alluded to in the will of John 1, paid 57 pounds of tobacco in 1723 as quitrents for three years on 79 acres. He added to his land holdings in 1726 with a grant of 740 acres on Broad Run in the back country of the county. Later he got a grant of 208 acres on the Morumsco, a small creek between the Neabsco and the Occoquan. The new tract adjoined his own land and that of his son-in-law, Robert Church. (7)

Three months after that patent issued Moses was dead. His will dated in April 1729 and proved the following June bequeathed to his daughter Seth a "certain tract of land lying on Morrumpsco Creek adjoining the land given her by Capt. Thomas Harrison." Henry Peyton was given 500 acres, part of the Broad Run patent, and grandsons Thomas Church and William Morris were each devised 100 acres of that tract. Others receiving bequests were his wife, Margaret; his daughter Frances; and his granddaughter Margaret Church. He named as executors his widow, Moses Quarles, and Valentine Peyton. The will was witnessed by William Linton, Moses Linton, Benjamin Grayson, and Charles Morris. (8)

Henry Peyton was the son of Valentine (1686-1751) and Frances Peyton. Although Henry has not been proved to be a grandson of Moses, he could hardly be anything else. Moses Quarles was married to daughter Seth. Charles Morris was without much doubt the father of William and thus the widower of an unidentified daughter of the Lintons. Grayson was a friend and neighbor. William Linton was all but certainly a nephew, the eldest son of John 1. The witness, Moses Linton, has been thought by some to be a son of Moses 1, but in our opinion was the second son of John 1.

Moses's widow, Margaret Linton, executed a deed of trust to Moses Quarles in 1732 in favor of her granddaughters Jane Quarles, the daughter of Moses and Seth Quarles, and Margaret Church, the daughter of Robert and Margaret Church. Mrs.

Linton's inventory was recorded in 1734 according to the index of Prince William Will Book C, but it was among the torn-out first pages of the book. (9)

It has been suggested that the Widow Margaret was a daughter of Captain Thomas Harrison (1665–1746) based on the name of her daughter Seth and Harrison's gift of land to the girl. However, it is very unlikely that the Harrisons could have had a daughter old enough to be Seth Linton's mother. We conclude Captain and Mrs. Harrison were godparents rather than grandparents. The hypothesis that Margaret was the daughter of Edward Barton and so a sister of Mrs. John Linton 1 is discussed below under Moses 2.

William Linton (ca. 1702–1733)
(William 2, John 1)

In 1728 or 1729 William Linton, John's eldest son, married Susanna (Monroe) Tyler (1695–1752), the daughter of Andrew Monroe and Eleanor Spence. Her first husband had been Charles Tyler, who had died two or three years previously. After William's death she married Benjamin Grayson. She had children by all three spouses. Those by Linton were:

John (ca. 1730–1775).
William (ca. 1732–1770).

William was appointed a justice of Stafford in 1729 and when Prince William was formed from Stafford in 1731, he was on its first commission of peace. His service in the office was cut short by his death in 1733. His will was among the lost records, but his estate account was left. Its entries, begun in 1733, included payments for Frances Linton's estate, since William had been her executor. They went to brother Moses for his own share plus those of John and Letice (both still underage) and to George Brett for his wife Constance. (10)

The coincidence that two other William Lintons died in the region soon after this Prince William resident has caused some confusion among persons interested in the family. However, both the man who died in 1734 in Westmoreland County and the other deceased in 1736 in King George left wills that demonstrate they were distinct individuals, possibly second or third cousins of William of Stafford. (11)

John Linton (ca. 1730–1775)
(John 3, William 2, John 1)

Benjamin and Susannah Grayson raised all her children

including those by her previous marriages. In 1751 "John Linton the Younger of Dettingen Parish, the son of William," acknowledged receiving his share of his father's estate from Grayson, his guardian and stepfather. The youth got four Negro slaves, thirty pounds, and a third of the land owned by the estate. His mother was due her dower rights to a third of William Linton's properties. The remaining share belonged to John's brother William. (12)

The term "Younger" generally was used to refer to the youngest of three men of the same name, but in some documents it was apparently just a synonym for Junior. In this case the oldest John Linton was the uncle of John the Younger, but the intermediate "John Jr.," if he existed, has not been identified. The four extant records of a John Linton Jr. between 1749 and 1758 all seem to apply to John, the orphan of William. They were as witness to a sale of land to his stepfather Benjamin Grayson, as plaintiff in a suit against Daniel McCarty in Fairfax court, as a customer of the Colchester store of the Glassford Company, and in a poll for burgesses of Fairfax County.

Two other John Lintons, probably intermediate in age between the Prince William pair (John 2, John 1 and John 3, William 2), are known. John, the son of William of Westmoreland, in 1745 bought land in that county that had once belonged to his father. The other John, grandson of William of Westmoreland, was underage when his father, Anthony Linton, died in Stafford County in 1739. No record after that date has been found that referred to a John who could be identified as the son of Anthony. (13)

John, the grandson of John 1, was the first Linton of the third generation to be born in Stafford. In 1752 he married Elizabeth Elliot, the daughter of John and Sibella Elliot. The couple had four children who survived to adulthood:

William.
Sibella (1761-1821), m. Burr Peyton.
John Augustine Elliot.
Ann (1765-1815), did not marry. (14)

On the John Henry map of northern Virginia published in 1770 a small circle marked the plantation of the "Lintons" (John and Betty) near the southeasternmost edge of Occoquan Bay. Very likely the property had been inherited from John's father and grandfather.

John fell into serious financial straits in the 1760's. Probably they were not so much caused by his own mistakes and bad business judgment as by his loyalty to his half-brother, Benjamin Grayson Jr. At least Linton's original difficulties resulted from co-signing notes for Grayson, who was unable to cover the debts. Linton was able to avoid bankruptcy (Grayson's fate) only by selling off most, if not all, of his inheritance. His sales began with 270 acres, a third of a tract on Cockpit Point granted to his father in 1730. Then he mortgaged the 509 acres that his grandfather had patented in 1727, "together with all corn now growing on (his) plantation in Prince William and all wheat." Later he was forced to sell this land. Next he mortgaged "39 head of sheep, 30 head of black cattle, 7 beds and their furnishings, 60 head of hogges, five horses, and four slaves to secure a six-months loan from John Brett (probably his cousin, the son of George and Constance Brett). Evidently he was unable to pay off the loan, for the four slaves were not included among fifteen sold outright the next year. After losing so much land, farm stock, and slaves, he apparently was reduced to running an "ordinary" in Colchester. (15)

William Linton (1758–1806)
(Wm. 4, John 3, Wm. 2, John 1)
&
John Linton (1762–1822)
(John 4, John 3, Wm. 2, John 1)

In the next generation the family recovered financially. By the turn of the century both sons of John 3, William 2 lived in the town of Dumfries and were prominent in Prince William's "oligarchy." Both were inspectors at the Quantico warehouse beginning in 1784; John was the county tax collector in 1800 and 1801 and the sheriff in 1805.

An example of the dispersal of the Linton family from their "ancient seat" along the Potomac is found in an 1807 document, by which John Linton Jr. and Thomas A. Linton, both of Natchez, Mississippi, gave a power of attorney to (their uncle) John Linton Sr. of Dumfries to cede to William A. Linton, their brother, all their rights to the estate left by William Linton, their deceased father, as well as some land left them by their grandfather, Thomas Atwell. (16)

William Linton (ca. 1732–1770)
(Wm. 3, Wm. 2, John 1)

William Linton began to appear in the records in 1757, often associated with the Grayson family. In 1761 a patent issued to a William Linton "of Prince William" for 128 acres on "Plum Tree Gutt" on the south side of the mouth of Occoquon Bay. We know of no William who might have been the grantee other than the son of William 2. Yet in the same year he was licensed to keep an ordinary at Colchester, the port on the north (Fairfax) side of the Occoquan. The inn was on a lot rented from his half-brother, Benjamin Grayson Jr. From 1765 to 1770 he was a vestryman of Truro parish, and from 1763 to 1770 he was one of the inspectors at the Colchester warehouse. He died intestate in 1770 leaving his wife, Mary, maiden name unknown, but no children. (17)

Moses (ca. 1705-1752)
(Moses 2, John 1 (?))

A Moses Linton was one of the original vestrymen of Dettingen Parish elected in 1745, but he resigned after three years because he had moved out of the parish. In 1749 he was named to the commission of peace of Fairfax, but declined at first because of deafness. However, the next month he took the oath as a justice. In 1750 he censused the titheables from the "lower end of Cameron Parish upwards," proving he resided at the time in the area that later became Loudoun.

In his capacity as a Fairfax justice of the peace, Moses arrested an Edmond Linton and Hester Smith as "vile characters and harborers of rogues and horse stealers." Edmond was fined for his "crime." Hester (sometimes spelled as Esther) was evidently not without charms. The widow of Jacob Smith, she married Edmond next, and after his death took a third husband.

Much perplexity about the parentage of the justice Moses has been caused by his sale of 26 acres on Morumsco Creek to Benjamin Grayson in 1748. The lot was described as part of 250 acres sold by Martin Scarlett to Edward Barton in 1685 and willed by Barton in 1711/12 to Moses Linton and Ann Linton. "Ann Linton died in her infancy, and the said Moses Linton surviving is now party to these presents." Susanna, the wife of Moses, released her dower rights to the property. (18)

The problem arises from the statement that the seller's sister Ann died in infancy, but Ann, the daughter of John 1 and Ann (Barton) Linton, was still alive in 1751. The inference is that Moses Linton (the seller) was the son of Moses 1 rather than of John 1. As far as we know this deed is the sole basis for marking the wife of Moses 1 as Margaret Barton, the sister of Mrs. John Linton 1. The conclusion seems logical, but it does not fit well with other records. As reported above, the will of Moses 1 does not even mention a son, let alone make him a bequest or appoint him an executor.

210

One possible explanation of the dilemma is that the Moses Linton who witnessed the will was indeed a son indicating his conformity with its provisions. However, a difficulty with that suggestion is that Moses Linton, the son of John 1, was alive in 1738 when he was paid by the executors of his dead brother William for shares in the estate of his dead sister Frances. Not once in the records is any distinction made between two supposed Moses Lintons, residing contemporaneously in the same part of Prince William County, such as terming one Junior or noting that one is the son of ----. We prefer to believe that John (1) had a daughter Ann who died as a baby and subsequently gave a second daughter the name. Such a reuse was not an uncommon practice in those days.

We had hoped that a lease Moses Linton made late in 1751 of 330 acres, "the land and plantation on which (he) lately dwelt on the Bay of Occoquon" might shed light on the unresolved question, but it disclosed nothing about the prior ownership of the tract. The lease "for the full term and space of the natural life of the said Moses Linton" was granted to John Graham with the proviso that during each fishing season Linton would be allowed "a sufficient quantity of fish for the use of his family." (19)

The lessee did not enjoy use of the property for long, because Moses Linton died intestate in less than a year. In October of 1752 the Fairfax court ordered an inventory of his estate and recorded that his widow Susanna gave the near-maximum bond of 1000 pounds as his administratrix. (20)

Moses and Susanna had two proved children and probably a third:

Catherine (1748–?), m. 1766 Joseph Lewis.
John (1750–1836).
? Moses (ca. 1752–?), probably died young.

There has been much speculation about the maiden name of the widow Susanna. Several researchers have placed her as a Harrison going as far as to identify her with the daughter of Colonel Thomas Harrison of Fauquier.

We now know that she was the young Susanna (Hancock) Linton, who less than a year after Moses's death was remarried to John Berkely. The key to her antecedents is a deposition made in a chancery suit brought by Susanna and her second husband against William Hancock and George Brett in the court of Loudoun County in 1763. It reads:

> ----*Letice Langfit aged forty-six years*-----*saith that Susanah Hancock now wife to*

the complainant John Berkely had willed to her by
Rich'd Britt two negroes to wit Sesor & Flora &
Scarlet Hancock one of the excr. of the sd. Britt
had the two said slaves in his possession ---- eight
years ---- that the sd. Scarlet Hancock rec'd for
several years five hundred & thirty pounds of
tobaco due yearly for rents ---- after the sd.
Hancock deceased his widow which was wife to
the defendant [William Hancock] had the sd.
slaves in possession two years & rec'd the yearly
rents ---- ye said Susanah was allway very meanly
cloathed such as plad Virginia cloath & imployed
at leading of the horse to plow & other services &
was four years old or thereabouts when she first
went to live with the said Hancock ---Susanah
had some schooling but of little consequence &
farther saith not.

Signed: Letice (her mark) Langfit. (21)

The slaves Flora and Cesar were included in the inventory
of Moses Linton's estate. (By law anything belonging to his
wife at the time of their marriage had become his property.)

Who were the parents of Susanna Hancock? Richard Brett's
will which might have answered the question directly has not
survived. However, the Langfitt deposition states that Susanna
went to live with " the said Hancock" when she was about four.
A careful reading of the deposition shows that "the said Hancock" refers to Scarlet, not William who is termed "the defendant." Susanna probably lived with Scarlet most of the eight
years that he had the two slaves in his possession.   Since
Scarlett Hancock died in 1741, Susanna was born not earlier
than twelve years previously, i.e., 1729. Thus she cannot have
been more than nineteen when her oldest child, Catherine
Linton, was born in 1748. (If she had been four in 1741 when
she went to live with William after Scarlett's death, she would
have been only eleven or twelve in 1748, when her daughter was
born.)

Scarlett and William Hancock were the sons of John
Hancock and his wife Katherine (Smith) Hancock, the stepdaughter of Burr Harrison Jr. John Hancock died as a resident
of North Carolina in 1740 leaving his eldest son Scarlett of
Prince William all his lands and personal estates in Virginia.
(22) If Susanna was his daughter as postulated, why would she
have been sent to live with her older brother instead of accom-
panying her father to North Carolina? Possibly the elder Han-

cock had moved to North Carolina intending to bring his wife Katherine and small daughter later, and then Katherine had died before she could join him. Alternatively, he had deserted his family. The latter might be the case, for in 1731 Katherine Hancock leased the land she had inherited from her grandmother Ann Green Scarlett and named her son Scarlett in the lease as heir to the property. Her husband was not a party to the transaction.

We conclude Susanna (Hancock) Linton Berkely was the daughter of John and Katherine (Smith) Hancock and the younger sister of Scarlett and William Hancock. (This is also suggested by her first child being named Catherine.)

Nevertheless, the family tradition that Moses Linton had married a Harrison might be correct. In 1752 William and Thomas, sons of Moses Linton, deceased, chose Burr Harrison (1699–1775) as their guardian.

For an orphan to make his own choice of guardian he had to be over fourteen. Since Susanna (Hancock) Linton Berkely was not more than nineteen when she married Moses Linton, she was apparently only a few years older than the boys. Thus, she could not have been their mother. Why then did they choose Harrison? He was certainly a friend of their father and the father-in-law of their uncle John Linton. He might also have been their uncle, if Moses Linton's unidentified first wife had been a daughter of Captain Thomas Harrison. The orphan, Thomas Linton, may have been named for his maternal grandfather. We do not know what happened to the boys, except that both died before 1775. (23)

John Linton (1750–1836)
(John 3, Moses 2, John 1)

John Linton, the son of Moses and Susanna, executed a document in 1775 which said in part:

> *John Linton of Loudoun County, the only surviving son and heir at law to my father Moses Linton ---- Gent., deceased, and eldest son and heir apparent to my mother as well ---- in consideration of my education and maintenance by John Berkely and Susanna his wife, my said mother and administratrix ---- of my father who died intestate ---- and for 300 pounds current money of Virginia ---- I release all my interest in ---- the estate of my father and mother ---- and of my deceased brothers and sisters. (24)*

This release confirmed the existence of older half-brothers, and that they (William and Thomas) had died before 1775. Since Moses Linton died intestate, under the law of primogeniture his oldest surviving son would have inherited two-thirds of his "real estate," the other third going to his widow during her lifetime. If that son died without "heirs of his body," his inheritance would have passed automatically to the next oldest son and so on. In other words the line of succession paralleled that still maintained for British royalty. The "personal estate" of John Linton's father, to which this document referred, would have been divided one-third to his widow during her lifetime and the balance equally among his surviving children who would gain full rights to their shares as they came of age. The rights of any who died intestate while unmarried and underage fell to their surviving siblings.

The 1771 Loudoun list of titheables had a John Linton with a Moses Linton (over sixteen) in his household, the only known reference to the latter. The John Linton could only have been the son of Moses and Susanna. We believe that the two were brothers. John was just twenty-one, and Moses must have been nineteen or twenty. Since no other John Linton was among the Loudoun titheables, we guess he and Moses were working the Loudoun farm he had inherited from their father. We presume Moses died while still a young man.

John married Ann Mason, a granddaughter of William and Elizabeth Berkely, who were the parents of John's stepfather. The couple had the following children:

John H. d. 1838.
Moses
Lewis
Benjamin
William m. Eliza Lyon Moran.
Martha
Susan m. William Moran.
Nancy d. 1862, m. Edward B. Edwards.
Mary m. (1)----Powell, (2) Dr. Polin.
Catherine m.----Taylor. (25)

Linton was commissioned lieutenant in the Loudoun militia in 1778 and captain in 1781. He continued to reside in Loudoun until 1818, when he moved to Springfield, Kentucky, to live near several of his children. He died there in 1836.

John Linton (ca. 1715-1759)
(John 2, John 1)

John Linton m. Jane Harrison (1726-1759), daughter of Burr and Anne (Barnes) Harrison.

At last we return to the groom of the wedding announced at the beginning of the chapter. John Linton, the youngest son and next-to-youngest child of the first John Linton, and his wife Jane Harrison, the oldest daughter and next-to-oldest child of Captain Burr Harrison, lived on the "quarter on the Riverside" inherited from his father. Quitrent rolls for Prince William showed him with two hundred acres from 1739 through 1760. In the last of these the entry is for John Linton with "& Burr Hn" added in a different handwriting.

The Proprietor's agents did not include a separate parcel of one hundred acres that Linton owned from 1751-1757 in the course of a history intertwining the Linton and Hancock families. It began in 1696 when Ann Scarlett gave her son Joshua Green "and the heirs of his body and in default of such heirs to his two sisters, Ann and Letice Green, a "neck of land between Occoquan and a small creek commonly called Morrumsco Creek" containing six hundred acres. When Joshua died without heirs, Ann and Letice received the tract and partitioned it into equal halves. Ann Green as Mrs. Edward Barton devised her share to her daughter Ann who married John Linton 1. When John died in 1728, he willed one hundred acres of the three hundred to their daughter Ann. He acted in accord with his legal rights as a husband, but apparently widow Ann forgot, misunderstood, or disapproved of the bequest. So in 1731 she sold William Linton, "her eldest son," the whole three hundred acres, noting it was where she was living at the time. Two months later William "leased" the three hundred acres back to his mother for the term of "her natural life."

In 1751 the daughter Ann Linton and her second husband, William Hancock (later the defendant in the suit brought by Susanna (Hancock) Linton Berkely), sold the one hundred acres "unto John Linton ---- which said tract of land the said John Linton and Jane his wife conveyed to Simon Hancock in 1757." (26)

John and Jane Linton died within days of each other in the early spring of 1759. Cuthbert Harrison, Jane's brother, noted in his family Bible: "Jane Linton departed this life April 3rd 1759." Burr Harrison, her father, gave bond for the administration of John Linton's estate at the April session of the Prince William court. He raised the four orphan children:

Ann d. 1798.
William (ca. 1745-?)
John (ca. 1747-?)

Sarah m. Robert Combs

According to H.T. Harrison's genealogy, Colonel Leven Powell (their uncle by marriage) often spoke of the Lintons in his letters with the deepest affection, "especially Miss Nancy" (Ann).

Sarah married her first cousin, Robert Combs, the son of her aunt, Elizabeth (Harrison) Combs. Sarah Combs was alive in 1825, but died before her husband. He died in 1842, when he was well into his nineties. They had at least five children living in 1825: John, Burr, Jane (married to Henry Glascock), Frances H. Brashares, and Sarah Ann (married to William Shacklett). (27)

William Linton (ca. 1747–?)
(William 3, John 2, John 1)

William Linton, "son of John Linton deceased of Prince William," obtained a grant of 400 acres on a branch of Cedar Creek and on the "drains of Buffeloe Meadow" in Frederick County in 1763. Two years later Captain Burr Harrison, William's grandfather, had the following recorded in Prince William: "I do hereby certify that Wm. Linton, an infant, is son and lawful heir of Mr. John Linton, deceased, for whom I made a survey of 400 a. in Frederick about 1751. Signed: Jno Baylis." (28)

The grant and the certification provide the last data that we have found that surely relate to this son of John 2 and Jane (Harrison) Linton. However, it is probable that he was the William Linton who purchased 312 acres on Broad Run in Prince William in 1781 from Elliot Monroe and who with his wife Euphemia sold 74 acres out of the parcel immediately and another 50 acres of it four years later. (29)

Robert Combs deposed in 1825 that the land he was living on had been placed in trust with the heirs of Colonel (Leven) Powell or William Linton or his heirs. We suppose Combs referred to his wife's brother.

John Linton (ca. 1750–?)
(John 3, John 2, John 1)

We know even less that is certain about John Linton, the younger brother of William. The trouble is that we have been unable to determine in some cases whether a record pertains to a descendant of William 2 or of John 2. For example, a John Linton sold 200 acres of a plantation "commonly known as

Shadding Bay" on the Bay of Occoquan to John Hancock in 1767. No release of dower rights by a wife accompanied the deed. (30). Thus, the seller was not John 3, William 2, unless his wife Betty had died between 1765 and 1767. Complicating the picture, in 1789 John Linton and Betty, his wife, sold William Davis Jr. the 120 acres on the Occoquan that had been bought in 1727 by "John Linton Sr." from James Bland, but according to Hayden the only John Linton (John 3, William 2) known to have a wife named Betty died in 1775. In 1791 a Betty Linton, now a widow, leased from William Downman 150 acres on the main road from Colchester to Dumfries for the rest of her "natural life." A Jabez Downman had land adjoining the "Shadding Bay" tract sold a quarter century earlier. When he died in 1774, John and William Linton had been two of the securities for his widow's administration of the estate. The two Lintons were very likely the sons of John 2 and Jane Harrison. (31)

On the basis of Hayden's 1775 date for the death of John 3, William 2, it appears that both he and John 3, John 2 had wives named Betty. If so, the latter John was the one who sold the 120 acres on the Occoquan. Without knowing when either one of the Bettys died, we are still in the dark about which John sold the Shadding Bay tract and which had been the husband of the widow Betty who rented land in 1791.

Patient work on land title searches in the area near the Potomac between Occoquan Bay and the Neabsco may answer some of these questions.

In the 1810 census four Linton men, all named John, were left in northern Virginia as heads of households. Two were in Loudoun and two in Prince William. One of the Loudoun men was John 3, Moses 2. The other, still spelling his surname with the antique "y" may have been his son, or, if not, a descendant of one of the Westmoreland "cousins" of his grandfather, John 1. One of the two in Prince William was John 4, John 3, William 2; we have not identified the other.

Notes:

1. St Z-116, 1701. County levy.
2. *Virginia Colonial Abstracts*, Vol. 19. Dorman, *Westmoreland Records*.
3. W O 1658-64, p.16a, 1662/3. Wm. Freake brought John Linton into this colony. W D 1665-1677, p.28, 1677/8. John Linton deposition.
4. Ibid., p.91a, 1671. John Williams to William Linton and George Harrison.

5. NN A-46, 1724. John Linton 382 a. on Accotink. NN B-95, 1727. 509 a. on Broad Run of Potomac. St D J-52, 1727. James Bland to J.L. 120 a. on main run of Occoquon, middle third of 1707 grant to William and James Bland and Francis Stone.

6. Section 309, Tayloe Papers, Va. Hist. Society, MSS 172118245. Will of John L. (abstracted in VG Oct. 1972, p. 97). Also original of deed from Anne L., widow of John L., for love etc. to daughter Frances L. If in default of heirs successively to son John, daughter Ann L., and finally daughter Constant L. All the tract where John Wallace now dwells containing 100 a. On Potomac riverside. Also similar deeds to son John and daughter Ann of the remainder of 300 a. that had originally belonged to Martin Scarlett. PW W C-339, 1742/3. John Gregg's guardian bond for Lettice Linton. Gregg was neighbor of the PW Lintons; therefore, Lettice was more likely the daughter of John L. than of Anthony. Her mother, Ann (Barton) Linton must have died. Her oldest brother William was dead, next brother Moses had moved out of the county, and brother John was probably too young to take the responsibility. No later information about Lettice has been found.

7. NN A-212, 1726. 740 a. on Broad Run (of Occoquon). NN B-171, 1728/9. 208 a. on Morumsco adj. own land and Robert Church. PW D M-59, 1749. Thomas Church, house carpenter of FX, sells 144 a. on Morumpsco taken up by Thomas Church in 1694, inherited by son Robert and then by seller, Robert's only son.

8. PW Land Causes 1754-1811, p.351. Will of Moses Linton copied for plaintiff, John Linton (1762-1822), in case of trespass on 500 a. of NN A-212 grant willed Henry Peyton, who had sold the land. It passed through various hands before the plaintiff bought it from Benjamin Dulany in 1804.

9. PW D 32, 1732. Margaret Linton to Moses Quarles. PW W C-7, 1734. Inventory of Margaret L. according to the index, but first seven pages of book are missing. The eighth page records a document of Sept. 1734. PW D Q-196, 1764. Deceased wife of William Tandy was a daughter of Moses and Seth Quarles.

10. NN B-152, 1728. William Lynton 166 a. on Bull Run. St W M-9, 1730. W.L. and wife Susanna administrators of estate of Charles Taylor (Tyler). PW C-432. Estate account of W.L.

11. W D&W 4-29, 1707. Wm. Clark of Cople Parish 100 a. to William Linton. Ri D 6-115, 1712. Sale by William Linton and wife Johanna. Ri D 9-573, 1739. Sale by

William L. to John Freshwater of land inherited from father William L. Ri D 10-99, 1745. John L. from John Freshwater land formerly belonging to father William L. (Sr.). KG W A1-127, dated and proved 1736. Names brothers Samuel, Thomas, James and sister Sarah.

12. PW D M-220, 1751. Receipt John L. to Benjamin Grayson.
13. St W M-261, pr. 1738/9. Anthony Linton will names wife Mary, underage children John and Letice. Wife was daughter of William Page. She m. (2) John Remy. Letice m. Joseph Carter in 1755.
14. Hayden is source of most dates in the table. PW W K-13, pr. 1815. Will of Ann Linton. Bequests to nephews John, Thomas, and William A. (sons of brother William) and John T. (son of brother John), nieces Mrs. Ann Gwinn and Miss Martha Peyton, sisters-in-law Mrs. Mary Linton (widow of William) and Mrs. Sarah Linton (wife of John), brother John, and sister Mrs. Sybella Peyton (wife of Burr Peyton).
15. PW D P-108, 1761. John L. and Betty sell 270 a. on Potomac at Cocke Pit Point granted father William L. and Mark Chilton in 1730/1. W.L. was surviving partner. L D E-1, 1765. John L. and Betty of PW sell 509 a. on Broad Run above Rocky Run.
16. PW 4-536, 1809. John L. Jr. and Thomas A. L. of Natchez grant William A. L. of PW all rights as heirs of William L. dec'd late of Dumfries in a house, furniture, and lot in Dumfries and 600 a. in PW and also all right in another tract lying near Broad Run "descended to us from our grandfather Thos. Atwell dec'd."
17. NN I-65, 1761. William L. 128 a. on Bay of Occoquon and Potomac River. Fx D F-73, 1764. William L. "of Colchester, ordinary keeper" from Travers Waugh. Deed missing, but known from order book to be for lots in Colchester. Fx Bond Book, p. 106, 1770. Bond for 1000 pounds for administration of estate of W.L. by John Hancock, William Elzey, and Sampson Turley, appointees of court.
18. PW D L-84, 1748. Moses L. to Benjamin Grayson 26 a.
19. PW D M-216. Moses L. of Cameron Parish to John Graham of Truro 330 acres lease for term of life of M.L.
20. Fx Bond Book, p.1, Oct. 1752. Susanna L. bond for administration of Moses L.'s estate. Fx O, June, 1753. As administratrix of estate of Moses L., Susanna Berkely and John Berkely have assets attached by Benjamin Grayson re suit against Thomas Church. M.L. had been guardian of Church.

21. Fx O Sept. 1756. John and Susanna Berkely against William Hancock and George Brett. L Chancery file M-2960, 1763. Continuation of suit after formation of Loudoun. Includes deposition of Letice Langfit. Letice was wife of Philip Langfit.

22. PW D E-238, 1740. John Hancock of North Carolina gives eldest son Scarlett of PW all his lands and personal estate in Virginia. PW W C-272, 1741. Will of Scarlett H. named wife Ann and children John and Ann. Son was bequeathed land in fork of Morumpsco Creek and 400 a. left Scarlett by Richard Brett, the man who had devised Susannah Hancock the slaves Cesar and Flora. KG D 1A-175, 1731. Katherine Hancock lessor of 160 a. Her son Scarlett, under 21, is heir to the land.

23. PW O p. 160, 1752. William and Thomas, sons of Moses L. dec'd, chose Burr Harrison as their guardian.

24. L D K-428, 1775. John L. release of rights to John and Susannah Berkely. Fx W J-175, 1809. John Berkely will names sons John Longworth, Scarlett (dec'd.), George and daughters Elizabeth Lewis, Susanna Lewis. Evidently wife Susannah had died before the testator.

25. *Pioneer History of Washington County, Ky.* is source of data on children. L W B-9, 1772. Will of Elizabeth Berkely (widow of the William Berkely who died in 1762). Bequest to granddaughter Ann Linton (daughter of Benjamin and Ann Mason and wife of John L.)

26. PW D A-228, 1731/2. Ann Linton, a widow, to William L. "her eldest son" 300 a. divided of estimated 600 a. of "that neck of land" between Occoquan and Morrumsco that had been "settled by Ann Scarlett on Ann Linton's mother and Lettice Smith, mother of Catherine Hancock, who is in possession of the "lower moiety" and Ann L. of the northern or upper half. PW D Q-474, 1767. Simon Hancock to John Tayloe 100 a. that had belonged in turn to Ann Scarlett; Ann Linton, wife of John L.; Ann Linton, daughter of John and Ann L. and wife of William Hancock; John and Jane L.; and the seller.

27. Fauquier Circuit Superior Court. Glascock vs. Combs, in Chancery, 1842-56, including copy of 1825 deed of trust from Robert Combs to Henry Glascock, is source of data on Robert Combs family.

28. NN M-147, 1763. William L. 400 a. in Fx on drains of Buffeloe Meadow.

29. PW D U-414, 1781. Elliott Monroe and wife Mary of Westmoreland to William L. of PW 312 a. where E.M. formerly dwelt, purchased of Thomas Dawkins. PW D U-

224, 1781. William L. and wife Euphemia to Bernard Hooe 74 a. on the Mountain Road adj. Newman Mathews, William Powell, and Benjamin Dulany. Part of tract purchased of Elliott Monroe. PW D W-360, 1786. W.L. and Euphemia to Bernard Hooe 50 a. part of tract purchased of Elliott Monroe. PW D X-79, 1787. W.L. and Euphemia to Alexander Bruce 195 a. on a branch of Broad Run, part of tract from Elliott Monroe.

30. PW D Q-423, 1767. John L. to John Hancock. Land bounded "on Bay of Occoquon, on land belonging to the heirs of the late John Linton Sr. deceased, on Mr. Jabez Downman's tract, and on Morumpsco Creek containing by estimate 200 acres commonly known by the name of Shadding Bay." Tayloe Papers, op. cit. Spence Grayson and John L. Sr. to Jabez Downman 26 a. on SW side of Morrumpsco, 1763..

31. John Glassford & Co., Colchester store, 1769. Both John Linton and John L. Jr. have accounts. Probably are John 3, William 2 and John 3, John 2. PW D X-237, 1789. John L. and wife Betty to William Davis Jr. 120 a. which John Linton Sr. had bought in 1727 from James Bland. This tract had been willed by John 1 to his daughter Constant who married George Brett. Unless the sellers were her heirs, how did they come to own it? PW D Y-71, 1791. Wm. Downman to Betty Linton lease during the natural life of lessee of 150 a. bounded on NW by the main road from Colchester to Dumfries. Witnessed by Wm. Linton and Jno. Linton. All other copies of signatures of any W.L. or J.L. showed the unabbreviated first name.

Chapter XIX

Calverts of Northern Virginia

Various members of the Calvert family, whose first representative came to Stafford County before 1690, lived between Quantico Creek and Powells Creek until well after the Revolution. (1) How closely the line in Prince William County was related to the direct descendants of Lord Baltimore has not been determined. The men were "planters," owners of land, but not powerful members of the Virginia gentry.

Like most families of their era, the Calvert males who survived beyond the age of thirty had a good many children. Very often the older sons were called George and John, making it difficult to tell who was who among contemporaries of the same name. In this chapter we attempt to clarify some of the relationships among those Calverts who resided in northern Virginia during the eighteenth century, but several genealogical questions remain unresolved.

George Calvert (? – ca. 1700)
(George 1)

The first Calvert to become a neighbor of the Harrison family on the southwestern side of the Potomac was the George Calvert who in 1690/91 witnessed the bill of sale of cattle from Richard Nixon to the immigrant Burr. Another mention of this initial George Calvert came in a 1695 grant for land bounded by a path to his home and that of Samuel Jackson; it placed Calvert's residence near the mouth of Quantico Creek.

To our knowledge these two are the only times that George 1 is cited in the extant Stafford records. Since there is no mention of him in Liber Z, we assume he died ca. 1700. (2)

222

Charles Calvert (ca. 1663-1731)

Before continuing with the descendants of George 1, we should note that Charles Calvert, a great-grandson of the first Lord Baltimore, grandson of Leonard Calvert (1610-1649), and son of William Calvert (1644-1733), lived for some years on the Machotick (now Machodoc) creek. A 1705 land grant to Charles provides the information that he had married Mary Howson, the daughter of Robert Howson.

When Charles returned to Maryland after Mary died, he left behind two young daughters in the care of Sarah Hewitt. Anne, the elder of the two, married Thomas Porter about 1715 and had children. Sarah married Nathaniel Jones before 1721. Her eldest son John Jones (ca. 1720-1762) sold Dr. Gustavus Brown in 1756 the share of Charles Calvert's land that had been inherited by his mother. (3)

George Calvert (ca.1690-1771)
(George 2)

A second George Calvert appeared in the Stafford records on the 1723 quitrent roll, on which he was billed for 417 acres. The next year he added through an original grant 92 acres on both sides of Powells Run. In 1731 with his wife, Constant, he deeded 100 acres to John Colverd of Prince William "in consideration of love, good will, and affection for our loving friend and brother." The lot was on or near Powells and adjoined land on which John was living. Signatures of the donors were copied George GC Colverd and Constant CC Colverd.

It has been inferred that George 2 and John 2 were sons of George 1, but the suggestion has not been corroborated. It could be that the John Calvert who received the bounty for killing a wolf in 1703 was their father.

The 1736 rent roll showed George with 400 acres, roughly equal to 419 + 92 - 100. That year he sold John Kincheloe 300 acres on Powell's Run, but apparently the deed was not recorded.

George's first wife, Constant, died before 1741, when his second wife submitted the estate accounts of Francis Stone, who had been her husband, signing them Esther Calvert. It has been suggested that Constant was the daughter of Edward and Ann Barton whose oldest daughter born before 1690 was named Constant. We know of nothing more than the coincidence of first names to support the hypothesis; the fact that none of Calvert's known children were given such Barton names as Thomas, Edward, or Nathan argues against it. The maiden name of Esther Stone Calvert is also unknown.

In 1749 John Tayloe leased 150 acres on the west side of the road to Quantico Mill to George Calvert, shoemaker, for his lifetime and those of his sons, John and George. In a deposition made in 1800, Humphrey Calvert, aged seventy-one years, named two more sons of George 2, i.e., himself and William, and reconfirmed that John and George were sons.

George 2 died in 1771. His will recorded in a lost book evidently named his widow, Esther; his stepson Thomas Stone; and Obed Calvert as his executors, for they were bonded for the administration of his estate. (4)

John Calvert (ca. 1695-ca. 1735)
(John 2)

In 1723 John Calvert, the brother of George 2, paid quitrents on 100 acres. The next year he and Jacob Gibson obtained a grant for 712 acres on Powells Creek and the North Run of Quantico. Later the partners divided the tract into halves. John 2 died before 1736, since he was no longer on the quitrent rolls in that year. (5)

George Calvert Jr. (ca. 1715-1782?)
(George 3, John 2)

The only Calvert on that 1736 list was George 2, but on the next extant roll, that of 1739, he was joined by George Calvert Jr., who paid on 406 acres. Then the latter sold John Gregg 306 acres on Powells Run described as half of the grant to Jacob Gibson and John Calvert dec'd, the father of the grantor. George Jr. had been living on the tract. His wife Ann released her rights to the parcel.

George Jr. had witnessed the will that Jacob Gibson wrote in 1734, making bequests to seven children, the youngest of whom was named Ann. It would not be much of a surprise to find that Ann Gibson later became Mrs. George Calvert.

George Calvert Jr., so termed to distinguish him from his uncle, was not on the 1752 quitrent roll, the next extant after 1739. However, he continued to reside in Prince William at least until 1761, when he voted in a poll for burgesses. Since no will or other record of his death was made in Prince William, he probably moved away, very likely to Culpeper County.

In 1798 a Culpeper deed from a John Calvert of that county acting as attorney for Sarah and Ann Calvert of Baltimore recited a long history. The tract had come into the Calvert family in 1777, when purchased by a George Calvert Jr. In 1778 the land was "made over" to an earlier John Calvert and then the next year by that John to George Calvert Sr. Afterwards it "reverted" to John as heir of George Sr., and finally by John's will was bequeathed to Sarah and Ann, "parties" to the 1798 deed. (6)

George 3, John 2 was perhaps the George Sr. of the Culpeper deed. George 2 died before 1777; his son, the other George 3, did not die until 1802. Of course, the Culpeper Calverts might not have originated in Prince William, but all the people mentioned in the deed had names commonly used by the Prince William family. A Calvert family living by the turn of the century near Upperville in the northern part of Fauquier came there from Culpeper.

Obed Calvert (ca. 1725-?)

An Obed Calvert first appeared in the Prince William records as witness to a 1749 deed. By 1751 he was a freeholder paying quitrents on 100 acres, an amount that he was shown as holding on the other remaining rolls through that of 1767. In 1769 a survey was made for him of 212 acres at the "head of Neabsco," adjoining his own land "formerly George Calvert's." It did not specify which George Calvert was that previous owner.

Therefore, the survey provides little help in defining whether Obed was a son of George 2 or John 2. An analysis of the rent roll data is also inconclusive in that regard. Obed's appearance on the 1752 roll coincides with the disappearance from it of George Calvert Jr. The latter had held 406 acres in 1739; after selling 306 to John Gregg, he had left 100 inherited from his father. No record of his disposition of the 100 acres survives; it may be that George Jr. transferred the plot to Obed.

However, the rolls also show in 1752 an equal decrease of 100 acres in the holdings of George Calvert Sr.; they drop from 400 in 1739 to 300. A note made by the collector beside the entry in 1752--"50 acres each to Humphrey and George Calvert"--probably explains the reduction. Yet no entry is made for either son in 1752 or on any subsequent roll. Thus, the collector's note may have meant their acreages were included in the 300 charged to their father. So conceivably it may have been George Sr. who was the source of Obed's 100 acres.

The rent rolls show that almost certainly Obed inherited 62 acres on the death of George Sr., whose holdings decrease from 300 acres to 67 in 1760 and 62 in 1767, while his sons John and William appear with 100/100 and 50/55 acres, respectively. Obed continues with 100. In 1773 George Sr. no longer figures;

John and William remain unchanged; but Obed is now charged with 374 acres. That number can be accounted for as 100 owned since 1752 plus 212 of his 1771 grant and 62 that exactly match those George Sr. had held in 1767, before his death.

In addition to the connection hinted at in the analysis of the quitrents, there is the fact that George Sr. (George 2) named Obed an executor of his will. The major block to concluding that Obed was the son of George 2 is that he is omitted from the sons named in the 1802 deposition by Humphrey Calvert.

We see two possible explanations of this complicated affair. Perhaps Humphrey did not include Obed because he had died before 1802, while the other four sons were still alive. Alternatively, Obed may have been the orphan of John 2, adopted by his uncle and considered by him more as a son than a nephew.

Obed seems to be the first Calvert with that given name. If true, it may have come from his mother's family. Since we did not make a specific search for earlier Obeds in the region, we can only note two contemporaries, Obed Cornwell and Obed Harris. Peter and Charles Cornwell were next-door neighbors of the Calverts and Calvert/Harris/Harrisons. So perhaps Obed Calvert's mother was a Cornwell. Similarly, the name of Calvert's wife is unknown. Looking for earlier men named Jesse might lead to her maiden name. (7)

On the last quitrent roll compiled in 1777, Obed Calvert is charged with 262 acres, Obadiah Jr. with 53, and Jesse with 59. The sum of 374 acres equals Obed's total in 1773. Jesse had been one of the chain carriers for the 1769 survey leading to Obed's grant on the Neabsco.

No record of the death of Obed exists in Prince William. Either it was in one of the lost will books or he moved away, possibly to live in his old age with an adult child. His sons, Jesse and Obed Jr., lived out their lives in Prince William. Jesse died intestate in Prince William in 1802; an order for the appraisal of his estate was minuted in December of that year with (his brother?) Obed heading the appraisers. We don't know if he left a widow or any children.

Another Jesse Calvert died in Prince William in 1815 leaving all his estate to his wife, Elizabeth, unless she remarried. In that case she was to have the use of only a third, and after her death the whole estate was to be divided equally among his children: Elias, Susan, Elizabeth, Nancy, Catherine, Aidy, Jesse, James, Presley, and Barrard. None of his daughters was married as yet.

Obed Jr. died in 1805. The first three or four pages of his will are missing, but the part that is left starts with bequests to his four "youngest" children: Samuel, John, Betsey, and Rhody (a son). Samuel was of age but unmarried; the last three were under age. Obed Calvert and James Peake were the executors. Jeremiah Calvert and Isaac Calvert witnessed the will. (8)

Humphrey (1729-1802)
(Humphrey 3, George 2)

Except for his deposition in 1802 and the note on the 1752 rent roll, the only mention of Humphrey Calvert that we have found in the Prince William records is that he voted in the 1761 election of burgesses in Prince William. (The other Calverts voting were his cousin, George Jr.; his brothers, George the Younger, John, and William; and Jacob.) As the owner of fifty acres, he would have been eligible to vote even if he did not make his home in the county. (9)

John (ca.1730-1788)
(John 3, George 2)

John Calvert m. (1) Susanna ---- , (2) Elizabeth ----. Children: Enoch, John, Chloe, Charlotte, Elizabeth.
A John Colvert co-signed the bond of Sarah Colvert for her administration of the estate of her husband, Thomas Colvert (alias Harrison), in 1754. He must have been over twenty-one and a property owner thought to have sufficient resources to back up his signature. Three years later John Calvert and his wife, Susanna, were sued in the Prince William court. In this period he was the only adult John Calvert residing in the county.
In 1779 John sent in his account for a year as guardian of Nancy Owens, the daughter of Joshua Owens. It included the expenditure of thirty pounds for board and schooling. Nothing in the report showed whether Nancy was a relative or not.
John 3 died in 1788. His inventory, which included six slaves, and the account of his estate sale were submitted by his administrators, John Redman and Elizabeth Calvert. Elizabeth Calvert, obviously his widow, bought most of the household goods. Other buyers included John, Francis, Zelah, and Thomas Calvert. (10)

George Calvert the Younger (ca. 1727-1802)
(George 3, George 2)

George Calvert had children: George, John, Cynthia, Levi,

227

Margaret.

Like some others in the family George Calvert the Younger was a part-time policeman. In 1755 he was paid for being a "patroller" and in 1761 for serving as a constable. That he followed the occupation of his father, George 2, is shown by his having the orphan Samuel Dobbins bound to him as an apprentice to learn the shoemaker's trade.

Partly because of the loss of many records and partly because he was a tradesman with few debts to pay or collect, other notices of this George Calvert were sparse. Nevertheless, the note made by the collector of quitrents in 1752 was confirmed in a 1785 deed covering fifty acres sold by George Calvert, who described the land as his part of a tract divided by his father, George 2, between himself and his brother Humphrey.

The inventory of his estate was ordered in 1803, but no will was recorded. The next year, Cynthia, who identified herself as a daughter of George Calvert, complained about the actions of the administrator of his estate, John Calvert. The outcome of this family squabble was not revealed. (11)

William (1732–1812)
(William 3, George 2)

William Calvert m. (1?) Caty Korn, (2) Hannah ----.
Children: Elisha (1758–1784), Basil (1760–1833), John (1762–1824), Landon (1764–1809), Gerrard (1765–1840), and William b. 1768.

William Calvert bought 117 acres on the north side of the North Run of Neabsco in 1779. He and his wife, Hannah, sold that land plus 65 acres given him by his father, George, to Arrington Wickliff in 1796. (12)

Jacob (ca. 1735?–1772)
(Jacob 4, George 3?, John 2?)

George Calvert, not otherwise identified, and Jacob Calvert were bonded for the administration of the estate of Richard Crupper in 1761. Shortly afterwards, John Crupper, the "orphan of Richard," was apprenticed to Jacob Calvert. Jacob voted in 1761, demonstrating he was of age and a landowner; yet he was not on any extant rent roll. Then in 1772 Sarah and Francis Calvert and their securities, "George Calvert of Deep Hole" and William Farrow, signed a bond as administrators of Jacob Calvert, deceased. (13)

These are essentially all the clues the Prince William

archives provide for fitting Jacob into the Calvert family. We guess that he was a son of George Calvert Jr. from the latter's association with Jacob Gibson. Even if the wife of George Jr. was not Ann Gibson as we have conjectured, Jacob Calvert could well have been named for the friend of his presumed father.

Nevertheless, we really don't know who was Jacob's father nor do we have much of an idea about how Francis Calvert and George Calvert of Deep Hole fitted into the extended Calvert family or why they acted as executor and co-signer, respectively, of the administrative bond. Francis was a buyer at the estate sale of John 3, George 2. In the listing of British Mercantile Claims he was put down for a debt incurred in 1776 with the notation "removed to North or South Carolina about 15 years ago," i.e., ca. 1785. George of Deep Hole was not designated that way again in Prince William, as far as we know. He was probably a son of either George Jr. or George the Younger. (14)

In 1803 another Jacob Calvert died. His will instructed that "my trusty slave Jacob who hath assisted me in accumulating the property I now possess be emancipated." His wife was to be executor and to receive all his estate, unless she remarried. In that case she was to have only half and the balance was to be shared equally by six persons headed by his brother John. (15)

That brother was apparently the John Calvert Jr. who owned 100 acres of the 1686 Brent Town Tract of 30,000 acres. He held it under Robert Bristoe's one-fourth share in the original patent, which had been inherited by a descendant of the same name who had died in England in 1776. When the Commonwealth of Virginia expropriated the properties of British subjects, it had to review the claims of Virginia citizens who had bought or leased parts of such tracts. So in 1780 the court decided in the case of the Bristoe land to "reserve" from confiscation Calvert's lot among others. Two descendants of the first Burr Harrison similarly affected were Timothy Peyton and John Farrow.

In 1768 this John Calvert had been surveyor of a road. The British Mercantile Claims file showed him with a debt due in 1776 and noted that he had removed to one of the Carolinas "about one year ago." (16)

It is by no means certain that the second Jacob and his brother John were sons of the Jacob who died in 1772. John was junior to John 3, George 2, but not his son. Most likely John 4, John 3 was the witness paid as John Calvert the Younger for seven days in court on behalf of John 3. John the

229

Younger would have become John Jr. after his father's death in 1788, and he was termed so in the British Claims, when he too "removed southward" about 1800.

Reuben Calvert (ca. 1735-1778)
(Reuben 4)

Reuben Calvert m. Sarah ----. She m. (2) Charles Dial/Doyle. Calvert children: Thomas and maybe others.

It would seem that the Reuben Calvert who took William Calvert's place as constable in 1763 was a birthright member of the Prince William Calvert clan, since he lived on Powells Creek in the area where the tribe had its "headquarters." Still, he is another that we are unable to place on the family tree, and an earlier Reuben had been born in Richmond County in 1703.

Reuben of Prince William was probably only a little younger than the "cousin" whom he succeeded as the law officer. He did not vote in the 1761 election, probably because he did not own the required fifty acres of land, (twenty-five if it had a house). In 1773 he purchased from Peter and Sarah Cornwell the 185 acres on the south branch of Powells originally granted to Burditt Harrison in 1730/1.

Reuben died in 1778. His inventory was recorded that year and so was his estate account presented by his widow Sarah. (We wonder if she was another Cornwell.) The account included a payment to William Calvert and a charge for the maintenance of his two youngest (unnamed) children. That his oldest son and heir was called Thomas was made evident when "Charles Dial and Sarah, his wife, formerly Sarah Calvert (widow) of Reuben Calvert dec'd and Thomas Calvert heir-at-law of the said Reuben Calvert and Mary Embly his wife" sold part of Reuben's 185-acre farm. In signing the deed Sarah's second husband made his mark, but Sarah "Doyle," Thomas Calvert, and Mary Embly Calvert all wrote out their signatures in full. (17)

In 1826 the land owned by a Reuben Calvert, no doubt a son or grandson of the man who died in 1778, was divided among his widow, Sarah C. Calvert, and his children, Alexander, Colin, Susannah (Mrs. Benjamin Tyler), Janet (Mrs. William Webster), Chloe Ann, Ruben, Sarah, Nancy, and Robert Alexander, the last five being underage. The properties were situated between the Occoquan and Neabsco, near the tract purchased by William Calvert in 1779.

Although no member of the large and evidently closely knit Prince William Calvert family "rose" to the positions of prominence and authority held by some of their Harrison neighbors, they still played a role in the development of Virginia. One example of the influence that they and people like them had on the structure of American society came in a petition sent to Virginia's new governing body in Richmond two months before the Declaration of Independence.

The petitioners, members of a group that would become the Occoquan Baptist Church, asked that they be allowed to worship God in their own way without interruption, maintain their own ministers, and be "married, buried, and the like without paying persons of any other denomination." If their request was granted, they promised to join with members of those other denominations "to promote the common cause of Freedom."

The forty-nine signers were all from the area between the Occoquan and the Neabsco, all men, all "ordinary" people challenging the ruling class and its institutions in the name of freedom and democracy. Five Calverts signed: Obed Sr., Obed Jr., William, Rolley, and Jesse.

Failure to define more exactly the identities of those individuals and other Prince William Calverts is primarily due to the loss of so many county records and to limiting the search to northern Virginia and the eighteenth century. Working back toward these data in time and place may clear up some of the uncertainties. (18)

Notes:

1. The 1810 census listed seven Calvert heads of households in PW: Catherine, Francis, two Johns, Reuben, Vincent, and William.
2. Md. Hist. 16-192. Major Nicklin's review of the Calvert family states George Calvert of Stafford was born in Maryland, a descendant of the first Lord Baltimore, and married Elizabeth Doyne. Nugent, *Cavaliers and Pioneers*, p. 146, 1643. 300 a. on Point Comfort Creek granted to John Calvert, brother and heir of Dr. George Calvert. Were they related to George 1 and John 1 of Stafford? St 1686-94 p.184, 1690/1. George Calvert witnesses sale of cattle by Nixon to Burr Harrison. NN 2-154, 1695. Grant to William Champ adj. George C.
3. W D 4-96, 1707. Confirms Charles is son of William Calvert. NN-3, 1705. Grant to Charles Calvert. St (lost) Liber M 1731-1739, Index, p. 34-35. Calvert to Porter. St D O-116, 1756. John Jones bond to Dr. Gustavus Brown.
4. NN A-43, 1724. 92 a. to George Calvert. PW D A-25, 1731. George Colverd and wife Constant for love to brother

John Colverd 100 a. between land of Elias Hore and others and the land where he "now liveth." PW W C-239, 1739. Will of Francis Stone. PW W C-302, 1741. Francis Stone estate account by widow Esther administratrix, who signs Esther Calvert. PW D M-1, 1749. John Tayloe lease to George Calvert. PW O p.105, 1753. George Calvert overseer of road to Quantico Church. PW D Q-623, 1760. George Calvert had sold John Kincheloe, the father of Cornelius Kincheloe, 300 acres on Powell's Run in 1736. Land now encumbered. Calvert agrees to relieve Kincheloe of any liability. PW W B-97, 1771. George Calvert dec'd. Widow Esther, Obed Calvert, and Thomas Stone give adm. bond with Foushee Tebbs and Thomas Blackburn securities.

5. NN A-345, 1724. Grant to John Calvert and Jacob Gibson. PW W C-35, 1734, pr. 1735. Will of Jacob Gibson. Wife Jane. Children: Abraham, Mary Parker, Jacob, Sarah Lambeth, Jann Turner, Isaac, and Ann.

6. PW D D-141, 1739. George C. Jr. sells John Gregg 306 a. F D 6-393, 1777. George Calvert of Culpeper 161 1/2 a. in Fauquier from Jesse and Mary Williams. F D 6-540, 1778. George Calvert of Culpeper to Martin Pickett land purchased of Jesse Williams whereon Calvert has a plantation. Signed: George Calvert Jr. and Lydia Calvert. C W D-117, 1794. George Calvert dec'd. C W D-139, 1797. John C. dec'd. C D T-298, 1798. John C. by virtue of power from sisters Sarah and Ann C. to William Deatherage.

7. PW D L-195, 1749. Obed Calvert a witness. PW O p.244, 1756. Obed C. a patroler. PW O 1759-61 p.87. Obed C. surveyor of road. Joyner, NN Surveys 3-96, 1769. Obed Calvert 212 a. on head of Neabsco adj. own land, formerly George Calvert's, and that of John and James Peake. PW D I-205, 1772. Obed C. 212 a. on Neabsco.

8. PW W H-508, 1802. Appraisal of Jesse Calvert estate. PW W I-53, 1804, pr. May 1805. Will of Obed Calvert missing pp.49-52 that include its first part.

9. PW Land Causes 1808-43, p.178. Humphrey Calvert deposition.

10. When children are listed without back-up data, the source is the G.H.S.King Papers. PW O p.244, 1756. John Calvert a patroller paid 50 lbs. tobacco. PW O p.262, 1757. Richard Sturman ag. John C. & wife Susanna. PW W G-61, 1779. John C. account as guardian of Nancy Owens. PW W G-395, 1788. Inventory of John C. includes 6 slaves valued at 265 pounds, cattle and other stock at 111 pounds,

total 599/5/0. PW W H–102, 1788. Estate sale of John C.
11. PW O p.313, 1753. Samuel Dobbins bound to George
Calvert the Younger. PW O p.19, 1755. George C. the
Younger a patroller. PW O p.211, 1760. Richard Grigsby
vs. George C. the Younger for trespass. PW D W–245,
1785. George C. to John Chick. No release by a wife. PW
W G–434, pr. 9/9/1789. Will of John Chick leaves this
tract to daughter Nancy (Chick) Powell. Children: Charles,
William, Reuben, Alis, Susanna, and Nancy all under age.
PW W H–524, 1803. Inventory of George C. ordered. PW
W, 1804. John Calvert, adm. estate of George C., father of
Cynthia. Fayette Co., Ky. W B–821. Will of Levi Calvert,
(son of George the Younger). Children include Peyton,
Jesse, and George.
12. PW O p.38, 1761. William Calvert constable in place of
John Calvert. PW D U–167, 1779. Robert Key to William
C. 117 a. part of tract granted Wm. Champe in 1712 on N.
run of Neabsco. PW D Z–82, 1796. William C. & wife
Hannah sell Arrington Wycliffe 114 a. bought of Key plus
65 a. gift from father, George C., in 1754.
13. PW O p.250, 1761. John Crupper, orphan of Richard, bound
to Jacob Calvert. PW Bond Book, p.102, 1772. Bond for
Jacob C. dec'd.
14. VG 20–263, British Mercantile Claims. Debt of Francis
Calvert due 1776.
15. PW W H–522, 1803. Jacob Calvert will, pr. April 1803.
16. PW Land Causes 1754–1811, p.99. The Bristoe litigation.
PW O 1762. John Calvert the Younger witness for John C.
PW O 1768. John Calvert Jr. surveyor of road.
17. Register of North Farnum Parish. Reubin Calvert, son of
Christopher and Anne Calvert, b. Nov. 1682. PW O 1763.
Reuben Calvert constable in place of Wm. C. PW Y–418,
1794. Charles Dial and Sarah, his wife, et al to Zachariah
Allen. VG 20–263, British Merc. Claims, Wm. Cunningham & Co., Falmouth Store. PW W G–7, May 1778.
Inventory of Rhuben Calvert. PW W G–31, 1778. Estate
acct. of Reuben C. PW Land Causes 1805–1849, p. 178,
1826. Division estate of Reuben C., dec'd.
18. A family of Calverts who lived on the Opequon in Fr from
1735 to at least 1760 bore no known relation to those of
PW. It included John who died before 1754 and his children Richard, Rebeckah, and Ann. V Jan–Mar., 1970.
Calverts of southern Fauquier are not related to those of
PW. Descend from Robert Covert of Md. Include Samuel
(of Culpeper), Charity (Calvert) Ford, and Levin.

Chapter XX

Other Harrison Families

In addition to the Burr Harrison family, there were unrelated (or not proved to be related) Harrisons in northern Virginia during the colonial period. Little is known of their antecedents in England, and in many cases the name of the immigrant ancestor has not been discovered. This chapter presents what we have learned about these other Harrisons, especially with regard to their genealogical data.

The first of these other Harrisons to arrive in Virginia's Northern Neck got there just before the immigrant Burr Harrison. In 1654 Mrs. Francis Harrison, a widow, obtained a grant of 1000 acres between Aquia Creek and a branch of the Chopawamsic; lands of Mr. Valentine Peyton and Capt. Giles Brent adjoined the property. Twenty headrights supporting the "devident" included her own and those of Dr. Jeremy Harrison. A patent issued in 1666 to Capt. Giles Brent, apparently for the same land, gave a slightly different history, reciting an original patent to John Harrison in 1655 transferred "for want of heirs of his body to his sister (-in-law) Mrs. Frances Harrison and for want of heirs of her body to" Brent. (1)

The two patents establish that neither John Harrison nor Dr. Jeremy (presumably the husband of Mrs. Frances) had direct heirs. Nevertheless, some researchers believe that they were related to the progenitor of a Harrison family who lived north of the Rappahannock in the latter part of the seventeenth century and had many descendants. Among its earliest members are thought to be Mathew Harrison, a witness in a Westmoreland court action in 1659, and John Harrison, plaintiff in a suit there in 1664. Thomas Harrison witnessed the signature of Elizabeth Mott, the "relict" of George Mott, in 1674. Soon after, Elizabeth married James Harrison, who sued in Stafford court in 1689 on behalf of Ellen Mott, an orphan. James, educated and well off, became a justice of Richmond County. He died in 1712 survived only by his daughter Jael, Mrs. William Williams. (2)

George Harrison (died 1713)

With the exception of James the fate of those early Westmoreland Harrisons is uncertain. However, much more detail survived concerning a George Harrison who in partnership with William Linton in 1671 bought from John Williams 450 acres at the head of the Yeocomico River. When he sold part of this land three years later, he was designated as a planter in the deed and was able to sign his name, indicating he had had some education. From then on until his death in 1713, George appeared with some regularity in the Westmoreland records. He and his wife, Elizabeth, the daughter of Peter Dunkin, had at least seven sons: Thomas, George, John, James, Peter, and William. Twelve known Harrison grandsons included the Jeremiah Harrison who died in Fairfax in 1751, naming in his will brothers Mathew and George and a son Mathew. (3)

The main reason for mentioning this family is that some Harrisons who were in closer geographical contact with Burr Harrison, and his descendants may have been related to it.

Thomas Harrison (died ca. 1690)

Two such Harrisons, Thomas and John, showed up in the Stafford records near the end of the seventeenth century. Thomas, possibly the Westmoreland man, appeared in 1685/6 when he bought land on Accotink Creek from William Greene. In 1692 he (or his son Thomas) sold the tract to John Holmes. In 1690 his estate was docked by creditors of John Harrison, seemingly one of his heirs. John was in such deep financial troubles that he had fled the county. (4)

Thomas Harrison (? – 1725/6)

Thomas Harrison m. Ann ———— d. 1725/6. Their children:
Catherine m. William Rowley of King George.
Jane m. (1) Joseph Winlock, (2) Robert English Jr.
Frances m. Joshua Davis of Stafford.
Anne m. ———— Griffith

A grant in 1695 of land in the Pasbetanzy area of Stafford (now Passapatanzy in King George), some twenty miles south of the Chopawamsic, noted the tract adjoined land belonging to

235

Thomas Harrison. Per the 1723 quitrent roll for Overwharton Parish (Stafford) Thomas Harrison paid on 350 acres, and in the following year's list of tobacco tenders he and three Negroes and a Negro boy were looking after 27,000 plants in the section of the parish from its lower end (the Pasbetanzy) to the south side of Potomac Creek.

The wills of Thomas Harrison and his wife, Ann, were recorded on consecutive pages of lost Stafford Book K. They died in 1725/6 survived by four daughters, known from later documents by which each disposed of her inherited share of her father's 350 acres. (5)

While the antecedents of Thomas of Pasbetanzy are unknown, he may have been the son of the man who bought the land on the Accotink. Either through that Thomas or independently, some link to the Westmoreland family may have existed, since the Pasbetanzy was near the seventeenth century border of Stafford with Westmoreland. Definitely, he was not the son of George nor the father of Thomas and Burditt Harrison of the 1729 grant on Pohick Creek.

William Harrison (ca. 1675-1724)
(William 1)

William Harrison m. Sarah Halley (1680?-1778), dau. of Henry and Sybil. Their children:

William (1703-1745).

Sybil (1705-1787) m. 1725 Hugh West.

George (1707-1748/9).

Sarah (1708/9-1789) m. (1) Thomas Triplett, m. (2) John Manley.

Mary (ca. 1715-?) m. (1) John Browne (2) John Peake.

Much more closely associated with the family of Burr Harrison was the Captain William Harrison who was the partner in the West-Harrison-Pearson-Harrison Hunting Creek grant of 1707. He has even been assumed by some to be a son of the first Burr. However, no proof exists of that relationship, which appears to be based on William's association with Burr's son Thomas, his residence in the general area, his age being in the range of Burr's known sons, and perhaps on his having a daughter named Sybil, the same as Burr's daughter, Sybil Whitledge. (More likely, William's daughter was named for her maternal grandmother, Sybil Halley.)

William Harrison appeared first in the Stafford records in 1700, when he was paid the bounty for killing two wolves. He was not yet a militia captain in 1702, but became one later. In that year he was enrolled in Captain (later Major) John West's company of Dragoons. Since the county militia was organized on a geographical basis, at the time William probably lived nearer to Captain West than to Captain Thomas Harrison, that is, north of the Occoquan rather than in the vicinity of the Quantico.

All efforts to determine where Harrison came from originally and how he came into possession of his property in the northern part of Stafford have failed. The warrants for his first land grants were not issued until 1704. Possibly he was living on a "quarter" belonging to his father, or he may have leased or bought land and later sold it. The fact that no trace of a bequest, lease, purchase, or sale has been found could be attributable to the irretrievable loss of almost all Stafford deeds of the time.

Harrison's patents were primarily for land north of the Occoquan in what is now Fairfax County, the one exception being for 190 acres on Powells Run. (6) Perhaps he lived at some time near that creek. The Halleys, his wife's family, had land on the Neabsco, the next creek north of Powells. However, they also owned land on the Accotink. Some spouses of his children came from one neighborhood and some from the other.

Harrison purchased two of his properties in partnership with Richard Watts of Westmoreland. Neither was directly on the Accotink, but both were close by. By coincidence the 14,114 acres on both sides of the Accotink and Pohick granted Cadwallader Jones and David Jones in 1677 included among 282 transportees a William Harrison and a Richard Watts. (7)

Within a few years William had accumulated 3300 acres, his share of patents from the Proprietors. The 1723 quitrent roll showed him holding 3302. He would have owed 792 pounds of tobacco on that acreage, but he paid only 500, the balance being in dispute with Col. Lee, the collector.

William Harrison died in 1724, as proved by a grant of 281 acres on the Potomac and Sugarlands Creek made the following year to his widow Sarah on behalf of his elder son, William. The survey had been requested by William Sr. (8)

His will and inventories, which might have shed light on his origins, were recorded in the lost Stafford Book K. His widow presented an additional inventory and estate account in 1734, signing as Sarah S Lewis, executrix.

Sarah (Halley) Harrison Lewis was sixty-eight years old in 1749, the year Thomas Lewis, her second husband, died. She was almost one hundred years old when she died in 1778.

The riddle of the ancestry of Captain William Harrison has

237

intrigued researchers. In addition to the idea that Burr Harrison was his father, it has been suggested that he was the son of William Harris of the Harrys-Baxter-Harrys patent of 1669. A main objection to that proposition is that William Harris was never called Harrison in any Stafford document. It seems implausible that the literate Captain William Harrison would have chosen to change his surname. The hypothetical father-son relationship remains without supporting evidence.

Another conjecture is that he was the son of the Thomas Harrison who purchased the Accotink land that later became the property of Major John West, whose son Hugh married William's daughter Sybil. Again nothing which would uphold the theory remains in the records, but neither is there anything to disprove it.

At any rate he seems to be related in some way to the "Westmoreland Harrisons." Note his connections with Westmoreland people such as Richard Watts, the likelihood that his wife Sarah Halley spent her early childhood in that county, and the congruence of his sons' names, William and George, with those used by the Westmoreland family. However, after so many searchers have failed to uncover definitive records, success now is going to require both perseverance and a bit of luck.

William Harrison (ca. 1704–1745)
(William 2, William 1)

William Harrison m. (1732) Isabella (Triplett) Hore. Their children:
Susannah m. 1750 Robert Slaughter.
Sarah m. 1756 John Monroe.
Margaret m. 1757 Edward Blackburn.
Mary m. John Waller.

A clause in the 1716 will of Major John West bequeathed a "young horse to Will Harrison Jr." The lad was the elder of two sons of Captain William Harrison.

William (Jr.) was one of the members of the commission of peace named for Prince William when it was divided from Stafford in 1731. The next year he married Isabella (Triplett) Hore, a daughter of William and Isabella (Miller) Triplett. His bride was the widow of Captain Elias Hore, who had died two years previously, leaving two sons and two daughters. (9)

The couple soon moved to Stafford County, where Harrison was made a justice in 1737. In 1742 he became an inspector at the Aquia warehouse.

238

Harrison died in 1745 survived by Isabella, his step-children, and four daughters. His widow was named executrix and guardian of her children. She did not marry again, though she survived her husband by eighteen years. (10)

George Harrison (ca. 1707–1749)
(George 2, William 1)

George Harrison m. Martha Cooke? She m. (2) John Posey.

Neither of the sons of William Harrison Sr. had sons to carry on the Harrison name. William Jr. had only daughters, and his brother George had no children.

George and his wife, Martha, lived in Fairfax County next-door to the church which gave its name to the present-day city of Falls Church. Harrison was a prominent communicant of the church and was named a vestryman of Truro Parish in 1743. His property, most of which was inherited from his father, adjoined the West-Harrison-Pearson-Harrison tract. (11)

When George died in 1749, his will bequeathed everything to his wife, Martha, for her lifetime. On her death the estate was to pass to the son of his sister Sybil, John West Jr. The widow Martha soon took John Posey for her husband. (12)

Charles Harrison of Stafford.

In 1700 a Charles Harrison of unknown lineage showed up in the Quantico area of Prince William, near the plantation of Burr Harrison Jr. In 1704 he witnessed a deed of sale by Thomas Baxter, the son of the deceased partner of Burr Harrison Sr. Only one other reference to Charles as a resident of Stafford survived. In 1712 he obtained a grant for 425 acres at the head of the north run of Quantico Creek, bordered by a path from Samuel Jackson's to the Quantico Mill. That path figured in the patent obtained by Thomas Harrison and Abraham Farrow a few years previously. (13)

Because of his living so close to the sons of the immigrant Burr, one is tempted to think that he was their brother. Still, the fact that none of the known grandchildren or great-grandchildren of Burr Sr. was named Charles argues against the idea.

Between 1726 and 1748 a Charles H (his mark) Harrison witnessed three deeds, all for land in the Quantico area. Probably he was the literate man's son, deprived of schooling by being orphaned at an early age. If this presumption is correct, he rather than his father was the Charles Harrison charged with 190 acres in the 1723 rent roll. (14)

Various John Harrisons

As we have seen, men named John Harrison have been contemporaries of the descendants of Burr Harrison from the latter part of the seventeenth century throughout the eighteenth century. Some of them may have been descended from the immigrant Burr.

They include: John who escaped his debtors in Stafford in 1690; John who witnessed the lease from Thomas Harrison of the Retirement in 1723; John, according to Hayden's *Virginia Genealogies* the son born in 1744 to Cuthbert Harrison; and John who was a neighbor of the Harrisons in southern Fauquier at least from 1760 to 1773 and for whom Colonel Thomas Harrison held cash to pay part of his debt to John Quarles. This last John Harrison lost custody of his daughter Elizabeth in 1764, because he was failing to provide for her education. (15)

Perhaps the most intriguing of the John Harrisons was one born in 1771, reportedly in Fairfax near what is now Alexandria and later resided in Loudoun, probably in the eastern part that was returned to Fairfax in a boundary change in 1798. He moved to Kentucky in 1794 with his younger brother Thomas and their wives, both from Loudoun families. In that year his oldest son, Burr J., was born. His second son was named Cuthbert.

Judging from the names of John's sons, it seems likely that the family descended from the immigrant Burr Harrison. The puzzle is how. It is barely possible that they were descendants of Thomas (1665-1746). More probable is that they were in the line of the Calvert alias Harrisons or of the Thomas and Burditt Harrison of the 1729 land grant on Pohick Creek. (See Chapters VII and XV.) (16)

In summary, George Harrison of Westmoreland must have innumerable descendants living today, many of whom bear the name of Harrison. The genes of Thomas Harrison of Passapatanzy and of William Harrison Sr. have been perpetuated through their daughters and granddaughters, but their Harrison name disappeared in one or two generations. The other Harrisons covered in this chapter could well have a multitude of descendants presently, even including some who have inherited their surname, but so far as we know, no one has been able to trace his ancestry back to any of them.

Notes:

1. Nugent, *Cavaliers and Pioneers*, p. 302, patent 3-319, 1654.

Mrs. Frances Harrison 1000 a. Ibid., p. 565, 5-532, 1666. Capt. Giles Brent 1000 a.

2. See J.F. Dorman's abstracts of Westmoreland deed, will, and order books, Beverley Fleet's of Richmond records, and G.H.S. King's *Marriages of Richmond County*. St 1689-93, p.79, 1690. James Harrison on behalf of Ellen Mott, orphan of George Mott. NN 5-25. Purchase of land by James H. in 1683.

3. W 1665-1677, p. 91a, 1671. John Williams to Linton and Harrison. W 1690-98, p.134, 1694. George Harrison and Elizabeth, his wife, acknowledge deed to Wm. Ramey. NN 2-271, 1697. Grant to George H. NN 3-90, 1704. Peter Dunkin by will gave to daughters, who with their husbands, George H. and Dennis Cornwall sold land in the forest of Nominy. Fx W A-384, 1750/1. Will of "Jeryah" Harrison signed Jeremiah H. names wife Ann, son Mathew, brothers George and Mathew. *National Genealogical Society Quarterly* 53-3, 1965. Descendants of George Harrison. The G.H.S. King papers contain a wealth of genealogical data on this family. Several members of it were contemporaries of Burr 4, Thomas 3, Thomas 2 in Fairfield County, South Carolina. George and Thomas Harrison in Fk before the Revolution may have been of this lineage.

4. St 1689-93 p.126, 1690/1. Wilford vs. Harrison. John H. "absented himself out of this county." St 1686-94 p.208, 1691. Mr. John Harrison debtor to George Andrews. St 1689-93 p.158, 1691. John H. late of this county indebted to George Andrews. Since Harrison had left Stafford, Andrews got a judgment against estate of Thomas Harrison. St 1686-94 p.20, 1685/6. Wm. Greene, planter to Thomas Harrison, planter, on Accotinicks Run, land formerly belonging to William Greene the elder, father to this William.

5. NN 2-213, 1695. Richard Bryan 200 a. on Indian Cabin Branch adj. Thomas Harrison. (In Pasbetanzy area.) St Z-464, 1708/9. Thomas H Harrison appraiser of estate of Jacob Gardner. St Index Liber K 1721-31. Thomas Harrison's will - p.210; inventory - p.225. Ann Harrison's will - p. 211; inventory - p. 226. St D J-517, 1728. Robert English Jr. and wife Jane sell 80 a. in Overwharton bequeathed Jane by will dated 10 Nov. 1725 of her father, Thomas Harrison. PW D B-431, 1735. Joshua Davis sells 328 a. to Edward Barry; wife Frances relinquishes dower rights. O D 6-?, 1783. David Griffith and wife Mary sell land they inherited from his mother Ann, dau. of Thomas Harrison who d. 1725/6.

6. St Z-53, 1700. William Harrison received the bounty for trapping one wolf and shooting another. (He also received bounties for wolves in 1701 and 1703.) Bockstruck, *Virginia Colonial Soldiers*. Op. cit. NN 3-146, 1706. 266 acres on Dogues Run. The permit to make the survey was issued the same day as that for the grant to the West-Harrison-Pearson-Harrison syndicate. (NN 3-153, 1706.) NN 4-2, 1710. 190 acres on both sides of the main run of Powells Creek. NN 5-46, 1714. With Richard Watts 384 acres on Holmes Run a little to the southeast of the syndicate's tract. NN 5-48, 1714. With the Rev. Alexander Scott, rector of Overwharton Parish, 1340 acres on Holmes Run. NN 5-49, 1714. With Richard Watts 2032 acres lying between Difficult Run and Accotinck Creek. On today's map the tract would be bisected by Rt. 123, Chain Bridge Road, just south of the town limits of Vienna.

7. *Cavaliers and Pioneers*, NN 2-191, 1677. Lt. Col. Cadwalader Jones and Mr. David Jones, 14,114 a. on both sides of Accotink and Pohick. Transport of 282 persons incl. William and Jane Greene, William and Mathew Harrison, Wm. Smith, Richard Watts, and Edward Hanston (Humston?).

8. Index to lost St Liber K, 1721-1730, p.99 "Harrison's will," p. 144 "Harrison's inventory," and p.261 "Harrison, William additional inventory." Fx O 1749-1754, p.49, 1749. Sarah Lewis renounces benefit of will of late husband Thomas Lewis and asks for her (dower) rights according to law. Fx O 1749-1754, p.57, 1749. Adm. of estate of John Manley granted to widow Sarah. Fx D G-388, 1768. Division between half-brothers Thomas Triplett and Harrison Manley, sons of Thomas Triplett and John Manley, respectively. F D 5-347, 1772. Col. Richard Henry Lee of Westmoreland to John Peake 174 a. near Turkey Run during the natural lives of himself, wife Mary, and son William Harrison Peake.

9. St W M-20, pr. 1729/30. Will of Elias Hore names wife Isabell, sons Elias and William. Isabell and brother James Hore are executors. St W M-304, 1740. Estate acct. of Elias Hore presented by William Harrison. PW D M-90, 1750. Susannah Harrison witness to division of land between William and Elias Hore (her two half-brothers). Tract had belonged to their father Elias Hore.

10. LR p.99, 1742. William Harrison made inspector at Aquia. Fx O p.455, 1753. Isabella Harrison, guardian of Margaret, Sara, and Mary H., "infants," and Robert and Susannah Slaughter are codefendants in suit. L D C-355, 1762. Edward Blackburn & Margaret, John Monroe & Sarah, to

John Trammell. Their combined half-share of undivided rights to 281 a. Sugarland tract. L D D-397, 1764. Sarah S Lewis, widow of William Harrison to John Trammel. William H made survey but died before patent was granted. Sarah transferred the patent to son William H. (Jr.) who died leaving four daughters, who sold their rights to Trammell. Sarah sells her dower rights to the Sugarland tract.

11. Fx D B1-424, 1748. The plat for a division of 214 a. between George Harrison (son of William) and Michael Ragan shows a house built by Capt. (William) Harrison. He may have lived there near Falls Church in 1723.

12. Fx W A1-260, 1748/9. Will of George Harrison. Fx O p.37, 1754. John West Jr. as adm. of George H. vs. John and Martha Posey.

13. St Z-210, 1703/4. Charles Harrison a witness to deed from Thomas TB Baxter. NN 4-63, 1712. Charles H. 425 a. at head of N run of Quantico on its S side and to north side of path from Samuel Jackson to the Quantico Mill. A Charles Harrison appointed overseer of a road in Northumberland in 1696 may have been related.

14. St D J-268, 1726. Charles H Harrison witness to deed of Margaret Beall to Edward Berry. PW D B-438, 1735. Charles H Harrison witness deed of Peter and John Cornwall of 100 a. on Neabsco to John Tayloe. PW D L-72, 1748. Charles H Harrison witness deed of William and Mary Butler to Joseph Butler of land that adjoins "Horsington's patent" on Powells Run.

15. John Harrison was named at least seven times between Feb. 1760 and Nov. 1773 in F minute books, including July 1764 re custody of Elizabeth and March 1770 as witness for Mary Harrison ag. Robert Ashby. Possibly he was a grandson of George Harrison of Westmoreland.

16. Johnson, *The Harrisons of Virginia, Kentucky and Indiana.*

Appendix A – Statistical Data

Fairfax County List of Titheables for 1749

Totals: Whites 1122 Truro Parish   1207
         Blacks   913 Cameron Parish   828
         Total   2035 Total   2035

(White -- Males of 16 and older.)
(Blacks -- Both sexes of 16 and older.)
(Cameron Parish became Loudoun County in 1756.)

Slave Ownership of Resident Landowners

Blacks/Household	Household		Blacks	
	#	%	#	%
None	468	71	0	0
One	43	7	43	7
Two	38	6	76	13
Three to Six	53	8	105	17
Seven or More	24	4	389	63
Total	626	100	613	100
Non-Residents	30		300	
Grand Total	656		913	

Slave Ownership by the 19 Justices of Fairfax

Four to Six	5		22	
Seven or More	14		271	
Total	19	3%	293	48%

Col. John Colville had 29 black titheables; Major Lawrence Washington had 27; next most among residents Catesby Cocke with 14. By far the biggest slaveholder was the Honorable Thomas Lee of Stratford Hall in Westmoreland, who held 67 black titheables in Fairfax County. Lord Fairfax, whose home was in Frederick, had 15 of the total black titheables and 10 of the whites (one or more overseers plus indentured servants).

The only Harrisons in the county were Thomas (1 white, no black), Samuel, a Quaker, (1 white, no black), and a widow, Mrs. George Harrison, (a white overseer, and 4 blacks).

Analysis of Religious Affiliation

Denomination	Truro	Cameron	Total
Anglican Church	1117	675	1792
Quaker	0	91	91
Roman Catholic	45	31	76
Presbyterian	45	19	64
Anabaptist	0	6	6
Other dissenters	0	6	6
Total	1207	828	2035

Noted as often or sometimes coming to church were one Quaker, three Presbyterians, and 27 "Papists." Ten titheables were noted as former Papists.

The Reverend Charles Green who compiled the list of titheables made the following comments:

> *In 1738 when Cha Green came up as minister of Truro Psh was titheables -- 621. Increased in eleven years -- 1414 [to 2035]. The Quakers live all in Cameron or the upper parish & scarsely one of them ever came to church in my time except Elisha Hall. Before the Parish was divided there was four churches in it 2 whereof now are in the parish of Cameron. At Goose Creek church I never had one communicant. The several times prepared to administer the Sacram' at Rocky Run Church built ab't 3 years since about [original torn] ---- at the two churches in the Lower Parish the falls Church & Pohic Church about 120 constant communicants. [Signed] Cha Green*
> *The country born negros are chiefly baptized.*

The numbers tabulated for the Anglicans are for titheables who did not claim affiliation with another denomination. Presumably all of them were baptized.

Elisha Hall, the only Quaker who ever went to church, was also the only one of the sect to own slaves. He had ten black titheables. None of the Anabaptists or other dissenters owned slaves. Clearly the dissenting churches appealed primarily to the small farmers in the back-country. Although some of their adherents came from Virginian families, most had immigrated from Maryland and Pennsylvania.

Appendix B - Other Families

The Bullitt Family

PW rent rolls for 1736 and 1752 list Capt. Benjamin Bullitt with 1423 a.; for 1754 have Capt. Benjamin B.- 461 1/2 a., Benjamin B. Jr. - 400 a., Thomas B. - 400 a., and Joseph B. - 461 1/2 a. No Bullitt on later rolls since all reside in Fauquier. F Tax lists 1787. Joseph Blackwell's (Southern) District: Cuthbert Bullitt, non-resident 0/19/25/20/54.   Joseph B. 0/5/9/2/7.

Joseph Bullitt
(Joseph 1)

Joseph Bullitt m. Elizabeth Brandt, dau. Capt. Randolph Brandt.

Chas. Co. Md. Liber 6-226.   Will of Capt. Randolph Brandt, dated Dec. 1697, pr. Feb. 1698 (or 1698/99).

Chas. Co. Md. Book Q-1 Reverse, Births and Marriages. Joseph Bullett, the son of Joseph and Elizabeth Bullett of Mattowoman, born 15 Jan. 1688/9. Benjamin Bullett, son of Joseph and Elizabeth B. of Mattowoman, born 28 April 1693.

Benjamin Bullitt (1693-1766)
(Benjamin 2, Joseph 1)

Benjamin Bullitt m. (1?) Sarah ----, m. (2) Elizabeth Harrison, dau. Capt. Thomas Harrison, m. (3) Sarah Burditt? Children: By Sarah - Joseph; by Sarah or Elizabeth - Thomas, Benjamin, Seth (dau.), Cuthbert; by Elizabeth - Elizabeth; by Sarah Burditt - William, John, George, Benoni, Parmanus, Burwell.

St D J-101, 1723/4.   Richard Foote of St Paul's Parish

247

lease to Benjamin Bullitt of Overwharton, 200 a. woodland commonly called Cattaile Pond, N side Cedar Run, "99 years to be compleated" if said Benjamin, wife Sarah, son Joseph shall so long live. Part of great tract of 30,000 a. commonly called Brent Town. (It has been suggested that wife Sarah was Sarah Elizabeth Harrison.)

PW W C-176, 1741. Benjamin B. and Thomas Harrison Jr. are Edward Sute's executors & guardians of his two orphan daughters. Widow named Elizabeth.

PW O-70, 1757. Giles Burditt chose Humphrey Burditt in place of Benjamin B., his former guardian.

F W 1-108, 1766. Will of Benjamin B. pr. October 1766 names sons Joseph, Thomas who gets land in Md. where father Joseph is buried, dau. Seth Combs, son Cuthbert, dau. Elizabeth; six sons William Burditt alias Bullitt, John Bullitt, George, Benoni, Parmanus, Burwell, all less than 18; wife Sarah.

Joseph Bullitt (ca. 1723-1792)
(Joseph 3, Benj. 2, Joseph 1)

Joseph Bullitt m. Barshaba Norman. Children: Susanna, Mary, Priscilla.

F Marr. Book 1-83, 1779. Joseph Bullitt consents to marriage of dau. Mary B. to Randolph Statlard. Ibid. p.133, 1783. Joseph B. consents to marriage of dau. Priscilla to Philip Redd.

F W 2-249, 1792. Will of Joseph B., dated 11/17/1792. pr. Dec. 1792 names wife Barshaba Norman now Bullitt; dau. Susanna Redd and her sons, Joseph Bullitt Redd and Permerus (?) Redd; dau. Mary Steatard (?) and her son Joseph Bullitt Steatard; dau. Priscilla Redd and her son Joseph Bullitt Redd.

Thomas Bullitt (ca. 1725-1778)
(Thomas 3, Benj. 2, Joseph 1)

Thomas Bullitt. Child: Sarah Bronaunt, dau. of Martha Bronaunt. Sarah m. Clement Trigg.

F D 4-360, 1771. Thomas Bullitt to John McMillion, 400 a. on Elk Run, had been gift from father Benjamin, plus negroes and cattle. To be void on repayment of 500 pounds.

F W 1-321, 1778. Will of Thomas B. dated 1775 pr. 1778. Bequests to brother Joseph, sister Seth Combs, wife of Cuthbert Combs; Benjamin Harrison; and Sarah Bronaunt, "natural daughter of Martha Bronaunt." Sarah was to have 400 a. out of Bullitt's property on the Kanawha and 5 pounds annually until she was eighteen for her "maintenance." Brother Cuthbert was the residual legatee and executor.

Thomas Bullitt was commissioned ensign and then lieutenant in 1754 in the Virginia Regiment commanded by Washington. He was on Braddocks' expedition and at Fort Necessity and was one of the officers who signed the "address" to Washington on the colonel's retirement in 1758. Bullitt stayed on and served in the Cherokee War in 1761. He was appointed surveyor for Brunswick County and surveyed large tracts in West Virginia and Kentucky including the sites of Charleston and Louisville.

Seth Bullitt (ca. 1727-1819?)
(Seth 3, Benjamin 2)

Seth Bullitt, dau. of Benjamin 2, m. Cuthbert Combs before 1759.

Benjamin Bullitt Jr. (ca. 1730-1757)
(Benj. 3, Benj. 2, Joseph 1)

PW Bond Book p. 29, Nov. 1757. Thomas B. and Cuthbert B., executors of Benjamin Bullitt Jr. give bond with Thomas Harrison, Cuthbert Harrison, and John McMillian (Sr.) as sureties.

Benjamin Jr. was killed in the French and Indian War.

Cuthbert Bullitt (ca. 1733-1791)
(Cuthbert 3, Benj. 2, Jos. 1)

Cuthbert Bullitt m. Helen Scott. Children: Alexander Scott, Thomas James, Sarah, Helen Grant, Sophia, and Frances.

F M May 1759. Appointed Fauquier County Attorney.

F D 7-485, 1783. Benjamin Harrison to Cuthbert B. of PW 235 a. on branches Licking and Elk Runs, bounded by Capt. Thomas B. plantation on road to Falmouth.

PW W G-533. Will May 1791, pr. Oct. 1791. Names children: Alexander; Thomas, who gets land on Quantico Neck, all legator's land in Fauquier, and 1500 a. on Pleasant Run and Beach Fork in Ky.; Sarah; Helen; Sophia; and Frances. Grandson Cuthbert, son of Alexander, is left 750 a. in Ky. Executors are wife, sons Alexander and Thomas, son-in-law William Gerrard, and friends Thomas Blackburn, Alexander Henderson, George Graham, the Rev. Thomas Harrison, and John Pope. Witnesses: Thos. Harrison Jr. and Cuthbert Harrison (sons of Colonel Burr), Thos. Ball, Thos. Harrison of Thomas (son of

Rev. Thomas). PW W H-215. Will of Helen B., July 1795, pr. July 1797. Names daughters Sarah Barnes, Sophia B., Helen Grant Huie; sons Alexander Scott B., Thomas James B.

PW W I-14. Will of Sophia B. Names sisters Frances Gerrard, Sarah Barnes, Helen Huie, brother Thomas James B., and nieces and nephews.

Elizabeth Bullitt

Elizabeth Bullitt b. ca. 1750, dau. of Benjamin. F Marr. Book 1-39, Feb. 1771. Bond for marriage of William Grigsby and Elizabeth Bullitt. Thomas Harrison gives consent for Elizabeth. Benjamin and Mary H. are witnesses.

Our genealogical problem with the Bullitt family stems partly from this marriage bond and partly from the Cattaille Pond lease. The V 23/24 Harrison genealogy states that Elizabeth Harrison, the sister of Col. Thomas Harrison of Fauquier, married Benjamin B. in 1727, died in 1742, and was the mother of the Bullitt children from Joseph through Elizabeth. However, when Elizabeth Bullitt married Grigsby, she was not yet twenty-one (i.e born after 1749), since she needed the consent of Col. Thomas Harrison, her guardian. Furthermore, Joseph B. was born before 1724, and his mother was named Sarah.

We do not know the original sources for the genealogy's dates for Elizabeth (Harrison) Bullitt. Nevertheless, clearly Benjamin 2, Joseph 1 did marry a Harrison, considering among other indications the names of his children: second son Thomas (named for maternal grandfather?), daughter Seth (almost exclusively a name of Harrison women), son Cuthbert, and daughter Elizabeth.

Our preferred hypothesis to resolve the incongruities is that the mother of Joseph and probably other children was Sarah Harrison. After Sarah's death (in 1742?), Benjamin married her younger sister Elizabeth, who possibly was the widow of Edward Sute. Elizabeth (Harrison) Bullitt could have been born between 1710 and 1720, i.e., ten to twenty years after her oldest brother, Burr, and still have been between thirty and forty when daughter Elizabeth (Bullitt) Grigsby was born.

William Bullitt (ca.1752-?)
(William 3, Benj. 2, Joseph 1)

PW O p.82, 1765. William Bullitt and William Harrison, witnesses for Benj. B. ag. Richard Dixon. Sh O p.2, 1772. William B. an undersheriff.

We wonder whether a 14-year-old could be a witness in a civil suit or at twenty-one a deputy sheriff. Was William born before 1752 or were there two William Bullitts?

F M Nov. 1774. William B. appt. guardian to George, Benoni, Parmines, and Burwell B. in room of Thomas and Cuthbert Bullitt.

John Bullitt (ca. 1755–?)
(John 3, Benj. 2, Joseph 1)

F M July, 1782. Benoni, Parmonous, and Burwell B. by Cuthbert B., "best friend," ag. Sarah and John B.

Burwell Bullitt (ca. 1759–?)
(Burwell 3, Benjamin 2, Joseph 1)

Burwell Bullitt m. Nancy ----. F Minute and Deed Books from 1797 to 1799 show Burwell Bullitt in financial trouble, mortgaging his property for time to pay debts, and eventually losing at least some assets.

The Fowke Family

Gerrard Fowke (1636?–1669)
(Gerrard 1)

Col. Gerrard Fowke
(Gerrard 2, Gerrard 1)

Col. Gerrard Fowke m. Sarah Burdett, dau. of Thomas Burdett and Verlinda (Cotton) Burdett.

Chas. Co. Md. Liber Q, Reverse, Births and Marriages. Gerrard F. of Portobacco was joyned in the holy state of matrimony unto Sarah Burdett, the youngest daughter of Mr. Thomas Burdett late of this county, dec'd., the 31st day of December, 1686. Gerrard F., son of Gerrard and Sarah F. of Nanjomy, born 16 October, 1687. Anne F., dau. of Gerrard and Sarah F., b. 13 Jan. 1689/90. Frances F., dau. of Gerrard and Sarah F., b. 2 Feb. 1691/2. Katherine F., dau. Gerrard & Sarah F., b. 8 April 1694.

NN 5-185, 1718. Gerrard Fowke 1032 a. on Pasbetanzy. St D J-421, 1727. Gerrard Fowke of Durham Parish, Chas. Co., Md. to Chandler Fowke, his son, of Overwharton for paternal love 1030 a. granted Gerrard F. in 1718.

Chandler Fowke (ca. 1695-1745)
(Chandler 3, Gerrard 2)

Chandler Fowke m. Mary Fossaker, dau. of Richard Fossaker and Mary (Withers) Fossaker.

St W M-427, May 1745. Chandler Fowke's will names wife Mary and children, Gerrard, Chandler, Richard, Elizabeth Anne, and Susannah.

Chandler Fowke (1732-1810?)
(Chandler 4, Chandler 3, Gerrard 2)

Chandler Fowke m. Mary Harrison, dau. of Thomas and Ann H. Children: Frances (1762-1835), Ann Harrison (1760-1787), Catherine (1765-1842), Nelly (1768-1841) m. John Latham, Thomas Harrison (1770-1843) m. Susan Baker, Jane (1772-1848), Sarah (1774-1851), Susanna (1776-1853), John Siddenham (1778- ?), Dorothea (1781-1843?).

F Marr. Book 1-1, 1759. Chandler Fowke to marry Mary Harrison. Consent by Thomas H. Witness Burr H., (Mary's brother).

PW D H-194, 1794. Elizabeth Brazier is daughter of Mary Fowke and has a daughter Sarah Harrison Cannon.

Gerrard Fowke (ca. 1730-1781)
(Gerrard 4, Chandler 3, Gerrard 2)

Gerrard Fowke m. Elizabeth Dinwiddie, (per Hayden).

F W 1-426. 1781. Will of Gerrard F. names son Chandler executor.

F D 6-134, 1774. Chandler Fowke apprenticed with approval of mother Mary to Wharton Ransdell. (Chapter V.) Was he Chandler 5, Chandler 4 or Chandler 5, Gerrard 4? Only proved Chandler of the fifth generation was the son of Gerrard 4, but his mother was presumably named Elizabeth. But if he was the son of Chandler and Mary (Harrison) Fowke, why wasn't his father the one who approved the arrangement?

The Gibson Family

Jonathan Gibson (? - 1729).

Jonathan Gibson m. Elizabeth (Thornton) Conway (1674-1732/3). Children: Jonathan, Sarah, Alice, Rachell.

KG W A1-82, 1729. Will of Jonathan G. names children.
KG W A1-93, 1732/3. Will of Elizabeth G. names son
Francis Conway, daughters Alice Catlett, Sarah G., and Rachel
G., and exec. son Jonathan G. (President James Madison was
grandson of Francis Conway and great-grandson of Elizabeth.)

Jonathan Gibson (ca. 1700-1745)
(Jonathan 2, Jonathan 1)

Jonathan Gibson m. Margaret Catlett.
PW D B-?, 1734. Thomas Furr sells Jonathan Gibson land
in Hambleton Parish.

Jonathan Gibson (ca. 1725-1791)
(Jonathan 3, Jon. 2, Jon. 1)

Jonathan Gibson m. Susannah Harrison, dau. Thomas and
Ann Harrison. Children: Thomas, John, Jonathan Catlett,
Benjamin Harrison, Ann Grayson m. 1787 Joseph Blackwell,
Susanna Grayson m. Wm. B. Taylor, and Mary.
PW Quitrents 1751. Jonathan G. Esq. held 1050 a.
O D 12-429, Nov. 1757 Jonathan Gibson to Arsalon Price,
200 a. Susannah Gibson relinquishes dower rights.
NN I-377, 1780. Capt. Jonathan Gibson of Fauquier 56 a.
on Elk Run adj. Gibson formerly Furr.
F W 2-204, dated 1788, pr. Sept. 1791. Names three
youngest children Jonathan Catlett, Susanna Grayson Gibson,
Mary; sons Thomas, John; dau. Ann Grayson (Gibson) Black-
well, niece Margaret Adie; granddaughter Margaret Catlett G.
Executors: Benjamin Harrison, sons Thomas, John, and Jona-
than Catlett.
F Marr. Books 1-117, 1782. Thomas Gibson to Charlotte
Beale.
Ibid. 1-127, 1783, John Gibson to Ann Eustace.
Ibid. 2-9, 1795, John Gibson to Elizabeth Harrison.
F D 13-439, 1788. Thomas and Charlotte Beale Gibson to
brother Jonathan Catlett G. a tract of land given Thomas by
grandfather Thomas Harrison adj. plantation of Benjamin Harri-
son. John Gibson Jr. a witness.
F D 45-488, 1846. Jonathan C. Gibson of Oldham Co. KY
power to John G. Gibson of same county to sell land and a
slave in Fauquier inherited from mother Mary G. (Grandsons of
Jonathan and Susanna G.).

The Gillison Family

James Gillison (ca. 1748–ca. 1800)

James Gillison m. 1768 Ann Harrison (dau. Col. Thomas and Ann Harrison). Their Children: John, Margaret, James, Benjamin Harrison, and Mary.

F Marr. Bk. 1-28, 5/17/1768. James G. and Benjamin Harrison bond for marriage J.G. and Ann Harrison. Consent by Robert Gilchrist for J.G. "of Caroline County a minor whose guardian I am." Consent by Thomas H. for dau. Ann. Witnessed by Jonathan Gibson & Elizabeth Bullitt.

F D 4-198, 1771. George Grant to James Gillison of Hamilton Parish 171 1/2 a. on Marsh Run.

F D 6-349, Mar. 1777. James G. and wife Anne to John Berryman 8+ acres in Hamilton Parish adj. said Gillison.

F D 6-359, Mar. 1777. James & Anne G. to Peter Bower of KG 333 1/2 a. on Marsh Run adj. Corbin and ."main" road.

F D 6-349, Mar. 1778. James & Ann G. of 1st part, Benjamin Harrison & Jonathan Gibson of 2nd part, and John, Margaret, James Jr., Benjamin Harrison, and Mary Gillison, children of said James & Ann. 220 pounds plus slaves in trust for the support and education of the children and any other that may be born in future.

F M Aug. 1788. Jonathan Gibson, security for James Gillison's debt, ordered to pay.

F Tax list 1787. James G. in southern district 00000 and Mrs. Mary Gillison and John G. 15554. All live close to each other in the southeast corner of the county. We don't know why James has no property (everything in trust to avoid creditors?), and we don't know who Mrs. Mary and John are.

F M Nov. 1795. James G. & Ann ag. Benj. Harrison. Ibid. Mar. 1798. Abates by defendant's death.

F W ?, 1803. James G. apportionment. No heirs named.

Elizabeth Gillison

F M Marr. Book 1-80, 1779. Capt. Thomas Helm Jr. to Elizabeth G., consent by Jonathan Gibson.

F M Nov. 1795. Thomas Helm & wife Elizabeth, late Elizabeth Gillison, ag. Benjamin Harrison, executor of Jonathan Gibson dec'd.

John Gillison (Jr) (ca. 1769 – ?)
(John 2, James 1)

F D 10-233, 1790. John G. Jr. witness deed Thomas Helm to Thomas Gibson, trustee for Elizabeth (Gillison) Helm. Is the John Gillison of the tax list John Sr.?

F M Nov. 1795. John G. a deputy sheriff. (Probably Jr.)

The Humston Family

Edward Humston I (? – 1686)
(Edward 1)

Fleet, Northumbria Collection, 19-A-4, 1662/3. Edward H. has servant Jane Smyth.

St Rec. 1664-68 p.94, 1668/9. Edward Humston power atty. from Abraham Flood.

St Rec. 1686-94 p.70, Feb. 1685/6. Inventory of estate of Mr. Edward Humston.

St P-161. Deed from Withers Conway for tract that Capt. John Withers, grandfather of W. C., bought of Edward H. Gent. in 1681, part was tract granted E.H. in 1667 and part bought of Robert Howson in 1667 on horse road that goes to Jordan's Bridge.

Edward Humston II (ca. 1675-1727)
(Edward 2, Edward 1)

Edward Humston II m. Lucy Gregg, dau. of Thomas and Lucy Gregg. Children: John, William, Edward III, Thomas, Lucy.

NN 3-61, 1704. Edward H. 200 a. sold by Robert Howson to Edward H., father of grantee, on N. side Upper Machotique Dam, adj. Richard Pierce, Robert King, John Alexander.

NN 3-126, 1705. Edward H. – survey disclosed grant of 200 a. really contained 489 a. Regrant for the 489 a.

St Z-327, 1706. Edward H. sells from 489 a. grant, 63 a. to Joel Striplin and 92 a. to Richard Fossaker.

St W K, Index 1721-1730, p.289, ca.1727. Humston's adm. bond.

St D J-3, 1722. Edward H. and Edward H. Jr. witnesses.

Edward Humston III (ca. 1705-ca. 1790?)
(Edward 3, Edward 2)

Edward Humston III m. Sarah ----. Children: Jane, Edward IV, Thomas.

St D J-515, 1728. Edward H. of St. Paul's Parish, son and

heir to Edward H. late of Stafford for love and affection to brother Thomas H. 211 a. on S. side Upper Machotick, part of tract of 337 a. granted in 1667 to Edward H., grandfather of said Edward H.

St W M-25, 1731. Will of Lucy Gregg Jan. 1730/1, pr. Mar. 1730/1, appoints grandson Edward H. executor.

St Z-6, 1699. Lucy Gregg witnesses a deed to William Fitzhugh. Z-46, 1700. L.G. witnesses a sale by son Thomas Gregg. Z-357, 1702. L.G. a witness to will of George Brent. Apparently she did not need to make her mark in signing.

St Rec. 1686-94 p. 43, 1687. Thomas Gregg aged 50 years or so. (Wife Lucy probably b. ca 1650, m. ca. 1665.)

St W M-50, 1731. Edward H. guardian of Priscilla Heabeard.

PW Rent Roll 1752. Edward H. 236 a. (None in 1736.)

KG D 2-54, 1736. Edward H. of St. Paul's Parish, Stafford, planter, to Thomas Grigsby 168 a. all tract which Thomas Gregg by will dated 7 March 1710 gave to Edward H. and Lucy his wife and after their death fell to Edward H. the Younger. Sarah Humston relinquishes dower rights.

PW Bond Book, 1756. Lucy Peake and William Peake, adm. of John Peake dec'd., with securities Edw. Humston, Richard Rixey, and George Calvert.

KG D 4-360,1758. John Humston's wife was daughter of Francis and Sarah Woffendall. Was the wife of John's brother Edward a Woffendall daughter also? Her name was Sarah.

KG D 4-364, 1758. John Humston, ship carpenter, to Edward H. of Hamilton Parish, land in KG left by Thomas Gregg by will in joint tenancy to Edward and Lucy H., latter sister to Gregg and mother to John and Edward, parties. Said Lucy being survivor willed to William and John H. William has not been heard of, land has fallen to John and by him now conveyed to Edward. Edward Humston Jr. a witness.

F D 1-123, 1760. Deed of trust from John Crump to Thomas Harrison and Cuthbert Harrison witnessed by Edward H., Martin Hardin, and Edward H. Jr.

F D 2-103, 1764. Deed from John Morehead to son John M. witnessed by Edward H.

F DB 5-508, 1774. Deed John Hudnall to Charles Morehead witnessed by Edward H.

F M May 1762. Edward H. and Edward H. Jr. appraise est. of Thomas Seaman.

F M Oct. 1768. Edward H. appraised estate John Morehead.

F Tax list 1787. Edward Humsted (sic) owns 15 slaves.

Thomas Humston (ca. 1707–1731/2)
(Thos. 3, Edw. 2, Edw. 1)

St D J–?, 1727/8. John Quarles, James Bland, and Thomas Humston witness deed from John Connell to Hugh West of 100 a. on Pohick Cr. St W M–48, Mar. 1731/2. Inventory of Thomas H. dec'd.

Edward Humston IV (1737–1821)
(Edward 4, Edw. 3, Edw. 2)

Edward Humston IV m. 1769 Susanna Quarles. Children: Edward V, Thomas, John.

F Marr. Book 1–31, 1/30/1769. Edward H. & Thomas O'Bannon bond for Edward H. marr. to Susanna Quarles. Consent for Susanna by (Col.) Thomas Harrison.

F D 6–40 1774. Lease Lord Fairfax to Edward H. 150 a. for lives of him, wife Susanna, & son Edward. (Near land of William and Jane (Humston) Harrison.)

F M July 1787. Edward H., one of the commissioners of this county, takes oath on his list of taxable property. Also noted as commissioner in 1789, 1795, and 1796.

F Tax list 1787. Edward H. 1/10/11/8/17. In own district. The one aged 16–20 is (son?) Thomas H.

F M Jan. 1793. Burr Harrison vs. Edward H. Sr. (Presumably refers to Edward IV.)

F Marr. Bk. 2–238, 5/1/1801. John Morehead and John Humston bond for marr. of Morehead and Susanna H. Consent by Edward H. Teste: John H. and Thomas H.

Thomas Humston (ca. 1772 – ?)

F Marr. Book 2–271, 1802. Thomas Humston bond for Andrew Foley and Elizabeth Mallory. Ann Mallory consents.

F M Dec. 1796. Thomas H. witness to will of Samuel Morehead.

V 40–79. Note on Harrison-Humston-Mallory says Philip Mallory Jr. m. Lucy Humston, dau. of Edward IV, no source given.

Edward Humston V (ca. 1770 – ?)
(Edw. 5, Edw. 4, Edw. 3)

The Humstons moved from Fauquier to Shenandoah about 1800. The Sh Grantor Index of Deeds 1772–1820 has following: 1783 Edward H. (IV) to Jacob Miller. 1813 Edward H. Sr. (IV)

from Thomas H. 1814 Edward H. (V?) to Thomas H. 1814
Nathaniel H. (?) to Edward H. (V?) 1814-1818 Thomas H. four
deeds.

The Peyton Family

Valentine Peyton (ca. 1628-1665)

Son of Henry of St. Dunstan's-in-the-West, London, England. In Va. by 1654. Married Frances Gerrard, no children.
Colonel and Burgess for Westmoreland. W 1-227, bought land
adj. Capt. Brent on Aquia. Will proved Westmoreland 1665.

Henry Peyton (ca. 1630-1659)
(Henry 1)

Henry Peyton (1656 - ?)
(Henry 2, Henry 1)

Philip Payton (? - 1727)

In 1679 had land on Machotick in St and later on Aquia.

Gerrard Peyton

NN 5-127, 1716. Land in Westmoreland

Valentine Peyton (ca. 1685-1751)
(Valentine 2, Henry 2)

Valentine m. Frances Linton, dau. of Moses and Margaret
Linton. Children: Henry, Francis, Craven, Valentine, John, and
Eleanor m. William Powell.
Burgess PW 1734-40.
NN 4-54, 1711/2. Warrant to Valentine P. assigned to
Capt. Wm. Downing.
NN A-159, 1725. 253 a. on Broad Run to Valentine P.
NN C-142, 1731. 130 a. on Gravelly Br. of Occoquon.
Found later to have 230 and replaced by NN F-164.

John Peyton (1691-1760)
(John 2, Henry 2)

John Peyton m. (1) Ann (Waye) Young, widow of Bryan

Young, m. (2) Elizabeth Rowzee. Children: by (1) Ann Waye m. Thomas Harrison, Yelverton, Henry;, by (2) John R., Valentine.

Burgess St 1734-40.

NN F-222 and F-236, 1745. 287 a. and 1290 a. on NW side of Pignut Ridge.

St W O-375, 1760. Will of John P. names children, brother Valentine, and grandsons John Peyton Harrison and Valentine Harrison.

Henry Peyton (ca. 1718-1781)
(Henry 3, Valentine 2, Henry 2)

Henry Peyton m. (1) Anne Thornton, dau. of Thomas Thornton, (2) Margaret ----. Children: Timothy, Mary m. ? Matson, John, Frances, Betty m. ? Martin, Thomas (under 21).

PW D P-299. Sale of 79 a. by John Ballendine recites that Henry Peyton sold in 1755 all tract on S. side of Occoquan near the falls being the "plantation whereon Valentine Peyton and Frances his wife lived and died, including the Occoquan warehouse.

F D 4-82, 1770. Henry Peyton of PW for love of son Timothy P. 254 a. on branches of Little River, part of a grant to Thomas Thornton of Lancaster who devised it to Anne T. who married Henry P.

PW Bond Book p.145, 1781. John Peyton Jr. executor of Henry P. dec'd.

PW W G-119, 1781. Will of Col. Henry P. names children and grandson Robert P.

John Peyton (ca.1720-1774)
(John 3, Valentine 2, Henry 2)

John Peyton m. Seth Harrison, dau. of Burr and Ann (Barnes) Harrison. Children: Valentine, John, Frances m. cousin, John P. Harrison.

PW D Q-279, 1765. John Peyton and wife Seth of PW mortgage to Burr Harrison 300 a. on N side Broad Run of Occoquan inherited from father Valentine.

PW Bond Book p.111, 1774. Seth Peyton, Valentine P., and John P. executors of John P. dec'd.

Craven Peyton (ca. ? - 1781)
(Craven 3, Valentine 2, Henry 2)

Craven Peyton m. Ann Harrison, dau. of Burr and Ann

(Barnes) Harrison. Children: Craven, Burr, Valentine, Robert?

Francis Peyton
(Francis 3, Valentine 2, Henry 2)

Justice Loudoun during Revolution.

Yelverton Peyton (ca. 1735–1794)
(Yelverton 3, John 2)

Yelverton Peyton m. Elizabeth -----.   Children: Elizabeth m. John Peyton Harrison (his second wife). Justice F 1759, moved to St in 1761. Justice St 1771.

Valentine Peyton (ca. 1755–1786)
(Val. 4, Craven 3, Val. 2)

Valentine Peyton m. Sally ----.   Children: Craven, Prudence, John, and Robert.

PW Bond Book p.175, 1786. Burr P. executor of Valentine P.

PW W G-336, 1786. Will of Captain Valentine P. names children and appoints brother Burr executor.

Burr Peyton (ca. 1750–1814)
(Burr 4, Craven 3, Valentine 2)

Burr Peyton m. Sibella Linton, dau. of John and Elizabeth (Elliot) L.

Other Peytons not placed:

Robert paid quitrents on 350 a. from 1760 to 1773.
Robert killed in Revolutionary War.
Henry Lieut. in Va 1st Reg., Light Dragoons.
Henry Jr. of Fauquier in 1790's.

The Quarles Family

John Quarles (ca. 1695–ca. 1729)
(John 1)

John Quarles m. 1722 Ann Grayson, dau. John and Susanna Grayson. Children: John, Betty, Moses.
Sp Marr. Book, p.1, 1722. Marr. of John Quarles. Bride's

name not given.

Index to lost St W K (1721-30), p. 33-, (ca. 1729). John Quarles's Inventory.

Moses Quarles (? - ca. 1740)
(Moses 1)

Moses Quarles m. Seth Linton, dau. of Moses and Margaret Linton. Known Child: Jane m. Wm. Tandy.

PW D B-32, 1732. Moses Q. from Margaret Linton. Roger Q. a witness. (See Chapter XVII.)

Caroline O (1746-54), p. 78, 1747. Jane Q. being admitted to choose a guardian made choice of Roger Q.

PW D Q-196, 1764. Benjamin Grayson sells "land originally taken up by Moses Linton, devised in his will to Seth Quarles and by her to her dau. who married Wm. Tandy" and by deed in 1755 to Grayson.

James Quarles
(James 1)

James Quarles m. Elizabeth Minor.

Roger Quarles

Roger Quarles m. Jane ----. Sons John and William.

Aaron Quarles

PW O p.119, 1753. Aaron Quarles vs. Moses Linton.

John Quarles (ca. 1723 - ?)
(John 2, John 1)

John Quarles m. Ann dau. James (1) and Elizabeth Quarles. Children: John, Henry, James Grayson, Elizabeth Minor, and another dau. who m. Wm. Cowne.

F O p.53, 1759. John Q. vs. John Harrison.

Betty Quarles (ca 1725-1773)
(Betty 2, John 1)

F W 1-220, 1773. Bequests to Elizabeth Minor Quarles, dau. of John Quarles, and to brother John Quarles.

Moses Quarles (ca. 1727-ca. 1755)

(Moses 2, John 1)

PW D L-217, 1750. Moses Quarles' receipt to guardian Thomas Harrison for full payment of share of estate of John Quarles.

Susanna Quarles (ca, 1753 – ?)
(Susanna 3, Moses 2?, John 1)

F Marr. Book 1-31, 1769. Bond for marriage of Edward Humston and Susanna Quarles. Thomas Harrison gives consent.

Abbreviations and Bibliography

Genealogical Numbering System:

In chapter headings and appendices the number after a given name of a family member represents the generation to which he belongs, counting as (1) the first known generation of residents within the Fairfax Proprietorship. The line of direct male descent from that first generation ancestor is shown by the order of son to father relationships. For example:

> Burr Harrison (1738–1822) of South Carolina
> (Burr 4, Thomas 3, Thomas 2, Burr 1)

was the son of Thomas Harrison who was the son of Thomas Harrison who was the son of the immigrant Burr Harrison, and

> Burr Harrison (1734–1790), Merchant
> (Burr 4, Burr 3, Thomas 2, Burr 1)

was the son of Burr Harrison who was the son of Thomas Harrison who was the son of the immigrant Burr Harrison.

Magazines:

T   ---- Tyler's Quarterly Historical and Genealogical Magaz.
V   ---- Virginia Magazine of History and Biography.
VG ---- The Virginia Genealogist.
W (1) ---- William and Mary College Quarterly, Series 1.
W (2) ---- William and Mary College Quarterly, Series 2.

Counties:

Au ----	Augusta	N ----	Northumberland
C ----	Culpeper	O ----	Orange
F ----	Fauquier	PW ----	Prince William
Fk ----	Frederick	R ----	Richmond
Fx ----	Fairfax	Sh ----	Shenandoah (Dunmore)
KG----	King George	Sp ----	Spotsylvania
L ----	Loudoun	St ----	Stafford
La ----	Lancaster	W ----	Westmoreland

Official Records:

D ---- Deed Book
M ---- Minute Book
O ---- Order Book
W ---- Will Book
NN---- Northern Neck Land Grant

Volume (or Book) and page numbers are shown as in the following examples:

Sh D B-8. Shenandoah Deed Book B, page 8.
V 23-322. Virginia Magazine, Vol. 23, page 322.

Copies of Original Documents:

Palmer, Wm. P., ed. *Calendar of Virginia State Papers, 1652-1781*, Vol. 1. New York: Reprinted Kraus Reprint Corp., 1968.
Des Cognets, Louis Jr. *English Duplicates of Lost Virginia Records*. Princeton, NJ: by the author, 1958.
Dettingen Parish Vestry Book, Prince William County, Virginia, 1745-1790. Dumfries, Va: Historic Dumfries Inc., 1976.
Hillman, Benjamin J., ed. *Executive Journals of the Council of Colonial Virginia*.
McIlwaine, H.R., ed. *Journals of the House of Burgesses*.
Henning's Statutes at Large: A Collection of all the Laws of Virginia.
Maryland Archives. Vol. VIII, Proceedings of the Executive Council.

Minutes of the Vestry of Truro Parish, Virginia, 1732-1785. Lorton, Va: Pohick Church, 1974.

Abstracts:

Dorman, John Frederick. *Westmoreland County, Virginia Records, 1658-1661, 1661-64.* Washington: by the author.
-----. *Prince William County, Virginia, Will Book C, 1734-44.* Washington: by the author, 1956.
Fleet, Beverley. *Virginia Colonial Abstracts.* Include Vol. 1 & 22 - Lancaster; 2, 3, 19 & 20 - Northumberland; 16 & 17, Richmond; and 23 - Westmoreland.
Gray, Gertrude E. *Northern Neck Land Grants, 1694-1742.* Baltimore: Genealogical Publishing Company, 1987-88.
Gott, John K. *Abstracts of Fauquier County, Virginia Wills Inventories, and Accounts, 1759-1800.* Marceline, Mo: Walsworth Publishing, 1972.
-----. *Fauquier County, Virginia, Deeds, 1759-1778.* Bowie, Md: Heritage Books, Inc., 1988.
-----. *Fauquier County, Virginia, Marriage Bonds, 1759-1854.* Bowie, Md: Heritage Books, Inc., 1989.
Holcomb, Brent H. *Fairfield County, South Carolina, Minutes of the County Court, 1785-1799.*
Johnson, June Whitehurst. *Abstracts of Prince William County, Virginia Bond Book, 1753-1782; Will Book C, 1778-1791; Order Book, 1769-1771; and Will Book H, 1792-1803.* Fairfax, Va: by the author.
Joyner, Peggy Shomo. *Abstracts of Virginia's Northern Neck Warrants & Surveys.* Portsmouth, Va: by the author, 1985-86.
King, George H.S. *The Register of Overwharton Parish, Stafford County, Virginia, 1723-1758.* Fredericksburg: by the author, 1961.
-----. *The Register of St. Paul's Parish, 1715-1798.* Fredericksburg: by the author, 1961.
Mitchell, Beth. *Beginning at a White Oak...Patents and Northern Neck grants of Fairfax County, Virginia.* Fairfax County Administrative Services, 1977.
Nugent, Nell Marion. *Cavaliers and Pioneers: Abstracts of Virginia Land Patents and Grants.* Vol. 1, 1623-1666. Baltimore: Genealogical Publishing Company, 1963. Vol. 2, 1666-1695, and Vol. 3, 1695-1732. Richmond: Virginia State Library, 1977 and 1979.
Sparacio, Ruth and Sam. *Abstracts of Virginia County Court Records.* Include seventeenth- and eighteenth-century

deeds and wills of Fairfax, King George, Loudoun, and Stafford counties and order books of Prince William and Stafford counties.

Military:

Bockstruck, Lloyd DeWitt. *Virginia's Colonial Soldiers.* Baltimore: Genealogical Publishing Company, 1988.

Brumbaugh, Gaius Marcus. *Revolutionary War Records, Vol. 1, Virginia.* Baltimore: Genealogical Publishing Company, 1967.

Clark, Murtie June. *Colonial Soldiers of the South, 1732-1774.* Baltimore: Genealogical Publishing Company, 1983.

Dorman, John Frederick. *Virginia Revolutionary Pension Applications.* Published by the author.

Gwathmey, John H. *Historical Register of Virginians in the Revolution, Soldiers, Sailors, Marines, 1775-1783.* Baltimore: Genealogical Publishing Company, 1973.

Russell, T. Triplett and Gott, John K. *Fauquier County in the Revolution.* Warrenton, Va: Fauquier County Bicentennial Commission, 1976.

General:

Boogher, William Fletcher. *Gleanings of Virginia History.* Baltimore: Genealogical Publishing Company, 1963.

Davis, Richard B. *William Fitzhugh and his Chesapeake World, 1676-1801.* Virginia Historical Society by University of North Carolina Press, 1963.

Groome, H.C. *Fauquier during the Proprietorship.* Reprinted for Clearfield Company by Genealogical Publishing Company, 1989.

Harrison, J. Houston. *Settlers by the Long Grey Trail, Harrisons and Allied Families.* Baltimore: Genealogial Publishing Company, 1975.

Harrison, Fairfax. *Landmarks of Old Prince William.* Republished Genealogical Publishing Company, 1975.

Meade, William. *Old Churches, Ministers, and Families of Virginia.* Republished by Genealogical Publishing Company, 1966.

Virginia Writers Project. *Prince William, the Story of Its People and Its Places.* Manassas, Va: Bicentennial Edition, The Bethlehem Good Housekeeping Club, 1976.

WPA Records. *Old Homes and Families of Fauquier County, Virginia.* Berryville, Va: Virginia Book Company, 1978.

Genealogies:

Harrison, Henry Tazewell. *A Brief History of the First Harrisons of Virginia.* By the author, 1915.
Hayden, Horace Edwin. *Virginia Genealogies.* Baltimore: Republished by Genealogical Publishing Company, 1973.
Hodges, Frances Beal Smith. *The Genealogy of the Beale Family, 1399-1956.* Ann Arbor, Mi: Edwards Brothers, 1956.
Johnson, Leona Grace Ellis. *The Harrisons of Virginia, Kentucky, and Indiana.* New Richmond, Wi: by the author, 1988.

All names are indexed through page 246. In Appendix B (pages 247–262), only names differing from the primary family name are indexed.

---- Alice 78 Ann 235 Burton 8 Elizabeth 227 260 Hannah 228 Jane 261 Jeremiah 157 Margaret 259 Mary Eliza 172 Nancy 251 Ruth 196 Sally 260 Sarah 230 247 255 256 Susanna 78 Susannah 227 Tim 157 Tom 139 Tomm 34 William 139

ADAMS, Gavin 101 178 Mrs Gavin 101

ADDAMS, Jno 2

ALCOCK, John viii Mariana vii

ALCOCKE, Thomas 11

ALEXANDER, 51 Elizabeth 22 Gerrard 99 John 22 30 63 100 255 Mary Stuart 86 Robert 22 30 93 William 86

ALLEN, 185 Caty 186 John 53 Zachariah 233

ALLENSON, Mary 39

ALLERTON, Isaac 20

ALSTON, Susan 159

ANDERSON, 11 David 4 5 27 Elizabeth 4 George 44 50 Seith 50

ANDREWS, George 241

ANDROS, Edmund 16

ARRINGTON, David 168

ASBURY, George 195

ASHBURNE, John 118

ASHBURNER, John 115 118

ASHBY, Robert 201 243

ASHTON, Laurence 146

ATHEY,Roxsey Ann 198 Willis 198

ATWELL, Thomas 209 Thos 219

AUNT BECC, 144 149

AWBRY, Francis 53

BAILEY, John 137

BAKER, Mr 11 Susan 252

BALL, Burgess 196 James 81 Sarah 78 Thos 249

BALLENDINE, John 259

BALLENGER, Alexander 56

BALTIMORE, Lord 222 223 231 Lord Baron, 152

BALTROP, Wm 2

BARKER, Leonard 53 201 Sharlett 175 181 Valentine 53

BARNES, Ann 54 83 103 109 110 120 203 259 260 Anne 215 Catherine 109 Frances 83 88 Mary 62 Mary Ann 109 110 Mary Anne 56 Mathew 83 88 203 Matthew 54 62 109 Mrs Sarah 250 William 113

BARRY, Edward 58 241

BARTON, 38 181 Ann 193 201 205 210 215 218 223 Ann Green 30 41 192 205 Anne 22 203 Benjamin 196 197 Benjamin Jr 197 Burr 191 194 195 197 201 Charles 191–194 201 Constance 192 Constant 192 201 223 Cuthbert 195 201 David 142 148 189 192 195–197 200– 202 Edward 30 41 192 201 205 207 210 215 223 Elisha 197 Elizabeth 189 194 196 197 200 201 Grace 191 200 James 191 195 197 198 202 Jane 198 202 John 196 197 202 Joseph 195 197 Kimbel 197 Kimber 197 Letice 201 Lettice 41 Levi 195 Levy 197 Lydia 191 194 200 Margaret 192 201 210 Maria 198 202 Martha 190 200 Mrs Thomas 37 Nathan 42 189 190 192 200 Nathan Jr 190 Peggy 198 Rhody 197

269

272

ROBERTS, James 91 100
ROBERTSON, James 64 77
ROBINSON, James 78
ROWLEY, Catherine 235 William 235
ROWZEE, Elizabeth 259
RUDDLE, Cornelius 112 Ingobe 112
RUSSELL, Ann 162 Anthony 134 Charles 162 Dorcas 159 James 159 Mary 162 Penelope 134
RUTHERFORD, Mary 115 Robt 177
SAFFORD, Elias 118 Nancy 118
SANFORD, Richard 100 Robert 100
SCARLETT, Ann 41 201 215 220 Ann Green 41 213 Jane 41 Lettice 41 Martin 41 210 218 Martin Jr 40 Mrs Martin 41
SCHOEPF, 170 Johann David 135 169
SCOTT, 73 Alexander 146 242 Elizabeth 70 86-89 101 Gen 124 Helen 249 James 58 70 72 71 86-88 101 197 James Jr 88 John 127 Nancy 86 Rev 196
SEALE, Anthony 70 71 Anthony Jr 182
SEAMAN, Thomas 256
SEBASTIAN, Benjamin 199 202 Priscilla 202
SHACKLETT, Sarah Ann 216 William 216
SHARPE, Horatio 152 161
SHORT, Frances 86 88 89 164 John 54 Mary 164 Seth 54 Sithia Elizabeth 51 54 Sythia Elizabeth 99 Thomas 86-89 164
SHUMATE, John Sr 75
SHURMAN, Elizabeth 26 John 26
SIMMS, John 193
SIMON, William 49
SIMONTON, John 160 163
SISSON, Mr 5
SLAUGHTER, Ann 116 117 119 Robert 238 242 Susannah 238 242 Thomas 118
SLAVE, Bristoe 144 Cate 92 Cesar 220 Dublin 143

SLAVE (continued)
Flora 220 Jack 80 Jacob 229 Pat 143 144 Peter 171 Sam 143 144 Samuel 168 169 Sylla 143
SMARR, 179 Andrew 93 178 183
SMITH, Edward 33 34 40 41 192 201 205 Esther 210 Hester 210 Jacob 210 Joseph 146 Katherine 34 40 53 60 205 206 212 213 Letiss 41 Lettice 220 Lettice Green 52 Lettis 174 Lettis Green 33 Lettiss 41 Mrs Jacob 210 Ralph 11 28 Samuel 65 79 Thomas 175 181 Thos 181 William 34 40 205 242
SMYTH, Jane 255
SNEED, Samuel 8
SNOW, Thomas 98
SOMMERS, 93 John 92 94
SOUTHARD, Ann 146
SPEED, Thomas 127
SPENCE, Eleanor 207
SPENCER, Nicholas 14 Secretary 17 18 20
SPOTSWOOD, Governor 48 59 62
STATLARD, Mary 248 Randolph 248
STEATARD, Joseph Bullitt 248 Mary 248
STEPHENS, Robert 183
STEVENS, Alice 78 James 78
STIPPLING, Thomas 70
STONE, Francis 218 223 232 Thomas 224 232
STOVER, Peter 114 118
STRAHAN, David 13 22
STRAUGHAN, David 37 39
STRAUGHN, 29 30 David 13 22
STRIPLIN, Joel 255
STRIPPLING, Thomas 70 71
STROTHER, Catherine 162 Catherine Dargan 153 Elizabeth 95 James 162 John D 162 Kemp 162 Mrs 153 William 153 162
STUART, Mary 14
STURMAN, Richard 232
SULLIVAN, John 119
SUMMERS, John 50 Mr 53 Mrs 53 Seth 50
SUTE, Edward 74 81 248 250
SWELLIVANT, Sarah 204

TANDY, Jane 261 William 218
  Wm 261
TANNAHILL, Sarah 127
TANNEHILL, Anne 128
TAYLOE, John 220 224 232 243
TAYLOR, Catherine 214 Charles
  218 Susanna 253 Wm B 253
TEBBS, Foushee 232
TERRET, Margaret 50 William
  50
TERRETT, 52
TERRIL, 153
TERRILL, John 152
THOMAS, Capt 45 David 79
THOMPSON, 78 Christopher 159
  Mathew 11 29 31 Sophia 159
  Wm 127
THORNKILL, Elijah 132
THORNTON, Anne 259 Elizabeth
  252 John 125 Thomas 259
THRAWLEY, Dorothy viii
TILLET, Giles 37
TRAMMEL, John 243
TRAMMELL, John 243
TRIGG, Clement 248 Sarah 248
TRIPLETT, Isabella 238 Isabella
  Miller 238 Sarah 236 Thomas
  236 242 William 238 Wm 136
TURLEY, 68 69 Mrs 49 Sampson
  67 176 182 219
TURNER, Jann 232
TYLER, Benjamin 230 Charles
  200 207 Eleanor 117 Sally 159
  Susanna Monroe 207 Susannah
  230 Wm 101
UNDERWOOD, John 200
VANBUSCARK, Michael 161
VANBUSHKIRK, 161
VAN BUSHKIRK, Michael 160
VANDECASTEEL, 42 Giles 35 37
  38
VANDERASTEAL, 42
VANDICASTILLE, 42
VAUHAN, John 2 Samuel 26
  William 26
WADDELL, John 201
WAGENER, Benjamin Harrison
  168 Beverley 172 Beverley R
  102 168 Beverley Robinson 168
  Beverly Robinson 99 Margaret
  102 168 172 Margaret S 168

WAGENER (continued)
  Margaret Short 99 102 Mary
  Eliza 168 Peter 168 172 Sinah
  172
WALKER, John 119 201 Richard
  158
WALLACE, Burr 199 Burr Jr 199
  Jane 199 John 199 218 Thomas
  199
WALLER, Charles 80 George 80
  John 238 Mary 238
WALLIS, 181 Burr 25 198 199 202
  Jane 199 202 John 25 189 198
  202 205 Mary 199 202 Thomas
  198 199 202
WALTER, Thomas 45
WARD, John 161
WARREN, James 102
WASHINGTON, 51 76 77 87 122
  158 249 Ann Gerrard Brett
  Broadhurst 28 Collo 10 Gen
  130 George 60 151 John 27 28
  Lawrence 245 Mr 71
WATERS, Elizabeth 135 Philem-
  on 133 135 137 138 187 Phi-
  lemon Jr 134 137 138 Thos H
  134
WATKINS, Griffith 175
WATTS, 148 Frances 175 181
  Francis 142 John 26 141
  Richard 237 238 242 Thomas
  142 143 201
WAUGH, 49 Elizabeth 29 Jno 17
  John 16 28 29 31 54 Mr 17 71
  Parson 17 37
WAYE, Ann 90 258 259
WEBB, Elizabeth 116 117
WEBSTER, Janet 230 William
  230
WEIRE, John 54
WEST, viii 15 53 65 242 Hugh 94
  100 236 238 257 Jno 17 John
  15 16 18 22 23 25 29 40 44 45
  49-52 64 237 238 John Jr 91 94
  100 239 243 John Sr 31 Mrs
  John 49 Sarah 25 Susanna
  Pearson 29 Sybil 236 239
WHEELOCK, Frances 129 James
  122 129
WHITE, Alexander 115 118 Ann
  112 Elizabeth 115 118

283